The Third Battle of Manassas

Managing Change and Growth in a Suburban Virginia School District

Manassas, Prince William County, Virginia

1973-1977

Milton Lee Pritchard Snyder, Ph.D.

The Third Battle of Manassas:
Managing Change and Growth in a Suburban Virginia School District,
Manassas, Prince William County, Virginia — 1973-1977

by Milton Lee Pritchard Snyder, Ph.D.
    Division Superintendent of Schools, Prince William County, Manassas, Virginia (1973-1977)

ISBN: 978-0-9967545-0-7

Newspaper articles in appendices are from the Potomac News, The Journal Messenger, The News, The Washington Post, and others. Newspaper articles were clipped and archived as photocopies when published. These recently were scanned and the text captured by optical character recognition software. Some photocopies were damaged, and text was cut off or missing in a few articles, these instances are noted in parenthesis in the text. The Journal Messenger and Potomac News have ceased to exist.

Book design and preparation for printing by Kathleen R. Weisel, Bellingham, WA (weiselcreative.com)

Maps: p. 2, sourced from https://en.wikipedia.org; p. 4, sourced from: http://nationalmap.gov;
p. 5, Map Data ©2015 Google.; p. 6, sourced 08/2015 http://mrgrimsleysearthscienceclass.wikispaces.com.

Cover photos: National Park Service's website at the Manassas National Battlefield Park.
Back cover: Fence source, Wikipedia, licensed under the Creative Commons by Billy Hathorn.

Milton Lee Pritchard Snyder, Ph.D.
1301 Spring Street
Seattle, WA 98104
miltsnyder@aol.com

• • •

If you are interested, my memoir was self-published in 2009-2012 and is available by doing an internet search for: *Maybe Milton Should Go Work in the Woods* by Milton Lee Pritchard Snyder, Ph.D.

Dedicated to the students of
Prince William County, Virginia,
and the people whose responsibility it is
to make their public education possible.

Contents

Appendix G: 2014-2015 . . . . **185**

Foreword

In 2009 I achieved a long standing goal with the publication of my autobiography, *Maybe Milton Should Go Work in the Woods*. In that volume, I recounted the events and the people in my life, including the history of my ancestors. However, a sizable portion of the volume described my professional career in public education. Most of my career was spent as a superintendent in a number of different school districts culminating in my retirement after eight years as the school leader of the Federal Way school system near Seattle, Washington.

In that book, I described my experiences in each of the school systems where I had served and the challenges I faced. One of those districts, Prince William County, Virginia (20 miles south of Washington, DC), presented some particularly unique challenges and opportunities which I felt warranted a more detailed accounting than I had been able to give in my autobiography. I served Prince William County as superintendent from 1973 to 1977—during a period of dynamic population growth and political upheaval which impacted both the governance and management of the school system.

Therefore, in March of 2014, I flew from Seattle to Washington, DC, and returned to Manassas, the county seat for Prince William County, to research and gather information about the events that occurred while I was there in the 1970s. I contacted as many former school board members, staff members, county supervisors and community leaders as I could for their remembrance of things that happened during my tenure there. I collected and assembled stories and documents from that period and interviewed former staff members in order to provide greater accuracy to my research. My purpose was to include available printed material from the past and to garner facts from leaders in the county who were active participants in the political scene more than 40 years ago. Much of the information will pertain to the period of disagreement between the governing board and the school board.

My purpose is to describe some of Prince William County's early history and the rapid population and business growth in the modern era that created the political turmoil and educational turbulence that marked this time in the 1970s. In addition, I wanted to share my recollections of the activities, successes, and sometimes failures of leaders in the county during this formative period, and the impact of their actions on the school system. These are my individual views concerning the actions of the school board, county supervisors, and others associated with the schools and with the county government during the years I served as superintendent of schools.

It is a record of events unfolding; a synthesis of personal experience, news, battles, and the rapidly shifting perspectives about those exciting years as a school leader in a dynamic and challenging environment. I've chosen to convey my impressions as they occurred more than 40 years ago, and I think most of them are true; but some of them could be wrong because of the frailties of memory and the fog of history. Out of that cauldron of experience, I learned that it is easy to criticize people in charge. It is much harder to be the person in charge.

Finally, I wish to acknowledge those who helped in the formation of this book. Dr. William L. Helton, Ph.D., my former deputy superintendent, was particularly helpful in reviewing and offering suggestions in the development of the document. His research and work is reflected in this book, especially in the sections dealing with the history and demography of the county and with the chronology of events during my four-year tenure as superintendent. He was named superintendent of schools in Prince William County following my resignation.

I am also thankful for the insight and advice provided by the former chairman of the school board, Ellis Hawkins, with whom I had a long conversation before he passed away in 2014. He clarified some events and relationships that I had not fully understood at the time.

I am also grateful to former school board members Regis Lacey and Bill Dunn and to former Virginia Department of Education staff Helen Warriner-Burke, Pat Burke, and Dr. Jerri Mills Sutton, Ph.D., for sharing their memories of the 1970s in Virginia education; as well as all others too numerous to mention who were courteous, kind and helpful in recalling the events of 40 years ago.

As always, my greatest acknowledgment is to my wife, Dr. Dolores J. Gibbons, Ed.D., who read each of the various stages of the manuscript and has supported me in every other way.

Manassas, in the title of the book, has special meaning for my family. In addition to my living in this historic and beautiful city, Great Grandfather, Captain Sampson Snyder (8/19/1840 to 3/6/1910), served in the Civil War and represented Northern troops as Captain of a West Virginia Militia Group.

Essays about the Third Battle of Manassas

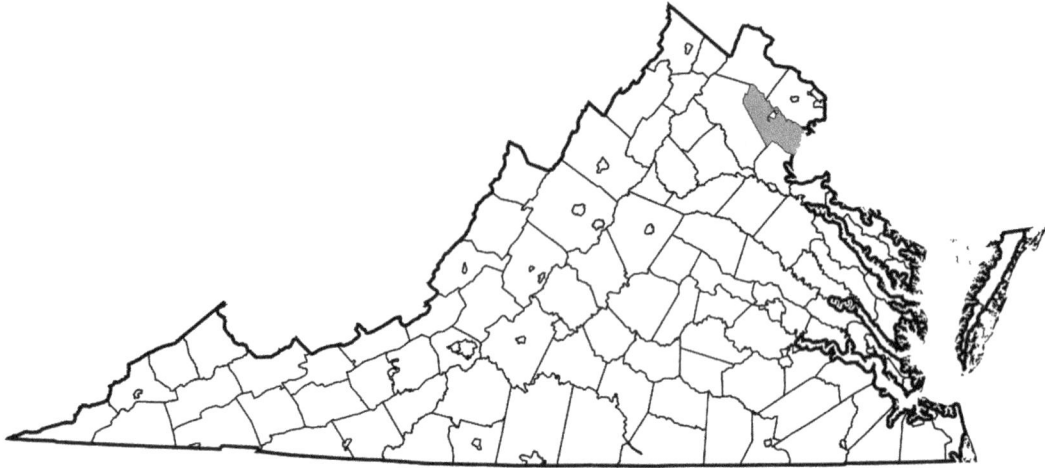

Essay 1.   Background

In March of 2014, I boarded a United Airlines 727-200 flight in Seattle, Washington destined for Dulles Airport near Washington, DC to return to Manassas, Virginia in Prince William County where I had served as schools superintendent 41 years ago. The reason for this trip back to Virginia was to research and gather information in order to recall some of the County's history during that nineteen seventies period. It was a time of divisive disagreement among the leaders of the county governing body. After an election to change the form of county government, the majority of the members on the new Board of County Supervisors, when it took office in January 1972, wanted to dismiss all the current policy boards, including the school board, and appoint their own new board members. This new Board of County Supervisors not only attempted to replace serving school board members but also to assume total control of school district policy formation, management and fiscal affairs.

I planned to meet and speak with former school board members, various school leaders, including a former member of the Board of County Supervisors, school associates and previous staff in the school district who remember our many accomplishments during the time I served as Superintendent. Also, I collected old news pieces and interviewed some former staff members who worked in the schools in the 1970s in order to give greater accuracy to this document. My purpose in the writing was to include available printed material from the past and garner facts from leaders in the county who were active participants in the political scene over forty years ago. Much of the information will pertain to the period

of disagreement between the governing body and the School Board. The majority members of the Board of County Supervisors planned to take over control of the school district, replace school board members with new appointments, cut school funds and slow down the costs of running the schools as a result of rapid student enrollment growth in the county. My purpose is to describe some of Prince William County's early history and the rapid population and business growth that in the modern era helped to create the political turmoil in this period.

In addition, this document will review pertinent details about the political conflict between the county boards and describe some of the repercussions that the conflict had on the schools. I will also describe the upheaval when a long-serving superintendent of schools left the district, and I will expand on the process of a sitting school board searching for a replacement superintendent. I also will review the events leading to the decision to hire a new superintendent. Finally, I will describe my term of service from my viewpoint as division superintendent of schools from 1973-1977. My purpose is to show the accomplishments, successes and failures of leaders during this period because my recollection of accomplishments of teachers, district administrators and school board members prompted the writing of these essays. These are my individual views concerning the actions of the school board, the superintendent, and individuals associated with both the school and county leaders during the years I served as superintendent of Prince William County Schools.

Prince William County Geography, Demography, and History

To help in my recalling my memories of Prince William County, William L. Helton, Ph.D., a native Virginian and my former deputy, and a former assistant state superintendent, agreed to assist in reviewing the geography of the area and in describing the political and demographic issues in the county prior to my assuming the position of superintendent on July 1, 1973. He has helped to provide background for the local political scene and the foundations of the period of crisis, which I call the Third Battle of Manassas. Dr. Helton had served the Prince William County school district for a number of years prior to my accepting the position of superintendent. Following is a summary of our description of the history of Prince William County and the political situation that existed prior to my arrival in 1973.

Prince William County is located in Northern Virginia about 20 miles south of Washington, DC and is bordered by the Potomac River on the east side and by the Bull Run Mountains in the west. Its land area covers 348 square miles and the county is included in the Washington-Arlington-Fairfax Metropolitan Statistical Areas and currently is one of the highest income counties in the nation.

Prince William County was created by the Virginia General Assembly in 1731 during the Colonial period and is named after Prince William, third son of King George II of England. The

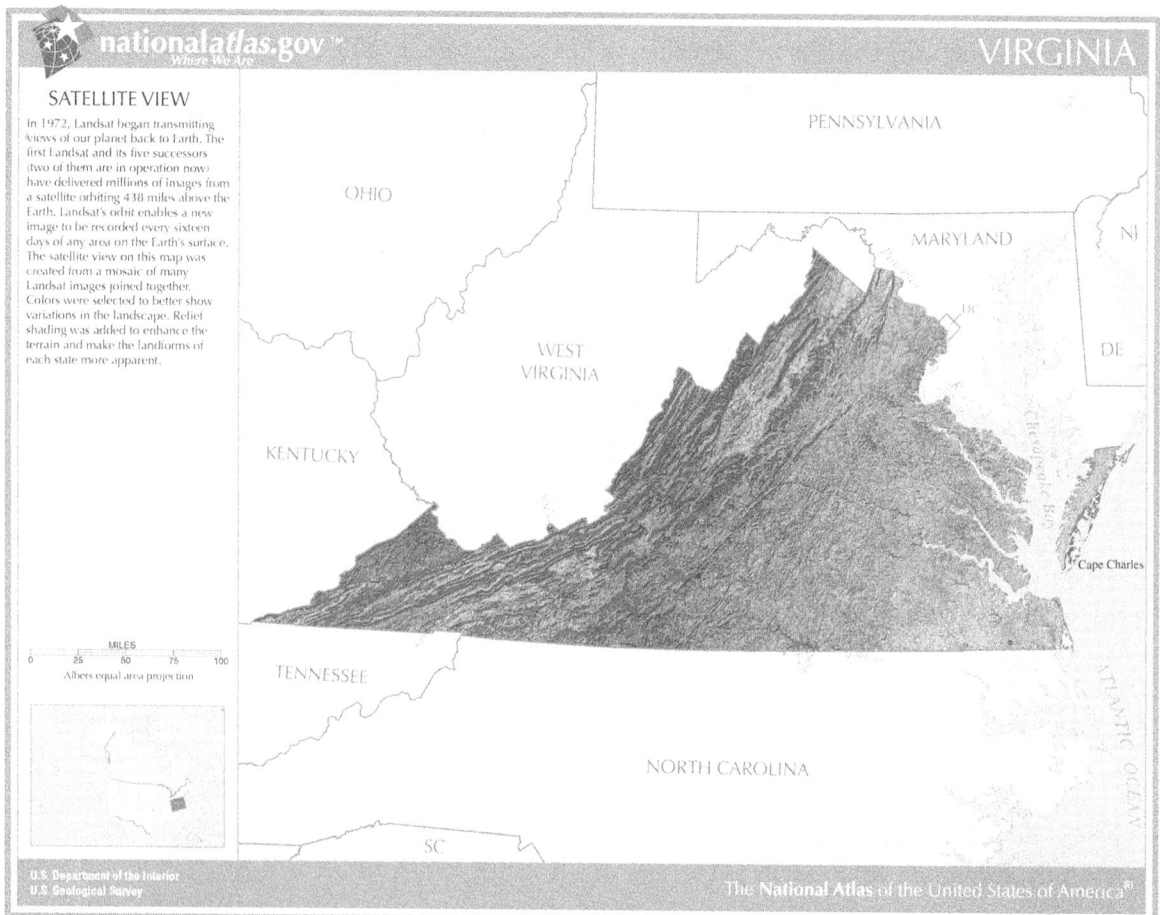

Map sourced from: http://nationalmap.gov

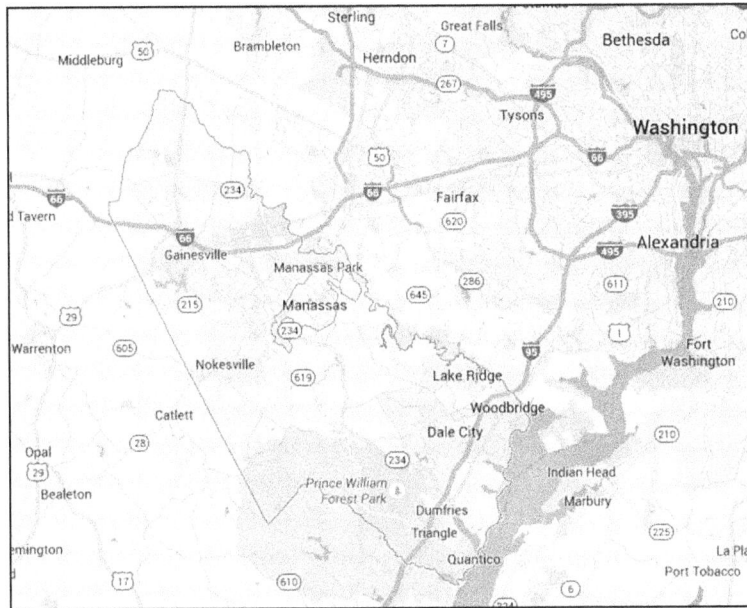

Map Data ©2015 Google.

county seat is the city of Manassas, where two of the great battles of the Civil War occurred and are known in history as the First Battle of Manassas (1861) and the Second Battle of Manassas (1862). (I have humorously referred to my four years in the county as the "Third Battle of Manassas.")

Until the middle of the 20th century, the county had a mostly rural and agricultural economy. However, in the period after World War II, the population began to double, from 22,612 in 1950 to 50,164 in 1960. It doubled again in 1960 to 111,102. By the time I arrived, the population had increased to 125,000. By the time I left, 42,500 students were enrolled. In 2014, over 85,000 students were attending Prince William County Public Schools.

Because of the open farm land and excellent transportation corridors of I-95 and Route 1 running through the eastern end of the county, as well as I-66 passing through the western side, the developers began building affordable housing units which attracted young families to move into the county in ever-increasing numbers. In addition, the Capitol Beltway made Prince William an easy commute to practically anywhere in the greater Washington, DC, area.

Many of these families had jobs recently created by the growth of the military and the federal government in response to the threat posed by the Cold War. The Quantico Marine Base was located in the eastern end of the county and nearby military installations included Fort Belvoir, Fort Meyer, Andrews Air Force Base, the Washington Naval Yard, the Pentagon, and other agencies such as the CIA and the FBI—all were located in or around Washington, DC.

As the population grew in Prince William County, so did the demand for the institutions and services to support the new arrivals such as better roads, water/sewer, police, fire and especially more schools to relieve the overcrowding in the existing schools. As the demand for better services increased, so did the pressure for increasing the local tax dollars to pay for these services.

The more rural population resisted the demand for any tax increases to support these services as demanded by the newly arrived population. Since

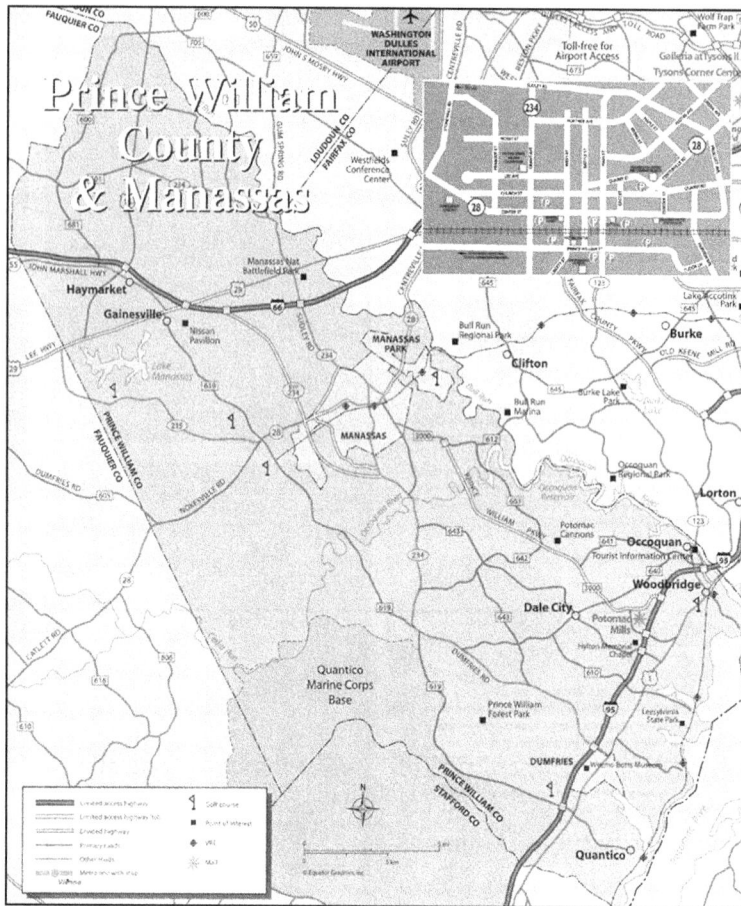

Sourced 08/2015 from http://mrgrimsleysearthscienceclass.wikispaces.com

there were no large taxable industries or businesses located in the county and 18.8% of the land area in the county was federally owned, nontaxable land, the real estate tax became the chief source of funding for local services. Thus, the political tensions heightened over the need to increase the tax rate to support the services required in the newly urbanized areas of the county.

These tensions were reflected in the November 1971 elections for the governing body known as the Board of County Supervisors, in which both the rural and rapidly urbanized districts expressed their dissatisfaction with the current situation in the county. The big issues were providing services for rampant development and increasing support for overcrowded schools and the resulting effect on the tax rate.

In addition to the supervisors' election, a referendum for changing the traditional organization of county government to the county executive form of government was on the ballot. This change of government structure was approved by the voters to take effect on January 1, 1972. As it was interpreted and implemented by the four majority members of the newly elected seven-member Board of County Supervisors, this change was to result in a monumental legal battle over the control and governance of the schools that finally had to be decided by the Virginia Supreme Court. Other legal challenges arose as the four-member majority of county supervisors dismissed other policy boards and appointed their own political supporters.

The new Board of County Supervisors that assumed office on January 1, 1972 included:

Charles Colgan - Gainesville District
Vernon Dawson - Occoquan District
Roy Doggett - Manassas District
Alfred Ferlazzo, M.D. - Dumfries District
Ralph Mauller - Brentsville District
Don Turner - Neabsco District
Scott Winfield - Coles District

Four of the supervisors (Doggett, Mauller, Turner and Winfield) colluded to form a majority alliance that voted as a block on most issues, while the three other supervisors (Colgan, Dawson and Dr. Ferlazzo) formed a minority alliance in opposition to the majority group. The four supervisors, led by Chairman Scott Winfield, implemented major changes in the county's governmental operations immediately after assuming office on January 1, 1972.

In the first official actions, they fired the county executive and ordered all the locks changed on county offices. They dismissed all department heads and all previously sitting board members on all county boards and named their replacements. They also proceeded to appoint themselves, members of their families, and political supporters to membership on various official boards, such as the welfare board, the planning commission, the water authority, and the school board. They ultimately would be criticized for hiring a grossly inexperienced county executive and making some questionable appointments to county boards and commissions. Their actions were opposed by minority board members Colgan, Dawson and Dr. Ferlazzo, who were continually outvoted.

The news media soon labeled this group of the four majority supervisors as "The Four Horsemen of the Apocalypse" from the Book of Revelation in the Bible, symbolizing destruction, famine, pestilence, and death. I gained a better appreciation of this label as I worked with them during my term of office as superintendent of schools. For this reason,

I decided to designate the period as the Third Battle of Manassas, as I struggled to manage the school system.

Prior to this change to the County Executive form of government in 1972, school board members in most of Virginia had been appointed by a School Trustee Electoral Board whose members were appointed by the district court judge, who had been appointed by the Virginia General Assembly.

Under the new County Executive form of government, this process was changed so that the Board of County Supervisors had the authority to appoint the members of the school board. The four-member majority (the so-called "Four Horsemen") of the newly elected board interpreted the change in county government as giving them the power to dismiss the previously appointed school board members and replace them with members of their choosing. Therefore, they had proceeded to name their replacements for the new sitting school board in January 1972, and to dismiss the school board members previously appointed.

The "old" sitting school board filed a legal challenge to this action arguing that the school board members had the legal right to serve out their terms to ensure continuity of services to students and to prevent disruptions in the legal obligations where the board had contracted with personnel and vendors. Thomas Beane, an attorney and school board member, provided leadership in challenging the board of supervisors' action in dismissing him and other board members, and the local circuit court judge agreed. This court ruled in favor of *not* removing the sitting board members because of the dangers of the disruptions it would cause in the school system and the legal problems in honoring binding contracts and in dispensing public funds.

Therefore, until the Virginia Supreme Court decided the issue of *which* board had legal authority for the school system, there was a period of uncertainty on the actions of the school board until the final binding decision that legally verified the legitimate status of the "old" board appointed prior to the election. The minority of three county supervisors continued to protest against the futility and expense that the majority were wasting in attempting their removal of the "old" school board members.

The exchanges between the two groups became very heated, as shown by this report describing one of the meetings: Dr. Ferlazzo shouts to Ralph Mauller, "You tell me to shut up one more time, and I'm going to invite you into the back room and beat your head in, young man!" Mauller had just told Dr. Ferlazzo to "Shut your mouth..." during an argument over the lawsuits against the "old" school board.

A newspaper editorial writer commenting on the lack of decorum during meetings of the Board of County Supervisors observed that "...any sense of a serious meeting taking place... is often reduced to a joke session or erupts into an argument which looks like it might need to be sanctioned by the American Boxing Association." Another newspaper opinion said that a recall was needed for some members of the new board of supervisors who had created "utter chaos" in county government and treated those who were unfortunate enough to appear before them with unmitigated arrogance.

At another supervisors' meeting, one member of the "Four Horsemen", Manassas supervisor Roy Doggett, protested the presence of the press at meetings, and said he "...did not want the press twisting around questions that I ask to make me look stupid."

Chairman Scott Winfield was increasingly criticized for not maintaining parliamentary order and control of the disruptive and rambling discourses during the supervisors' official meetings. As a result, they redundantly were dubbed the "Four Headless Horsemen without a head."

Despite legal opinions from the local Commonwealth Attorney and the Virginia Attorney General warning against the futility of appealing the lower court's decision, the majority four members of the board of supervisors appealed the decision to the Virginia Supreme Court. A year later, in January 1973, the Virginia Supreme Court upheld the local judge's original decision that the so-called "old" school board was the legally constituted school board.

The Supreme Court stated that the County Executive form of government required the County Supervisors to mandate the appointment of the school board members in office on December 31, 1971, either for four-year terms each or, at the supervisors' option, for staggered terms. As these terms expired, the supervisors were free to appoint "new" or reappoint "old" members as they deemed advisable.

After much wrangling and attempts to block the court's ruling for more than three months, the supervisors on a split four-three vote (with Chairman Winfield abandoning his fellow "Horsemen") finally appointed a school board with staggered terms. The school board members and their terms were as follows:

> Ellis Hawkins - four years
> William Dunn - four years
> John Pattie - three years
> Clay Wood - two years
> Thomas Beane - two years
> Paul Arrington - one year
> Paul Boots - one year

It was this board that awarded me a four-year contract to serve as Division Superintendent of Schools in Prince William County, Virginia. Over time the board of supervisors replaced the old board members who had hired me with their own choices, and most of these replacement board members held views which were different from those of board members who had appointed me.

Members of the "new" school board that had been appointed by the newly elected Board of County Supervisors in 1972 and negated by the Supreme Court's decision were:

> Homer Akers - Gainesville District
> Paul Boots - Brentsville District

John Roy Doggett - Manassas District
  (son of Supervisor Roy Doggett)
Regis Lacey - Neabsco District
E.M. Lynn - Occoquan District
Jacqueline Mullen - Coles District
George Stringer - Dumfries District

A new state law adopted by the Virginia General Assembly prohibited the appointment of close relatives of members of the board of supervisors from serving on school boards. Since his father, Roy Doggett, was a member of the Prince William Board of County Supervisors, the new law made John Roy Doggett ineligible to accept a school board appointment.

After Paul Arrington's term expired for the Manassas District, Roy Doggett named Robert Boyd, a guard at the Lorton Federal Prison, to replace Arrington on the school board in March 1974.

Regis Lacey, a neighboring Fairfax County School administrator who resided in Prince William County, became eligible for appointment by Don Turner, the Neabsco District Supervisor; but Brentsville District Supervisor Ralph Mauller raised objections and wanted to reappoint Paul Boots, who was no longer in the Neabsco District but was now in Mauller's district because of redistricting.

Mauller continued to challenge Lacey's appointment by seeking to have the Virginia Attorney General declare Lacey ineligible because he was a school employee in Fairfax County, which Mauller thought created a legal conflict of interest with his school board duties in Prince William County where he lived. The Attorney General's opinion declared that no conflict existed, and hence, Mr. Lacey could assume his school board seat.

In addition to the upheaval and uncertainties created in the county over the political changes in leadership, long-serving school superintendent Stuart Beville resigned before finishing his four-year term and accepted a position at Virginia Tech University. To assist in the search for a new superintendent,

the school board hired two consultants, Dr. George Holmes, Executive Director of the Virginia School Boards Association and a professor at the University of Virginia, and Ray Reed, retired superintendent of Arlington, Virginia County Schools and former Deputy Superintendent of Public Instruction for the Commonwealth of Virginia.

The school board appointed Herbert Saunders, the Assistant Superintendent for Personnel, to serve as Interim Superintendent for 60 days, with a one-time extension of 120 days while the search for a new superintendent was conducted. He had worked in the school system for more than 30 years after arriving in 1939 as a teacher and coach at Osbourn High School in Manassas. He served as a principal in several different schools, and in 1963 assumed his duties in the personnel office.

During this period, all school superintendents had to meet the graduate education and experience requirements established by the State Board of Education to be placed on the eligibility list for superintendents. Superintendents were appointed for four-year terms and their appointment had to be approved by the State Board of Education. State law required that all appointments be made in the 60-day period preceding May 1, or the State Board was empowered to make the appointment for the local school board from the eligibility list. Mr. Saunders lacked the necessary graduate work to be placed on the eligibility list for superintendents.

However, in January 1973, Bill Wright, the finance director and clerk of the school board for the school system, informed the board that the 120-day period the state Board had approved for Saunders would expire on February 10, 1973. Although the deadline for applications for the superintendent's position was January 15, 1973, the board did not have enough time to review all applicants and complete the necessary interviews for a permanent superintendent to be selected. Wright also quipped that from the description of the job in the superintendent search brochure, nobody but Moses would be qualified for the position, and Moses had not applied. He said that there were about 50 candidates, with three applicants from within the school system.

Mr. Saunders informed the board that he had contacted staff in the Virginia Department of Education to explain the legal problems of the dispute over the appointment of the two conflicting local school boards and the uncertainties of the Supreme Court's decision and the conflicting actions of the Board of County Supervisors in interpreting the legal status of the school board. To resolve the issue, the Prince William County School Board requested that the State Board of Education place Saunders' name temporarily on the Eligibility List of Qualified Division Superintendents so he could serve as a permanent superintendent for a brief period to complete the remainder of the unexpired term of Stuart Beville, the former superintendent, through June 30, 1973.

The State Board of Education approved the request with the stipulation that Saunders would only be qualified to serve as permanent superintendent until June 30, 1973. In addition, he was approved as qualified for service only in Prince William County, and his name would be removed from the eligibility list after June 30, 1973. Following approval by the State Board of Education, the Prince William County School Board named Saunders as Division Superintendent of Schools to complete the unexpired term of Stuart Beville.

After this action, Mr. Saunders advised the board that the word "interim" would be removed from his title and that a portion of his salary would be reimbursable by the state, as it was for all permanent superintendents. As a result of this unique action on the part of the State Board of Education, Saunders served the brief period from February 10, 1973, to June 30, 1973, as permanent superintendent of Prince William County Schools.

In some respects, Saunders may have had plans to become permanent superintendent of schools in Prince William County resulting from his actions in dealing directly with the State Board of Education and in changing his title from "interim" to "full-time" superintendent of schools in the county. Also, as I now view the situation, and, in my opinion, Herb Saunders may have believed that he could continue to influence his eligibility by being able to bypass the credentialing requirements of the State Board of Education and, perhaps, become the full-time Superintendent of Schools of Prince William County, Virginia, beginning July 1, 1973.

• • •

During my telephone conversation with Ellis Hawkins in March 2014, a few weeks before he passed away, Ellis told me that he had no intention to hire Herb Saunders as permanent Superintendent of Schools to replace Stuart Beville in the spring of 1973. He and the Prince William County School Board were unanimous in planning to seek a new Division Superintendent of Schools who had no political ties to Virginia or in Prince William County.

As a result, my goal in beginning the job as Division Superintendent of Schools in July 1973 was to provide equal educational opportunities for all students, and to design a strategic plan to educate students in a diverse multicultural student population in a year round school district and remain separate from the ongoing political problems existing in the county.

Essay 2.   1973-1977

My Years as Division Superintendent of Schools, Prince William County, Manassas, Virginia

In the summer of 1973, I arrived in Prince William County as the Vietnam War continued to generate widespread protests and demonstrations in Washington. The country was also becoming aware of the ramifications of the Watergate cover-up in daily revelations as reported in The Washington Post and in the investigations and testimony given in the Congressional hearings on the role of the White House in the scandal. After I relocated with my family in the southern suburbs of Washington, DC, each morning The Washington Post arrived in my driveway. For me, Watergate was a current-events interest and a local interest. The county was located only 25 miles south of the Capitol, and many of its residents were civilian or military staff employed by the federal government, and they had an intense interest in the ongoing crisis of this, the historic Constitutional struggle occurring in our backyard. As a result, it was an unusually riveting and exciting time to be in the Washington area.

During the first week of June 1973, I made an informal visit to the county to meet with school board members and top staff who would be working closely with me when I officially began my duties on July 1. I stressed to the news media that I was coming to the county with a completely open mind and that I looked forward to creating conditions in the school system for community involvement. In

an earlier trip, I had visited several schools and was impressed with the enthusiasm of the students and the obvious learning that was occurring.

At my first official school board meeting in July, members reelected Ellis Hawkins as chairman and Tom Beane as vice chairman. Both were long-time residents dedicated to the welfare of the school system and both had been steadfast in guiding the school board through a legal and political dispute with the Board of County Supervisors that had attempted to dismiss all of them from office in 1972 and install a new school board of its choosing.

The board appointed assistant superintendent Herb Saunders as Clerk of the Board to replace Finance Director Bill Wright, who had served for some time and wished to be relieved of his duties. The board appointed assistant superintendent Ernest Mueller as the Deputy Clerk. On my recommendation the board approved the employment of a secretary to assist the board and the superintendent in conducting board meetings and in maintaining the official minutes of the board. This was a new position for which current employees could apply, and it proved invaluable for providing an organized record-keeping system of board actions.

In my first days as schools superintendent, at a meeting with the Board of County Supervisors I quickly became aware that the struggle with the governing body was far from over when my supervisor of transportation, Fred Fluckinger, disputed a report made by an advisory committee to the supervisors that recommended the consolidation of the school bus fleet and school vehicles into a county motor pool under the control of the county executive and the board of supervisors. The supervisors' transportation advisory committee that proposed this consolidation was chaired by George Mullen, a political activist, and included supervisor Roy Doggett who had been supported by Mullen in the last election. This dispute would continue to surface later in my tenure when George Mullen was appointed to the school board.

In my first school board meetings, I quickly became aware of another contentious issue that would consume much of my future time and attention which involved the completion of Osbourn Park High School. Ranger Construction Company from Atlanta had been awarded the contract to build the new school, but was behind schedule. The school board had been negotiating with Ranger over the amount of time it would take to finish the project, but a satisfactory agreement had not been reached.

After reviewing the board agenda format, I made several changes which board members appreciated. They especially liked the placing of "citizens' time" at the beginning of each meeting, and both Chairman Hawkins and I urged citizens to attend and to express their opinions and concerns.

I presented a plan for streamlining the schedule for the preparation and presentation of the school board budgeting process. The timeline called for immediate internal development by the staff, review and changes by the board, holding a public hearing, revision as necessary and final presentation at a joint session with the board of supervisors since they controlled all the county revenue and set the tax rate. Board members were obviously pleased with the schedule and promptly approved it.

One of the most enjoyable duties of my job as superintendent was in welcoming new teachers to the school system and sharing with them my belief that they are the key to learning and that I would do

everything I could to support them in having a successful career. It was my pleasure to welcome 319 new teachers to the county at a meeting that I held in coordination with the Chamber of Commerce. Chamber members provided a kit of information and gifts and presented a program about the local community and economy. The teachers were also matched with a chamber member who would provide information about rental property, shopping, transportation, and any other information they might need in adjusting to their new community.

On school opening day in 1973, 34,400 students enrolled in county schools, and before the end of the school year, an additional 2200 would be added to the student population. I visited a number of schools on opening day and was impressed by the neat appearance of the campuses and the good order in which principals began the school year.

In September at a joint meeting of the school board and board of supervisors, the George Mullen/Roy Doggett transportation plan for the consolidation of the school system vehicles into a county motor pool controlled by the county executive and the supervisors was hotly debated. I presented a counter proposal to separate the school board and county vehicles as a more viable and workable solution, since the principals needed to work closely with school bus drivers in ensuring the safety of the children and since there was the obvious need to promptly respond to any breakdowns or problems buses might encounter on routes covering over 300 square miles from the Potomac River to the Bull Run Mountains. No action was taken, but eventually my proposal prevailed, and the school board was able to maintain its authority over its own transportation fleet, facilities, and staff.

Prior to my arrival the school board had approved a bond referendum proposal for $30,000,000 for converting all the school buildings to accommodate the year round school calendar, for constructing additional elementary schools, and for building another high school and for adding two new stadiums to the two high schools that didn't have them. But inflation had now become an important factor pushing costs much higher and forcing the board into coming back to the voters with yet another bond issue in the near future and risking bond exhaustion. Therefore, I recommended that the board not move forward until an outside review and cost updating of the bond proposal was completed.

I shared my concerns with the board about the adequacy of this bond proposal in meeting the county's future construction needs and felt that we should have an objective evaluation, in addition to my own assessment, before moving forward. On my recommendation the board contracted with Dr. Carol McGuffey, a nationally recognized facilities and educational planning professor at the University of Georgia, to study the county's school construction needs and the administrative organizational structure and report his findings and recommendations to the board.

After completing his study of the proposed $30,000,000 bond plan, Dr. McGuffey and his team reported to the board that my recommendation for the board to reconsider the bond was a "wise move" on the part of the new superintendent and that more study should be given to the conversion of all schools to a year round schedule, the additional space requirements for adding kindergartens, and the impact of inflation that was increasing as the Vietnam War continued with no peace in sight. However, the school board wished to continue with a separate bond referendum for the building of the two stadiums at the two new high schools that didn't have them in order to equalize facilities at all high schools.

Therefore, I moved forward to meet with citizens and parents to encourage support for a bond referendum on the November 6, 1973, ballot for $540,000 to build stadiums at Woodbridge and Osbourn Park High Schools since the other highs schools already had stadiums. When I appeared before the board of supervisors and made the case for placing the stadium bond referendum on the ballot (which required

the governing body's approval), only two of the so-called "Four Horsemen" voted against it, and I was able to convince the other five members of the board to allow the voters to make the decision on the stadiums in the November election.

Since the bond issue was now going to be decided by the voters, I appointed a chairman at each school to build support for the vote so each school would have equal facilities. I stressed the need for community involvement in the bond drive, and board chairman Ellis Hawkins remarked that, "In its previous actions, the board has received some criticism for a lack of citizen involvement on issues and objectives. I think this is a fine direction; one we should be following."

In October 1973, I announced the architects for the stadium designs. Roy Pentecost, who designed the new Stonewall Jackson High School and the new Osbourn Park High School, would design the stadium for Osbourn Park.

Phillip Brown, who designed the new Garfield High School and the new Woodbridge High School, would design the stadium for Woodbridge. Jack Saylor of the bond *ad hoc* committee remarked that in Dr. Milton Snyder, "You will see a big swing in the way the educational program is run in the future. Dr. Snyder is committed to the total involvement of the community."

In the fall of 1973, I announced my initiative to end the textbook rental system that had a long history in the county and said that I was totally opposed to it. I wanted to eliminate it for the next school year. I also announced to a gathering of parents that I would be working to initiate a public kindergarten system in the county in the next school year. I would continue my major endeavor to ensure the increased participation and involvement of parents in the making of school decisions and changes.

In November, the stadium bond issue passed by a 2,400 vote margin which was attributed in large part to the community involvement that I initiated. As I remarked after the results were in, "I can't say enough about those members of the *ad hoc* committees who did so much to put it over the top." The *ad hoc* committees were to continue to advise the board on plans for the facilities and would cease efforts after the new stadiums were dedicated.

In November 1973, board of supervisors' member Don Turner nominated Regis Lacey to replace Paul Boots on the school board for a term beginning on January 1, 1974. Supervisor Ralph Mauller objected strenuously and wanted to reappoint Paul Boots who had been redistricted from Turner's district into Mauller's district. But the other supervisors agreed with Turner's choice and approved Mr. Lacey's appointment.

Supervisor Roy Doggett nominated Robert Boyd, a prison guard, to replace attorney Paul Arrington on the school board for a term to begin on March 1, 1974. Boyd was a local political supporter of Doggett's in Manassas and had previously been Doggett's appointee on the Social Services Board.

As the winter of 1973-74 approached, we had to cope with an unanticipated energy crisis which would have a great impact on the operations and budgets of all school districts in the country. By the early 1970s, American oil consumption—in the form of gasoline and other products—was rising even as domestic oil production was declining, leading to an increasing dependence on oil imported from abroad.

Despite this, Americans worried little about a dwindling supply or a spike in prices, and were encouraged by policymakers in Washington, who believed that Arab oil exporters couldn't afford to lose the revenue from the U.S. market. These assumptions were demolished when an oil embargo imposed by Arab oil exporting countries led to fuel shortages and sky-high prices throughout much of the decade.

After decades of abundant supply and growing consumption, Americans now faced price hikes and fuel shortages, causing lines to form at gasoline stations in the county and around the country. Local, state, and national leaders called for measures to conserve energy, asking gas stations to close on Sundays and homeowners to refrain from putting up holiday lights on their houses. With the energy shortage and cutbacks on thermostats, long johns and sweaters were big Christmas sellers.

In dealing with this crisis, I described to the school board steps the schools were taking to conserve energy without disrupting our educational programs. The heat in all county schools was lowered to 68 degrees, all school vehicles were to travel no more than 50 miles per hour, all pep and spectator buses would cease, and principals were asked to eliminate half of all field trips. Other measures were taken to save on heat, lighting and gasoline. Schools that normally had interior lights on at night would be dark.

If energy supplies for the schools were cut further or the amount of fuel on hand was insufficient to last through the winter, then more drastic measures would be instituted. Contingency planning was underway to deal with these threats as well as any other problems that might arise as a result of the oil embargo.

In presenting my 1974-75 projected school budget, I had included $400,000 to supply free textbooks for the first time. I also added two planetariums at two high schools to enhance our science program. I explained that I had to increase the general services budget because of an 80% inflation increase in oil and gas supplies for the schools and school buses.

During one of my appearances before the board of supervisors, a local women's club was there and reviewed what they had observed afterward over lunch. One woman who had attended said, "They call public employees up there and then berate them. It's very humiliating."

Another observed that one of the supervisor's "...English was atrocious. Everyone reads it in the paper, but my husband always thought the supervisor was misquoted until he went to a public hearing once and heard it in person."

The women concluded that the supervisors "...

did very little homework. It's a shame; it consumes everyone's time."

After the supervisors had been in office for two years, one writer felt that the chances for local government stability were brighter, "...because the courts thwarted some of the more dangerous actions of some of the new board men—particularly an obvious effort to dominate the county school board. It helped ameliorate the so-called 'Four Horsemen' coalition which for a time appeared to gallop under a battle cry of 'Rule or Ruin!' Scorn was heaped on all who stood in their way."

This continuous barrage of criticism showed widespread dissatisfaction with the governing style of the "Four Horsemen" and seemed to be having some effect on the coalition because at the opening January 1974 organizing session, the board elected supervisor Charles Colgan as chairman and re-elected Don Turner as vice chairman. Colgan had not been a member of the "Four Horsemen" and had been a strong supporter of the county schools in opposing their actions. He later was elected to the Virginia State Senate where he became the longest serving member in the history of that body.

In March 1974 Dr. Carol McGuffey of the University of Georgia presented the findings from his study of the school construction needs in the county. He recommended building another high school, modernizing 38 existing schools to equalize educational facilities throughout the county, upgrading facilities for year round schools, and adding an inflation factor to account for future cost increases. Based on the recommendation from the county's financial advisors, he advised deferring the $40,300,000 bond to a later date because the county had $15,000,000 in bonds up for sale, and he didn't think it would be wise to put another bond referendum on the ballot until these county bonds were sold. He also observed that the board of supervisors should not continue to try to act as a "super board of education."

The board commended Dr. McGuffey for performing a thorough job of analyzing school needs.

A newspaper editorial commented, "It was indeed wise of Dr. Milton Snyder, the county schools superintendent, to bring Dr. McGuffey and his team of experts in before proceeding with a bond referendum. The report provides an excellent foundation from which the county can now determine its school construction course."

McGuffey and his team also made recommendations for school management restructuring to me and to the school board. He recommended that the areas of school services, finance, and school plant under Ernest Mueller be separated. Finance should report directly to the superintendent, and school services should be consolidated under a new assistant superintendent. Other changes were recommendations for the personnel department to eliminate the position of assistant superintendent and be reorganized under a director of personnel, reporting to the associate superintendent of instruction, Carl Riehm. I explained to the board that I would not be asking for increased expenditures for the new management staff, but that I would focus on moving existing personnel. Ernest Mueller resigned to become superintendent of the Pennsbury school district in Bucks County, Pennsylvania, a suburb of Philadelphia, and Herb Saunders remained as director of personnel.

In the spring of 1973, student unrest at Gar-Field High School required my attention and action. There were reports of fights, disorderly conduct, students demonstrating outside the building, drug problems, verbal abuse and disrespect for teachers, and calls to police for help. Ten policemen helped the staff break up fights and restore order by handcuffing students and taking them away in cruisers. I took swift action to protect students and staff by transferring the principal and hired Dr. David Myers from the Arlington County school system to serve as principal. We dispatched human relations counselors to assist in restoring order and discipline at the school which soon had a smooth transition to a year-round school schedule.

The new kindergarten program (for which I had

fought so hard) was finally in operation, opening in July 1974 in all the elementary schools that were on the year-round school calendar, and was off to a good start. Kindergartens opened on morning and afternoon shifts in order to have adequate space in each school and to provide a savings in hiring additional teachers.

In May 1974 we lost a strong supporter of the schools from the board of supervisors when Dr. Ferlazzo suffered a heart attack and subsequently had to resign for health reasons. He, Charles Colgan, and Vernon Dawson composed the minority members who had opposed the actions of the "Four Horsemen" in their attempt to take over the school system and replace the school board with their hand-picked supporters. A three judge panel appointed a former supervisor and stock broker, Andrew Donnelly, to complete Dr. Ferlazzo term of office.

At the school board organizing meeting in July 1974, Ellis Hawkins was reelected chairman of the school board and Tom Beane was also reelected to serve as vice chairman, but his term would expire during the next year. The new associate superintendent for school services, Mark Rothacker, was named clerk of the board to replace personnel director Herb Saunders, who had filled the clerk's position for the previous year.

The board was pleased to hear my report that the unrest at the new Gar-Field Senior High School had subsided under the leadership of the new principal, Dr. David Myers. The air-conditioned school had opened on an optional year-round school calendar. Dr. Myers explained that there were five attendance calendars in operation at Gar-Field with four of them being the 45-15 choices that were color coded as red, blue, green, and orange with one color always on a 15-day break while the other three occupied the school for 45 days. In addition, students had the option of attending on the traditional nine-month calendar with the three-month summer break. The optional aspect of the five school calendars was believed to be unique nationwide,

and both the board and I hailed the school staff, the principal, and the community on achieving this milestone of a successful year-round high school.

After completing my first year in office, I reviewed the four major goals that I had set for myself. My first goal was to advise the board on the thirty million dollar bond it had adopted before I arrived and had planned to place before the voters in May. Based on my recommendation and with the assistance of a thorough and objective study of current and future construction needs by Dr. Carol McGuffey and his team from the University of Georgia, I was able to present a revised bond proposal to the board that would take into consideration the inflation factor, the implementation of year round schools, and the addition of kindergarten space.

My second goal was to improve our communication with parents and citizens by establishing school planning councils consisting of parents, teachers, and administrators in each school that would develop school plans to be sent to the central office planning staff and consolidated into composite plan for the district to help the board in the development of policies and budgets. To reach my goal of improved communication, I directed that a series of school-community seminars be conducted in each school to determine school needs. Each school had seminars in which parents, teachers, and school administrators broke into small groups to wrestle with priority needs.

Groups then ranked on a prepared sheet the needs in order of importance until a consensus was reached and the documents were turned over to school principals. I spoke to each school with opening remarks by video tape and stressed that community involvement was essential as the schools belong to the community. I explained that the information would be compiled and used in budget development, in school goal-setting, and in the five-year plan.

My third goal was to have the school district meet the academic and school requirements that were in the state mandated Standards of Quality.

The Standards also required that we develop a five-year plan showing areas of improvement, and we completed the plan with the involvement of parents, teachers, and community.

My fourth goal was the implementation of a kindergarten program in all elementary schools, and although I encountered major resistance when I first proposed this goal, it soon became apparent that parents and citizens wanted it, and they wanted it now. The majority of the school board members strongly backed me, and the outpouring of overwhelming parental support soon overcame the opposition of some members of the board of supervisors. I consider the establishment of the kindergarten program in Prince William County as one of the greatest and most satisfying achievements of my career as a superintendent.

In October 1974, the Board of County Supervisors dismissed the county executive, J.J. Salovaara, with whom I had worked since I first arrived in Prince William County. He was replaced by Clinton Mullen who had impressed one supervisor as an aggressive manager "who comes on like a whirlwind." He had been a controversial figure in his 14 months as county manager in Powhatan County, Virginia, where he had resigned four months earlier after some supervisors reportedly expressed dissatisfaction with the direction he was taking in the county.

Probably the most time consuming and frustrating experience I had during my tenure in Prince William County involved the completing of the construction of the new Osbourn Park Senior High School, which was supposed to have been completed by December 1973, but was still unfinished in the fall of 1974.

The students who were to occupy the building were still being housed at the old Osbourn High School which was much too small for the increased enrollment, so there was an urgent need for a new and larger facility. As a result of the delay, the students at the old Osbourn building had to be placed on a double shift schedule. The "A" shift attended from 7:00 am until 12:00 noon. The "B" shift attended from 12:10 until 5:10 pm. Four mobile trailers and four Quonset huts were added to provide additional space. I had a great sense of urgency and responsibility to have the students in the new school as soon as possible.

Construction of the $7,600,000 contract to build the high school had been awarded to Ranger Construction Company of Atlanta in December 1971, with a completion deadline of December 1973. Ranger had completed about 75 percent of the work, but the progress had slowed to such an extent that it was already mentioned by the school board as a serious issue when I first arrived in July 1973. Only a crew of 10-12 workmen had been seen at the construction site over the past several months. The roof needed to be redone since it was only partially and incorrectly installed by Ranger. There was a substantial amount of work that was improperly done, and taking it apart and redoing it would take more time. The school was already more than a year behind schedule.

Dr. Paul Trautman, School Plant Services Director, estimated that there would be a need for $2,240,000 to complete the school. These funds would be in addition to the $1,800,000 still in the original funds allocated for Osbourn Park construction. The additional funds would need to be raised by obtaining a low-interest loan from the Virginia Public School Authority or from the county's general fund. In any case, the board of supervisors would need to approve the action. My prime goal was to get the school finished so that Osbourn High School students would not be on double shifts for another year.

The school board had employed Tremblay and Smith, a Charlottesville law firm, to advise on legal options that might be needed in dealing with Ranger. There was some discussion about Ranger's proposal for a new contract to finish the school, but I was opposed and gave the board my recommendation:

"In view of Ranger's history of performance here

and elsewhere, I cannot recommend a new contract with Ranger. There is no evidence available to indicate that a new contract will produce a completed project. All evidence is to the contrary."

As a result, the school board voted unanimously to terminate the contract with Ranger because of default on the agreement. I took steps to notify Ranger and its bonding company, Travelers Indemnity Company, of the board's decision. The board authorized me to secure the site, conduct an inventory of materials stored there, provide an estimate of cost for completing the project, and direct Travelers to bring the bond into full force and effect. The board of supervisors were briefed in a joint session with the school board.

The supervisors were concerned about the source of the additional funds needed. I explained that the funding would depend upon Travelers' decision to either concur or disagree with the school board's decision. Travelers' Indemnity Company held the bond for Ranger Construction, and under terms of the bond, Travelers must pay for completing the school unless it could prove that the school board breached the original contract. Supervisor Roy Doggett concluded the joint meeting by telling school board members, "Somebody must have screwed you all!"

Ranger responded to its dismissal with a lawsuit against the school board charging breach of contract, conspiracy, libel, and defamation of character. The federal suit asked for damages on each of three counts totaling $13,500,000. This action set off a complicated legal tangle in which everyone was suing everyone else with court cases pending in the local circuit court and in the Federal District Court. The gaggle of complaints was further complicated by subcontractors who were not paid for their work by Ranger. Two subcontractors had already sued Ranger, which in turn asked the courts to charge the money to the school board.

More suits kept being filed in the courts because Ranger had failed to pay a substantial number of subcontractors. Some had completed their work; others walked off the job. The school board won the first round in federal court when the judge approved having all the cases consolidated together under the purview of the federal court.

The school board counter-sued that construction problems at Osbourn Park High School were the fault of Ranger Construction. I officially notified Travelers Indemnity Company that the school board expected it to make good on its bond guaranteeing the completion of the school. The school board also asked the court to charge Ranger liquidated damages at the rate of $500 per day for every day of lateness, which had reached 400 days.

In order to resume and finish the construction of the school, I recommended the hiring of a construction manager who would be paid a salary and related expenses to coordinate and supervise the work and could hire subcontractors. This plan would get the job done faster and cheaper than a general contractor.

Despite the seriousness of all the legal actions occurring during this time, a lighter moment occurred one evening as the school board meeting was about half over when a U.S. Marshal entered the chambers to serve more suits related to the Ranger Construction legal controversy. As he looked into the half-full board chambers, the Marshal apologized, "I don't have enough for all of you; I'll just have to give out what I have." Then he proceeded to call each board member's name, and deliver the federal suits.

The Marshal had attempted to serve suits at members' homes earlier.

"Are you the one with the German Shepherd?" he asked Clay Wood.

"Yes, and I've got another one ordered," Wood quipped.

Bill Dunn laughed and said, "So that's why you looked so ripped up by the time you got to my house." The board had received so many legal papers over the Osbourn Park case that being sued had almost become routine.

The school board requested joint meetings

with the board of supervisors to assure that there would be sufficient funds available to complete the Osbourn Park project because supervisors must approve funds before construction could be restarted. This led to long debates and much shouting on the part of some of the more colorful supervisors. Although Travelers was the bonding agent for guaranteeing enough money to complete the building, that outcome was dependent on the school board winning its case against Ranger in federal court.

Supervisor Ralph Mauller, in another attack of "Mauller Mania," fiercely opposed approval of any funds for the project and railed against it saying it was "one of the wildest schemes" he had ever heard of. Supervisor Winfield complained about me, saying, "They made a mistake when they hired Dr. Snyder. He's not doing the job—when did he qualify himself to build schools? He's running a one-man show over there!"

However, Supervisor Colgan defended me in the fight for funds to finish Osbourn Park by blasting supervisors who were "overreaching without getting all the facts. I'm going to put my faith in Dr. Snyder as superintendent of schools. He's carrying the ball now—let him carry it. It disappoints me to see people acting like a bunch of children. To get the school completed is the big thing."

On the Osbourn Park joint meeting, a writer commented that "the outbursts of Winfield and Mauller on the Osbourn Park issue show both of whom are so obsessed by a mistrust of the school board that it discolors almost every effort for the two boards to work together."

I warned the supervisors that "any further delays beyond the current week will delay the opening of the new school next year by as much time as it takes to arrive at a solution." After another long debate, punctuated with shouting and much banging of the gavel in an attempt to keep order, the supervisors voted 5-1 to approve $2,100,000 to complete the school. Mauller opposed the action, and Doggett was absent.

I spoke to the supervisors and said, "I commend the supervisors for having the foresight and strength to move ahead in order to finish this building for boys and girls." At its next meeting, the school board voted to approve my recommendation to award a contract to CM Associates of Houston to oversee completion of Osbourn Park High School. Charles Martini became the construction manager for the project and quickly had 110 workers on the job. Martini projected that he planned to have the school ready for occupancy by August 15, 1975, in time for the opening of school that fall.

At another Board of County Supervisors meeting, members Mauller and Winfield of the "Four Horsemen" group complained about my salary raise the school board had approved. Winfield said, "what upsets me is that the school board increased Dr. Snyder's salary by $1,900 and gave him a new car." Winfield was also upset that the school board gave me a vote of confidence.

Mauller agreed and offered a motion that the supervisors be on record as saying that I was doing a "perfectly horrible job." Mauller's motion died for lack of a second.

In 1975 the towns of Manassas and Manassas Park announced plans to convert to city status if they didn't get tax relief from the county, probably in the form of revenue sharing. Their actions would become even more likely if the county had another large bond referendum for schools. Both towns decided to become cities shortly after making the announcement of their intentions.

This action would affect the composition of the county school board since Robert Boyd lived in the city and would have to resign from the Prince William County school board. He did resign and was later appointed to the new Manassas City School Board. To replace Robert Boyd on the county board, supervisor Doggett recommended Emily Rosenberg, who lived outside the new city of Manassas.

The food service in the Prince William schools was decentralized, with each school's cafeteria manager and principal operating independently, and in most cases, differently. Some schools ran a surplus in the funds they collected from the sale of school lunches while others had little or nothing left over. The cafeterias also had to ensure that they were meeting the federal guidelines governing standards for school lunches, as well as the requirements of the local health food safety laws and regulations.

Therefore, I instituted a plan to centralize all schools' food services under the direction of a supervisor and staff to ensure uniformity in school cafeteria operations and in meeting federal and local standards. Under the leadership of Associate Superintendent Mark Rothacker and Supervisor of Food Services Nellie Curtis, uniform accounting practices were developed and instituted so that cafeteria funds were accounted for and used to support the program and not for unrelated purposes, such as the example of one school using cafeteria funds to purchase an air conditioner for the teachers' lounge. It also centralized the funds so that they could be transferred from one school to another to help a school with needs that others did not have in the student population.

In 1975 we had several changes on school board membership. As I have mentioned, Emily Rosenberg replaced Robert Boyd. In addition, supervisor Scott Winfield replaced Tom Beane from the Coles District with George Mullen in March 1975.

Bill Dunn, school board member from the Gainesville District, announced that he would run as an independent from that district for the supervisor's seat of Charles Colgan, who had announced that he would run for the State Senate. In addition, Tom Beane, who had just left the school board, announced that he would run for the Virginia House of Delegates.

On my executive staff, Dr. Carl Riehm announced that he would accept a position in the Virginia Department of Education in Richmond as an assistant superintendent. He would be replaced by Earl Phillips, our director of secondary education. Director of personnel and former interim superintendent Herb Saunders resigned on June 30, after 36 years in the school system.

The new Manassas City School Board named Jim Leo, one of our middle school principals and former assistant principal and coach at Osbourn High School, as acting superintendent, who said that he was working toward meeting requirements for being placed on the State Board of Education's list of those qualified for superintendent.

In August 1975 I recommended, and the school board appointed, Ruby Strickland as the first African-American woman to serve as a school principal in Prince William County. She was appointed to the principal's job at Washington-Reid Elementary School. Strickland had served as assistant principal at Parkside School since 1972 and had worked in the school system since 1963.

The "Four Horseman" on the board of supervisors never missed an opportunity to complain about me. At a joint meeting of the Board of County Supervisors and the School Board to review the proposed schools budget for the next year, supervisor Winfield made a motion that he would be willing to vote to supply $60,000 to buy out the superintendent's contract. As before, the motion died for lack of a second. After the meeting, Clay Wood, a school board member of 24 years, announced he would be a candidate for the board of county supervisors from the Brentsville District currently held by one of the "Four Horsemen," Ralph Mauller, a constant critic of the school board and superintendent.

The long-delayed Osbourn Park High School project moved on to completion under the supervision of a construction manager as I had recommended. It was clear that the new school would be ready for occupancy in late August 1975, in time for the fall school term. Finally, I could announce that Osbourn Park High School was finished and ready for students on September 2, 1975. It is clear now that in replacing Ranger Construction, we chose the right path to ensure that the work was done on time and under the estimated budget.

As a newspaper editorial observed, "The school board, Dr. Snyder and his staff, and others who worked on the project have a right to be proud that they had the guts to gamble. They placed all their efforts and their votes on the line to serve students, and they won."

More than five years later—and after I had left—the school board finally was awarded $3,100,000 in a court settlement with Ranger Construction and its bonding company, Travelers Indemnity. A newspaper writer editorialized, "It is the ultimate vindication of the wisdom of former schools superintendent, Dr. Milton Snyder, as well as former school board chairman, Ellis Hawkins. There were many others involved, but these people led the way. They convinced others that the dangerous course of suing Ranger and completing the school alone was correct. Mr. Hawkins and Dr. Snyder set a simple goal—to get students into the building as quickly as possible, then fight the legal battle to its conclusion. We can, at least, say thank you. Thank you for the money, for the high school, and for the courage to take an unpopular and dangerous course aimed at providing education for students."

In 1976 I experienced some conflict among school board members in surveying parents on allowing the board to adopt mandatory year-round school programs. The school board policy required that no community would be placed on year-round school without community input and a formal survey. After the parents returned the forms, an outside agency would compile the results.

After the school administration had contracted with Virginia Tech (in a small contract of $2,000) to tabulate the results of the survey, new school board members Emily Rosenberg and George Mullen objected, as Emily Rosenberg growled with her teeth clenched in anger, "This staff is usurping the board's prerogatives." She had thought the staff would contact outside firms for bids and give the board a choice. I explained that the funds came from the contracting services of the budget and were budgeted for this sort of expenditure.

Mullen and Rosenberg did not agree and Mullen maintained, "we can't leave ourselves wide open for the staff to take a resolution of ours and go out and spend money."

I defended the staff and replied, "You have made two accusations against this staff which are not true. I will not permit the staff to be dealt with in this fashion." The board was informally polled and members were unwilling to stop the survey because of Rosenberg and Mullen's objections.

In November 1976 a newspaper editorial noted that my contract would expire on June 30, 1977, and that the school board should be prepared to make a decision on renewal prior to that deadline. It also noted that the political rumors included suggestions that there were deep divisions among school board members on the subject of my contract renewal. The editorial continued that "it would be a sad state of affairs if the school superintendent were to become the focal point of a political tug-of-war. Dr. Snyder's contributions to Prince William County are too great to be subjected to such treatment. He must be judged on his record of positive achievement. In our opinion, Dr. Snyder should be kept here if he will have us. We are indeed fortunate to have a man of his stature."

In December 1976 the school board discussed the renewal of my contract for a second four-year term. By a 4-3 vote the board expressed its interest to rehire me, even though the resolution had no legal effect, because under state law, a school superintendent can only be hired between March 1 and May 1 for the four-year contract period, which begins on July 1. Board members Beane, Hawkins, and Lacey had already indicated their support and Bill Dunn joined them in voting for my contract renewal. The opposition of George Mullen, Emily Rosenberg, and Herb Saunders was also clear.

Saunders' opposition dates from the time when his position as assistant superintendent of personnel was reorganized to director of personnel. He then retired and was later appointed to the school board to replace John Pattie, who had served 24 years. Saunders said that he voted against the resolution because he wanted to choose among candidates for superintendent who might apply for the job if it were advertised.

Lacey said in backing my reappointment that the board should look at my accomplishments "… including completion of Osbourn Park High School, development of comprehensive special education plan, expansion of year-round school program, implementation of a kindergarten program, and development of a program for the gifted and talented students. People of his caliber come only once in a great while. I encourage you to extend Dr. Snyder's contract for four more years."

By early 1977 it had become obvious to me that the 1972 change in the method of appointing school board members by the Board of County Supervisors instead of the School Board Trustees method was beginning to reflect the wishes of the "Four Horsemen" coalition of supervisors who had assumed majority leadership in 1972. Their attempt to dismiss the previously appointed school board was blocked by a Virginia Supreme Court decision in 1973. However, as the terms of old school board members expired, new ones were selected and appointed by the board of supervisors.

As the years went on during my tenure, the original board members who had hired me were replaced by the supervisors' choices. Two of the school board members who were replaced had served for 24 years each. Only one board member was left of my original board members. Tom Beane, who had been replaced by George Mullen, was again reappointed to another term. The other six old members were replaced by new ones which helped to create a different atmosphere and philosophy. This made it more difficult to reach consensus on goals and direction for the school system.

This change in philosophy was expressed by Mrs. Rosenberg, who had been appointed by one of the "Four Horseman," supervisor Roy Doggett.

She thought that she got her appointment "because I said I wanted to blow up the schools. I went onto the board with the idea that the schools were using too much of the tax dollar. We were put on the board because we had a negative attitude toward education." This attitude was reflected by some of the other new board members, who appeared to view the staff with suspicion and mistrust and seemed to hassle and belittle the staff over reports and agenda items.

At times tempers would flare among board members and concern for issues would give way to wrangling over procedures. Board approval and scrutiny was increasingly required on relatively small board matters to the point that it could be interpreted as micromanagement of the school system by individual board members. Some of the new board members frequently projected themselves like politicians by giving lengthy justifications for their votes on minor items.

After the vote of confidence on the renewal of my contract in December on a 4-3 vote, it was obvious that a deep division among school board members existed on the subject of my contract renewal. It appeared that some of the newly appointed board members reflected the same goal as often expressed by the "Four Horsemen" supervisors to end my contract.

A newspaper editorial expressed the opinion that, "If the school board is contemplating any replacement of Dr. Snyder, it would do well to consider that in making such a replacement, it will be dealing with an unknown quality. Snyder's knowledge and experience in running a school system must be the hub of any discussion. These positive qualities have been amply demonstrated during the period of his incumbency. We are indeed fortunate to have a man of his stature."

In March 1977, the Board of County Supervisors replaced two of the School Board men who had hired me, Ellis Hawkins and Bill Dunn, with Michael O'Donnell and Phyllis O'Toole. Tom Beane was the only board member remaining who had hired me in 1973. I did not know the views of these new board members, but I had to assume that at least one of them would probably reflect the same views as the "Four Horsemen" about not renewing my contract.

I had been the target of dispute for at least the past year as the newly appointed board members replaced the previous ones and increasingly made it difficult for the board to conduct its business in a timely and efficient manner. I felt that I had given my best effort in leading the school system as I was hired to do.

Now with my leadership thwarted, undermined, and challenged by some board members, I felt I needed to review the situation to determine what was best for my family and me, as well as the school system. Therefore, I conferred with board members—both those who supported me and those who did not—in an attempt to determine clearly where my future lay.

After much serious discussion and receiving a frank assessment of my situation as the board members viewed it, I made the decision to submit my resignation as school superintendent, effective June 30, 1977. In my statement to the board, I indicated that I was leaving for personal reasons, and informed them that, "at this time, it is impossible to consider a continuation of the contract for a new four-year period."

Tom Beane said, "It was with great personal reluctance and sadness on my part…" that he voted to accept my resignation. Regis Lacey also expressed his disappointment and said, "I think he pulled us through extremely difficult times and could have brought us much farther ahead."

A local newspaper commented on my resignation by noting, "The unwarranted abuse which bordered on personal vilifications at times would have forced a less strong individual to throw in the towel long ago. The protracted struggle… has done the county schools no good. All the citizens of the county will be the losers for his leaving the system, but those who will suffer most are the students whose interests have been the object of Dr. Snyder's efforts."

Essay 3.   Narrative and Afterthoughts

My Experience as Division Superintendent, Prince William County, Manassas, Virginia

July 1, 1973, I assumed my duties as the permanent division superintendent of the Prince William County, Virginia school district and stepped into the central office located in Manassas, Virginia. Herb Saunders returned to his previous job as the assistant superintendent of personnel. His short service as interim superintendent following Stuart Beville's resignation was over.

Reflecting back on Herb's change in roles, it must have been difficult, if not impossible, for him to fully accept that his role had diminished. But, at the time, I intended to exercise my powers and responsibilities as division superintendent of schools and he was expected to report directly to me. Later in this essay, I will elaborate further on my perceptions and reasons for the deterioration of our working and personal relationships.

It is important to note that prior to July 1973, not only had I developed plans for an orderly process for dealing with the county political conflict, but I also had marshaled a select outside team of experienced planners and leaders with deep experience in the fields of school planning. I will describe some of these basic strategies for "jump-starting" a working plan that we hoped would restore stability to the school system during this period of turmoil and disruption.

The honor of entering the schools of Prince William County in July 1973 as Division Superintendent of Schools was a meaningful event in my life. It was an honor 40 years ago and remains a high point to have served with such a fabulous group of students, teachers, parents and patrons, the best an educator could ever hope for. Being a former leader of a public school district that in 2015 enrolls over 85,000 students is a distinction which I will carry the rest of my life. It is my hope that the Prince William community will continue to support Superintendent of Schools Dr. Steven Walts, the school board, teachers and staff as they provide a quality education that all students deserve.

The pride of leading the Prince William County Schools during the nineteen seventies gives me an opportunity to review and discuss the numerous accomplishments that the staff, school board and my executive team accomplished during the period of 1973-1977. It would be my hope that our leadership as educators during that period might be remembered and recorded as providing an excellent educational opportunity.

One of the first plans I recommended to the school board was to initiate a process to seek opinions from patrons, parents, students, and staff about the on-going conflict and battle existing and revolving throughout the county and school district. The basic purpose of the study was not only to garner feelings and opinions from residents in the area, but also to assess parents and patrons about their feelings on education in grades kindergarten through twelve in the county and their willingness to support its planning and development. The plan was intended to contract with an outside team to conduct a series of face-to-face interviews with critics, Board of County Supervisors, teachers, district principals/administrators, and key patrons/parents and provide an objective report about their views and opinions on the status of the educational program in the county.

I arranged a contract with Dr. Carol McGuffey, Professor, University of Georgia School of Education and Facilities Planning, and Dr. James M. Thrasher, Professor of Executive Management at United States International University (now known as Alliant International University in San Diego, CA), to give direction and leadership to the assessment project. These two experts in education facilities planning were given the task to assess the opinions of parents, patrons, staff and responsible leaders in the county regarding their perceptions of the status and needs of the school system. The McGuffey and Thrasher survey teams intended to elicit the hopes/aspirations of residents and opinions on the factors hindering the promotion of education planning in 1973-1977. I will outline key information that the McGuffey team received in the interviews and the specific recommendations proposed regarding management issues in the school district and its relationship to the county government.

A second accomplishment, for which I am most proud, occurred in 1973 or early 1974. I appointed the first African American female principal, Ruby Strickland, to the position of elementary principal at Washington-Reid School in the Dumfries District. Ruby replaced Happy Boozer, former principal at the school, who needed to return to South Carolina to care for an ill relative.

A third issue, during my four years in the county, included the building and modernization of six high schools, as well as several middle and elementary schools. Intensive work was done with architects, construction staff, principals and instructional staff to design and complete educational facilities to meet the Standards of Quality curriculum being developed in Richmond in the Virginia Department of Education.

A fourth project involved the continued implementation and expansion of the year-round school program that the school district had begun in 1971 in order to meet the demands for housing the exploding school population. I also recommended schools be renovated for the expansion of year-round programs by installing air conditioning and ventilation systems in older schools of the county. In addition, I established a new color-coded, quarters system for families to be able to coordinate their children's attendance at middle, elementary and high schools in the district in order to manage vacations at the same quarter period. In the year-round program, students were in the schools for 45 days and then had a 15 day school vacation resulting in four 45-day sessions to provide the 180 days of instruction required by state law. By utilizing this plan, the buildings could hold one-fourth more students, and thus were used year-round. This plan helped accommodate more students in each building, and hence reduced the need to construct more schools.

A fifth and major attainment that I recommended and started in 1975 was kindergarten enrollments for students. The decision was a first for school districts in the Commonwealth. The Department of Education proceeded to follow the lead of Prince William in proposing kindergarten programs be started in all school districts in Virginia. The decision was met with a negative response from the "Four Horsemen" members of the Board of County Supervisors, who complained that money was unavailable to begin and offer programs for "play school." The county governing body opposed the program, but the school board was adamant in their support and kindergarten started on time in 1975 in Prince William County schools.

Ellis Hawkins loved telling me about the "Four Horseman" members berating him as school board chairman for being influenced by the superintendent into accepting a "play school" program designed in California. Two supervisors lamented that kindergarten programs would only provide freedom for mothers to be away from their children so they could play bridge during the day. I remember the hundreds of parents demonstrating on the streets in favor of opening kindergarten programs and their support in 1974-75 for my recommendations.

A sixth accomplishment was bringing a critical measure of transparency to the office of superintendent of schools in the county. I realize that parents, staff, and patrons recognized and appreciated the importance of being transparent regarding policies and issues being proposed for consideration. After leaving the county, I received numerous letters from parents, patrons, and county leaders, as well as editorials and news articles, commending me for being so open with information.

A seventh achievement of which I am extremely proud is the enhancement and strengthening of diversity throughout the schools. I take credit for increasing the number of women promoted to principal and district-level administrative positions, and for improving plans of integration and multicultural education. In addition, an increase in the number and percentage of minority staff in the school district was achieved. I provided leadership in continuing peaceful integration and in working relations through employee diversity and quality education for minority students in the district.

An eighth attainment during the four years was to manage a large public school system in a positive manner, despite the negative pressures exerted on our work by the three newly appointed school board members who were appointed by the "Four Horsemen" on the governing body. Herb Saunders, following his resignation from the school district, was appointed by the Board of County Supervisors to become a member of the school board. After he was appointed, he joined two other newly appointed members, George Mullen and Emily Rosenberg, which became a minority voting bloc against almost every positive issue that was proposed for the schools. The good news about his appointment was that the local news media began reporting on almost every move he and the other two attempted. Later in this document I will describe in detail an important plan Saunders created that affected me to a great extent.

The ninth achievement for which I am proud was the Osbourn Park High School construction project that took four to five years to accomplish. In fact, the final report of its success was printed after I left the district. Several news stories relating to the project are available to read in the Appendices.

The Ranger Construction firm had signed contracts to begin construction of the new high school more than a year before I arrived, and it became clear to me that the project was seriously behind schedule. As a result of my previous consultant work in facilities planning in Washington state and California, I realized that the project was in deep trouble and needed immediate corrective action. At the same time, the University of Georgia study was beginning for the county schools. I asked Dr. Carol McGuffey of the University of Georgia and Dr. James Thrasher, former Executive Director of Educational Management in San Diego, to review the problems of the Osbourn Park High School construction project and recommend solutions.

Based on the advice I received from McGuffey and Thrasher and based on my previous experience in California and Washington state, I recommended to the school board that it declare Ranger Construction in non-conformance with the contract stipulations and dismiss the company for non-performance. They appeared to have no intention of finishing the job on time and it appeared to me that they were delaying the project in order to submit requests for budget extensions and change order payments, and planned to petition the "Four Horsemen" at the county level to seek more construction money and to bypass the school board and the new superintendent.

We eventually sued the Ranger Construction Company for damages as a result of their mismanagement of the Osbourn Park High School construction project. After I left as superintendent, the school board and county board won millions of dollars in the lawsuit. Later in this document, I will expand on and quote comments of Board of County Supervisors about the Osbourn Park High School construction feud.

Also, I urge readers of this essay to read the materials included in the Appendices including editorials and news articles printed in the local Potomac News and The Journal Messenger newspapers during the entire debacle. Lynne and Herald Grandstaff and their editor, Paul Muse, of the Potomac News deserve Pulitzer awards for their coverage of the entire Osbourn Park construction episode. For example, here is an editorial quote from their newspaper on August 22, 1975, authored by Lynne and Herald. Their words were a true summary review of accomplishments of the school board and staff regarding the completion of the construction project.

> "THEY DID IT — Hurrah! Osbourn Park High School is finished. … Credit for the success is due to schools Superintendent Dr. Milton L. Snyder, his staff, the Prince William County School Board, expert advisors hired by the school board and those supervisors who had the wisdom to support their school board. For others, a meal of crow is in order; those who said the school could not possibly be finished in September [1975] and that cost overruns would be millions of dollars higher than the School Board estimated have been proven wrong.
>
> "At a time when owners in other areas were renegotiating to return Ranger [Construction Company] to troubled construction projects, the School Board dared to venture on its own to complete the building by September. A few members of the Board of Supervisors dared to support them. … When the school board took its proposal and financial requirements to the supervisors, Ralph Mauller called the proposal 'a wild trip' and predicted that the estimated $2.1 million additional money needed would turn into $6 million. …

> "From the very beginning, Supervisor Charles Colgan declared his intention of backing the School Board and its administration. Supervisor Andrew Donnelly quickly made it clear that he would not sit quietly by and let Mr. Mauller be the only vocal board member. His voice answered Mauller's tirades. … The School Board, Dr. Snyder and his staff, CM Associates and others who worked on the project have a right to be proud that they had the guts to gamble. … They all placed their efforts and their votes on the line to serve students, and they won."
>
> excerpt: *Potomac News*, August 22, 1975. Editorial.

Critics and Supporters in My Term as Superintendent of Schools

To set the stage regarding my critics and supporters during the period of my serving as Division Superintendent of Schools, it seems appropriate to restate the basis for the unrest of county residents at this time. Rapid population growth and large numbers of new students created tensions in the county. These factors were reflected in the November 1971 elections for the Board of County Supervisors. The big issues were rampant development, overcrowded schools and the effect these conditions had on the tax rate. As a school superintendent in this maelstrom, I represented the largest share of the tax rate. Growth of the student population in any community is cause for additional spending to support new schools, additional teachers, and more instructional materials.

In the midst of this tumultuous county environment, I did not fully realize the extent of the conflict that would come to exist between Mr. Saunders and me. I should have known at the time that "no way in hell" was Herb Saunders planning to turn the reins of the office of superintendent over to a newcomer from California. He may have failed to fully appreciate my background of growing up in the hills of Northern Idaho as the son of a logging contractor where "lumberjacks" fought fairly, but disliked losing. My experience in Korea during 1951-1952 as a 22-year-old 1st Sgt and Gun Sgt. in A Battery of the 300th Armored 105 Field Artillery Battalion taught me some basic skills about management and leadership when dealing with older US Army veterans. Senior Artillery troops disliked taking orders from a new, young leader.

The "Four Horsemen" governing board members opposed everything that the school board and I proposed, and in their dissent they were like bird dogs pointing at pheasants in a field of corn. To be fair, the three minority members of Colgan, Dawson and Dr. Ferlazzo supported the school board and me throughout the four years. The "Four Horsemen," Scott Winfield, Ralph Mauller, Roy Doggett, and Don Turner, were committed critics throughout my four-year term. As a lead critic, Chairman Scott Winfield suggested in 1976 that he would like to appropriate funds to buy up my contract as a result of my recommendations regarding the construction of the new Osbourn Park High School and removing Ranger Construction from the project.

One of the most important basic skills elected politicians, educational leaders, military officers and business leaders fail to learn or understand is the ability to conceptualize the larger implications of a problem. The majority faction of the county supervisors in 1972 became so fixed in their own views that they failed to seek advice from competent, professional advisors in the search for credible and accurate solutions. The "Four Horsemen" got so mired in the trees that they lost sight of the forest. The school board and the three minority county board members sought guidance from professionals in the field for the solution and won a creditable solution for the county citizens.

The story of Prince William County, Virginia, during the 1970s, if made into a movie, would spend a majority of film time on the critics, especially the "Four Horsemen." In more than 70 years of educational study, work, planning and managing, I must count the Prince William experience as one I shall never forget. The Third Battle of Manassas is one of the exciting management opportunities of my life. My goal in rewriting the scenes of more than 40 years ago is to show present-day citizens and leaders in the county the dangers and successes of candidates they elect to offices.

I remember the hundreds of times I met in the Board of County Supervisors' chambers to present school budgets, respond to questions from Mauller, Doggett and Winfield regarding rumors, parent complaints, student or discipline issues. The meetings always began and ended by Ralph, Roy and Scott posing questions to me and delivering long lectures on what I needed to do to resolve problems. It was always a circus scene, and I had to be careful about giving promises and reacting to their complaints with information that had no relevance to the disputes. As I stood at the podium before the governing body, I often thought of Abraham Lincoln when he said, "The best thing about the future is that it comes only one day at a time."

One major issue in 1975-76 (regarding critics of me personally) changed matters when the county board was able to begin replacing the school board members who had hired me, with their own appointees. The first two newly appointed board members were George Mullen and Emily Rosenberg, who announced to the media that they would follow the "Four Horsemen" to prevent me from receiving a second four-year appointment. Mullen was the husband of [the late] Jacqueline Mullen from Coles District. She was one of those named for the new replacement school board that the "Four Horsemen" had proposed following their election in 1971. The third new member to join the school board was Herbert Saunders, who had resigned from his position with the school district as a result of my decision to demote him for violating a major new hiring policy in direct opposition to my specific direction.

As a result, the county board majority "Four Horsemen" were slowly beginning to achieve their original goal of taking over control of the school district. Herbert Saunders, who was known as the

"Gray Fox" for his gray hair and long tenure in the district, returned as a board member to be in a position of power in the school district. He had come full circle from coach at Osbourn High School in 1939 to principal of several schools, to the assistant superintendent for personnel, interim superintendent, and now, member of the board of education. Although he was unable to return as the permanent superintendent, he had secured an appointed political position in which he could assist the "Four Horsemen" in carrying out their desire to keep me from receiving a new four-year contract as superintendent of schools in 1977.

I will expand on the maneuvers of the "Gray Fox" to remain in the power circle of the school district and to influence personnel appointments, promotions and major policy issues.

Additional Facts and Antics of the Critics Continue

In order to set the record straight about the political power measures being taken in the county following the election of the Board of County Supervisors, I believe it appropriate to list and expand on a number of political positions that were in the funnel of consideration prior to my arrival as superintendent in 1973.

Chairman of the school board, Ellis Hawkins, was instrumental in keeping me apprised of information, facts and the plans of key critics in the county. He had confidants that kept him informed on the "Four Horsemen" plans and especially on the "Gray Fox." From the beginning of my contract and as late as a month prior to his passing away in March of 2014, Ellis had always shared with me information on the details of Saunders' plans to become permanent Division Superintendent of Prince William County Schools. I recall vividly that, following my decision to demote Herb Saunders, Ellis and I met for lunch. We discussed the matter, but Ellis reminded me that Herb would not go down quietly. Mr. Hawkins supported me all the way.

What I heard Ellis say several times, and even

the last time we talked before his death, was related to the workings of Herb Saunders. He reminded me that the "Gray Fox" had tried to develop connections with a variety of power brokers in the county prior to the 1972 county board election. According to Ellis, Herb became associated with key members of the Board of County Supervisors and namely the "Four Horsemen," prior to and after their election. According to Ellis, county board members Ralph Mauller, Roy Doggett and Scott Winfield felt strongly about Herb Saunders assisting them in dismantling the power structure of the school district and returning control of schools back to the county. As a result, they would support Herb to become full-time superintendent.

In the ramifications of the University of Georgia interviews, Dr. McGuffey told Ellis and me that Herb Saunders would never relinquish power and control of hiring personnel and staff promotions. The Georgia team recommended that he must eventually be demoted, fired or allowed to resign. The superintendent must be in total control, since the school district cannot afford two people "calling the shots." One person must serve as superintendent, not two!

Ellis confided in me about a number of issues that pertained to Herb Saunders' past and his rise to power in the county over a period of some 30 years. In local communities high school principals can become influential leaders following their long service. For those who remain for a long period of time with students graduating and continuing to live in the community, principals become endowed with local political power and are viewed by former students and graduates as leaders in the school district. Following years of service as principal and assistant superintendent of personnel, Saunders used the personnel position to appoint new staff, promote loyal staff to principalships, and reward loyal associates with higher paying positions.

His power as the personnel officer allowed him to elevate special favorites and former associates into central office positions and the superintendent's office. Herb Saunders had become the voice and power broker of the Prince William Schools. He planned to retain the authority he had earned for his service to the school district for many years into the future.

In summary, here are the points and facts about the "Gray Fox" in addition to other related issues that Ellis shared with me after I left Prince William County to take a position in Oakland, California.

- Prince William wished to seek a new superintendent with no political ties to Virginia and Prince William County during the 1973 search.
- The opinion of some indicated that Herb Saunders planned to become the permanent superintendent when the new superintendent failed.
- Ellis Hawkins refused to support any plans to name Herb Saunders as permanent superintendent.
- Ellis had decided to make his own mark as chairman of the school board.
- The University of Georgia study team discovered a key plan regarding the "Gray Fox," which gave the new superintendent leverage.
- Herb Saunders arranged for Michael O'Donnell's appointment to the Prince William County School Board to replace William Dunn.
- Herb Saunders met and talked with members of the "Four Horsemen" before their election and after the resignation of Stuart Beville.
- Ellis Hawkins told me during our long telephone conversation in February 2014, prior to his death in March 2014, that the "Gray Fox" had continued to talk and bargain with the "Four Horsemen" after I assumed the job as superintendent of schools.
- The University of Georgia study team stated that I would serve one term only if Herb Saunders remained in power as assistant superintendent of personnel in the district and responsible for hiring new staff and promoting employees.
- Phyllis O'Toole replaced Ellis Hawkins and supported me.
- Regis Lacey, a member of the replacement school board, became a long-serving school board member, was reappointed numerous times and was a strong supporter of me.
- Tom Beane became chair of the school board and was a long-term supporter of me.
- The Potomac News Editor Paul Muse and staff writers Lynne and Herald Grandstaff served the citizens of the county with their objective reporting. They, along with other leaders in the county and Commonwealth, presented factual and positive news about school district accomplishments and all of the details of the "Four Horsemen" and other issues.
- Some of the superintendent's executive staff assisted in keeping the "Gray Fox" and county critic "wolves" away from the door of the superintendent.
- The school district, under my leadership, accomplished a great amount in a four-year span, largely because of the executive support of Bill Helton, Richard Johnson, Ed Thomas and a number of high-performing associates.
- Additional credits are extended to key staff associates like Paul Trautman, Director of Facilities, and Mark Rothaker, Assistant Superintendent for Finance.
- Ellis Hawkins said that certain county leaders were discussing in 1972 a plan for the towns of Manassas and Manassas Park to separate from the county government and become two cities. The plan also was to have separate school systems in the new cities. The "Four Horsemen" were tied into the planning in order to limit spending and reduce taxes in the county. Herb Saunders was viewed as a conduit and potential player in expediting the separation process. The separation finally occurred after my exit. The cities of Manassas and Manassas Park met a state deadline by separating before the Commonwealth passed

laws restricting future city districts from forming and exiting their counties.

- Numerous leaders in the county assisted me and the school district in fighting the "Four Horsemen," the "Gray Fox" movement, and critics.
- Ellis also reminded me (during our telephone conversation in February 2014) that some key executive secretaries in the school district during my term of office were also funneling information to Herb Saunders regarding fiscal matters and plans/proposals under consideration and being proposed for adoption by the school board. Confidential information also was included in the chain of information materials being forwarded.
- Senator Charles Colgan, a former member of the Board of County Supervisors, supported me from the beginning and during his service as Senator of the 29th state senatorial district that included Prince William County.

The aforementioned are highlights and are intended to reinforce some of the facts and issues that helped to shape the many accomplishment that occurred during my tenure in Prince William County while fighting the Third Battle of Manassas.

Commendations to Supporters/ Associates and Other Issues

I personally commend the many associates, key staff, school board members, parents, teachers, principals, patrons, and the three voting minority members of the Board of County Supervisors—who all promoted the cause of public education in the county during the 1970s.

- Accolades for their unbelievable leadership are listed in order that they know how much I appreciated their efforts.
- As I have previously written in this book, these special leaders in the battle deserve outstanding recognition for their leadership and

firm support during the turmoil of the battle in the 1970s.

- To the three voting minority members of the Board of County Supervisors, Charles Colgan, Dr. Alfred Ferlazzo, and Vernon Dawson, I give substantial recognition for their support.
- School Board members Ellis Hawkins, William Dunn, Regis Lacey, Thomas Beane, John Pattie, and Clay Wood were a positive force against the "Horsemen" throughout the "battle."
- Much commendation is given to the executive team composed of the deputy, Dr. William L. Helton, the assistant superintendent, Richard Johnson, and the administrative assistant to the superintendent, Ed Thomas.
- Additional recognition goes to Dr. Paul Trautman, the director of facilities, and Mark Rothaker, the assistant superintendent for finance.
- Local newspapers, the Potomac News and The Journal Messenger, also receive well-earned acknowledgment for their printing of factual news and supportive editorials.
- Paul Muse, editor, and Lynne and Herald Grandstaff, staff writers for the Potomac News, receive superior marks for objectively reporting the news and writing incisive editorials.
- During this Third Battle of Manassas my four years went fast, but each day brought a new challenge and fresh opportunity.
- There are many additional staff, parents, patrons, and teachers whom I want to commend for their efforts during the "battle" for educational opportunity they gave to all students during my term of duty as superintendent during 1973-77.

A fundamental measure of leadership is the stature and common sense of the leaders and their followers. I credit our accomplishments in Prince William County during the Third Battle of Manassas to an army of supporters.

Forty Years Later, Leaders Stand the Test of Time

My first award must go to all of the leaders who were a part of the Prince William County Schools' family during my tour of duty as Division Superintendent of Schools during the years of 1973-1977. My appreciation is extended to those who remained solid in our team throughout the campaign.

However, special awards for their support must go to the school board members who extended my contract in November 1976 for a second, four-year term as superintendent of schools. These board members were Chairman Ellis Hawkins and board members Thomas Beane, Regis Lacey, and William Dunn. They will be encased in my memory and soul forever. These four members also backed my decision to demote Herb Saunders, "The Gray Fox," for violating my decision regarding a hiring freeze on all staff due to major budget cuts imposed by the Board of County Supervisors. Herb Saunders, assistant superintendent for personnel, hired 17 music teachers without my authorization and I, therefore, demoted him. As a result, he resigned and retired and the "Four Horsemen" of the Board of County Supervisors appointed him to the school board to replace John Pattie, who had served more than 20 years. The University of Georgia study team, chaired by Dr. Carol McGuffey was correct in recommending that only one division superintendent of schools should exist, and I was the legally appointed superintendent at that time.

A second award is given to my executive team members composed of Dr. William L. Helton, Richard Johnson and Ed Thomas for their superior performance in assisting me in carrying out my duties as superintendent during 1973-77.

A third award must be extended to the Department of Education in Richmond, Virginia, to the executive staff for their support during the four years I served as Division Superintendent of Schools in Prince William County. The State Superintendent of Public Instruction and, of course, Dr. George Holmes, Executive Director of Virginia School Boards Association, were continuously supportive of me throughout my term.

Dr. Holmes had followed the entire battle in the county and had directed the search team that recommended me as superintendent. As a result of the superintendent search process, he had become very familiar with the former superintendent, Stuart Beville, and after Stuart's resignation, the interim superintendent, Herb Saunders. Dr. Holmes introduced me to a number of leaders at the Department of Education and the state superintendent recommended that I should contact Helen Warriner-Burke and Dr. Jerri Mills Sutton, who were associated as key staff of the state superintendent in 1973.

When I first joined the county as superintendent, Dr. Helton served as supervisor of social studies in the county, prior to being appointed associate superintendent, and had worked directly with staff members at the Department of Education. He had introduced me to Jerri Sutton, who served as chair of state accreditation of schools in Virginia, and she invited me to serve as a member of study teams. My early work with the accreditation teams assisted me in better understanding public education in the Commonwealth of Virginia.

I must give special credits to Dr. Jerri Mills Sutton who served as a trusted advisor, consultant, counselor, accreditation executive, and curriculum leader during my work as superintendent in 1973-77. Jerri presented a perspective of the South and the Commonwealth of Virginia of which I had limited knowledge and understanding. Her skills in conceptualizing and grasping the core problems of education in Virginia and in the South gave me a unique and positive outlook in dealing with those problems. Dr. Sutton was calm, cool, and collected in situations dealing with problem-solving conflicts. Her gifts of language and writing skills in analyzing the issues in conflicts were extraordinarily superior. This lovely lady, compassionate mother, superb presenter, skilled executive and excellent negotiator of problem solving was a unique advisor for me during my entire stay in Prince William

County. Dr. Sutton advised me on the culture of public education in Virginia. Her advice and input regarding the Virginia Department of Education in Richmond were critical to me during this period.

A fourth special recognition must be given to the writers and editors of printed media in the county during 1973-77. As some of the addendums show at the end of this essay, I must also commend those who created all of the words, stories and editorial positions taken by the local newspapers, the Potomac News and The Journal Messenger, regarding our accomplishments for schools during the "battle." Potomac News Editor Paul Muse and Lynne and Herald Grandstaff, staff writers, were instrumental in informing county residents of the facts about the school system during the period. The Journal Messenger also should receive credit, but their reporting about our work was less extensive, possibly because of their physical location in Manassas.

A fifth appreciation is extended to Senator Charles Colgan, who served in the seventies as a county supervisor from the Gainesville District and who currently, in 2015, is the longest serving State Senator in the General Assembly of Virginia. Senator Colgan, during the "Third Battle of Manassas," was a leader in representing the minority bloc of Board of County Supervisors who remained supportive of the school board and of our plans to construct the new Osbourn Park High School on time and within the planned budget. As a member of the Board of County Supervisors, he gave major support for the introduction of kindergarten programs in the county for the first time. Senator Charles Colgan presently serves as President *Pro Tempore Emeritus* of the Virginia Senate, representing the Prince William County area.

It would be a source of satisfaction for me to see Osbourn Park High School renamed as Senator Charles Colgan High School. As a Board of County Supervisor member in 1973-1975, Senator Colgan was a major and influential factor in supporting the school board's voting bloc of Hawkins, Beane, Dunn and Lacey to finance the school board's plan to complete the Osbourn High School construction project by assuming management of the construction and dismissing the contractor.

• • •

The final epitaph of leaving Virginia as superintendent occurred in November 1976, when four school board members, Ellis Hawkins, Regis Lacey, Bill Dunn and Tom Beane voted to renew a four-year extension of my contract, to begin on July 1, 1977. Herb Saunders, George Mullen and Emily Rosenberg voted against the motion. In January 1977, Don White was elected to the Board of County Supervisors, and he appointed Michael O'Donnell to replace Bill Dunn on the school board.

Ellis Hawkins told me at our February 2014 telephone conference call, one month before his death, that Herb Saunders made a deal with Michael O'Donnell to join with him, Mullen and Rosenberg to rescind the decision that the school board majority had approved in November of 1976 to extend my contract for an additional four years. As stated earlier, Tom Beane newly appointed chair of the school board, replacing Ellis Hawkins who had ended his four-year term, and O'Donnell met with me to announce the Saunders-led decision. As a result of my meeting with Beane and O'Donnell to hear the decision of O'Donnell's vote, I resigned as the Prince William County Division Superintendent of Schools and called Dr. Ruth Love, Superintendent of the Oakland City, California School District to accept their offer to become Deputy Superintendent of the Oakland, California School District. Herb Saunders had now come full circle!

Well, I was taught early by strong parents and grandparents to deal with adversity in a positive manner rather than appearing defeated. My Snyder Grandfather, John Wesley, reminded me to always keep my eyes steady while firing my 32-special rifle at elk and deer in the Northern Idaho mountains of the Pacific Northwest. I learned to be steady because the slightest blink of the eye could cause the shot to go skyward and miss the target. Following his advice, I knew to zero in on the target or problem and to use my instinctive skills in dealing with the conflict to bring the problem to resolution.

As a result, I accepted the Prince William board's decision and prepared to move on to Oakland, to look forward to new challenges and to new opportunities for service in a much larger, urban, West Coast school district that needed my skills and experience.

I reflect on the words of one of my favorite poets, Robert Frost, and saw him recite his poem, "The Road Not Taken" at President Kennedy's inauguration in 1962. I must quote the words of the last part of his famous poem:

"I shall be telling this with a sigh
Somewhere ages and ages hence:
Two roads diverged in a wood, and I—
I took the one less traveled by,
And that has made all the difference."

The road to Manassas was a great journey that actually prepared me for air flights to Oakland, back to the state of Washington at Federal Way School District and a return to Washington, DC, with AASA. Recently, after traveling the roads with 35 private technology companies as an executive consultant, I find that it has been a rich experience.

Traveling the highways of Virginia to experience the Third Battle of Manassas taught me a number of human behavior and technical skills and that has made all the difference.

My experiences in the Commonwealth during the period of 1973-1977 and again in 1988-1990 stimulated me to consider taking the road back to Virginia to meet with some former key associates and to compose an essay regarding our experiences during the Third Battle of Manassas.

• • •

So, back to the major purpose of my return to Virginia that occurred in March 2014: I invited a few former associates and former school board members to a dinner party at the Thomas Jefferson Hotel in Richmond on March 15, 2014: in order to honor them. The following were invited to attend:

- Ellis and Jane Hawkins - Woodbridge, VA
- Regis and Donna Lacey - Woodbridge, VA
- Bill and Mardy Dunn - Reedville, VA
- Richard and Callie Johnson - Warrenton, VA
- Dr. William and Cindy Helton - Fredericksburg, VA
- Dr. Jerri Mills Sutton - Beaufort, NC
- Helen P. Warriner-Burke and Pat Burke - Amelia, VA
- Senator Charles Colgan - Gainesville, VA
- Herald Grandstaff - Manassas, VA

The celebration of my return to the Commonwealth of Virginia, after 40 years, was an experience I will treasure and forever remember. This connection with special friends at the Jefferson Hotel was intended to be a true highlight for me personally and would cement old memories. However, I was saddened to learn that Ellis Hawkins had passed away. Jane Hawkins called me to report that she and Ellis had planned to attend, but he passed away one week prior to our Richmond event. May Ellis rest in peace and remain in our hearts forever.

In order to sum up our event, my essay is intended to report issues about the Third Battle of Manassas, and new information which I learned when Ellis and I talked prior to his passing. Ellis urged me to tell the true story.

It is my pleasure to recognize Ellis Hawkins for his long and tireless journey as Chairman of the Prince William County School Board. I am reminded of the "Song of Blessing" by Pete Seeger, so *t*hank you, Ellis Hawkins, for giving me a chance to perform as superintendent of schools in Prince William County and for your service to the student and parents of the county. Your BELL will ring forever in our hearts.

A Few Final Recommendations

- I propose that the school board name future schools in honor of the following former school board leaders:
  - Ellis Hawkins
  - Thomas Beane
  - Regis Lacey
  - William Dunn
  - Senator Charles Colgan
- I recommend that the names of the four school board members who fought the "battle" to construct the Osbourn Park High School during the year of 1973-1977 be posted in the building.

I take this opportunity to list some summary remarks about the conflict during the period of the 1970s to retain control of the school district at the policy and executive levels.

- Public schools should provide equal educational opportunity for all students in the K-12 grades.
- Public schools must remain free of political wars and searches for power.
- Parents and patrons of a school district should always be alert when selecting strong school board members who are dedicated to the importance and retention of the public school structure.

This book was designed to review and share some final facts that occurred during my tenure in Manassas, Virginia (1973-1977) and again in March of 2014 about the Third Battle of Manassas. So, as a result of my journeys and experience, I would recommend that we all should remember our roots, our experiences, learn from our mistakes, and conceptualize how our positive accomplishments occurred, and, most of all, remember those who contributed the most in our past and present to assist us in achieving our goals.

Always carry a list of hopes and aspirations in your mind, because they will help keep you alive and functioning. I learned a tremendous amount of human behavior skills while leading schools in Virginia that will help carry me through adversity for the remaining years of my life.

In ending this review of the past, I take this opportunity to make a final statement about my story of surviving my stay in Prince William County in 1973-1977. This story is being told as a personal legacy for my present and future descendants to study long after I have passed to a better place. Now that the words are in print and my story is told, I feel much better about the experience of serving as Prince William County school superintendent.

However, what helps make the story more interesting is that the "Gray Fox," Mr. Herb Saunders, helped make my stay in the county schools as superintendent an exciting ride. If the former personnel director had failed to exist, how could I have even attempted to write and recount an old story of 40 years ago? Perhaps it illustrates the truth in this quote from Winston Churchill, "You have enemies? ... Good! That means you've stood up for something, sometime in your life."

Yes, in Prince William County, Virginia, I think I had made an enemy in Herb Saunders, but our conflict was larger than a personal disagreement. In my opinion, he had waited to become the permanent division superintendent in order to replace Stuart Beville, who resigned in November 1972. However, he failed to earn credentials to qualify for the superintendent's position. So, as a result of the Supreme Court's decision to retain the old school board, he was forced to assist them in the search for a new superintendent. As a result, a Weippe, Idaho native, Milton Lee Pritchard Snyder, Ph.D., was named Division Superintendent of Schools for Prince William County in 1973-1977.

The positive effect on my moving on from the Prince William County Schools in 1977 was the opportunity to join Dr. Ruth Love, Superintendent of Oakland City Schools, to accept the position of deputy superintendent in the district. Following my work in Oakland, I returned to Washington state as Superintendent of Federal Way Schools near Seattle. I finished my work in Federal Way nine years later and traveled back east to Washington, DC, as Deputy Executive Director of the American Association of School Administrators, which represented superintendents and school administrators through the United States.

Mark Twain recommended: "Keep away from people who try to belittle your ambitions. Small people always do that, but the really great make you feel that you, too, can become great."

I believe that most of the people with whom I was associated during my stay in Prince William County were fabulous individuals. Twain was correct and reminds us to remain connected with positive human beings. The negative ones may do us harm!

Conrad Hilton suggested: "Success seems to be connected with action. Successful people keep moving. They make mistakes, but they never quit!"

The Prince William school board, my confidential executive team, and some key associates were responsible for helping to keep our focus in pursuing our mission to educate the 42,000 students. You all know who you were!

Eventually, there was an important local result of the Third Battle of Manassas. Today school board members are elected by the voters in the Commonwealth of Virginia rather than being appointed by the Board of County Supervisors.

All's Well That Ends Well.

William Shakespeare wrote the play, "All's well that ends well" in 1604-1605. My story was lived and played out during 1973-1977 in the Prince William County, Virginia public schools, which I recall as the Third Battle of Manassas. To paraphrase Second Timothy 4:7, "We fought the good fight, we finished the race, we kept the faith..." in our goal to provide the best education possible for the youth of Prince William County, Virginia, and I think we accomplished our goal.

Milton Lee Pritchard Snyder, Ph.D.
Seattle, Washington

Preface to Appendices

Webster's Collegiate Dictionary defines *appendices* as supplementary material attached at the end of a piece of writing, a bodily outgrowth or process. I have attached copies of editorials from the Potomac News, The Journal Messenger, and The Washington Post newspapers in order to lend credibility to my essays.

Given that the print or photocopy quality of many of the pieces was not easily readable 42 years after the printing presses have gone dry, I have had them scanned and used optical character recognition to glean the content.

I have attempted to describe the period of time in which I served as Division Superintendent of Schools in Prince William County, Virginia, during the 1973–1977 years. My words describe personal views of the "battle." However, the documents listed in appendices should provide clarity in that they are copied from news clippings of county, school district board issues, and opinions of individuals during the period. Selected copies are about key leaders who served during the "battle"

and shaped the future of relationships between school boards and county government leaders some 42 years later—at least it is my hope that this is happening.

Many of the leaders who participated in the battles of the 1970s have passed on to a better place and I honor their service to Prince William Board of County Supervisors and the Prince William School Board.

My sincere acknowledgments are extended to press leaders, school district staff, key associates and all of the students and parents who were a critical part of the political struggle during my stay as Division Superintendent of Schools in the 1973–1977 time frame.

May the political scene in Prince William County, Virginia, be more stable and the relationships between county, city and school board leaders be more productive and harmonious in tending to the business of providing the best educational program that all students and citizens deserve.

Appendix A:
1963 – 1973

An early story about Prince William County, Virginia, as written by a well-respected former County Board of Supervisors member during the period of 1973–1977 during the years that Dr. Milton Lee Pritchard Snyder served as Division Superintendent of Schools in the Prince William County School District.

As it was, as it would be

By Andrew J. Donnelly, former member at the Prince William County Board of Supervisors, located in Manassas, Virginia

In the fall of 1958, I packed my clothes, got behind the wheel of my Ford, left my parents home in northern New Jersey and headed south. I had graduated from Seton Hall University in South Orange the previous June and was due to report to the United States Marine Corps' Officer Candidate School in Quantico, Virginia for training.

As I traveled Route 1 through Woodbridge and Dumfries, encountering a complete absence of traffic and traffic lights, little did I know that, in the years to follow, the county would be my home for 40 years.

Woodbridge became my permanent home in 1963 and by this time traffic was becoming a problem, County services were in their infancy.

Law enforcement was provided by the sheriff. A county police department would not be established until the early 1970s. There were no parks or recreation services. The Poll Tax existed until eliminated in 1964.

Cecil D. Hylton almost singlehandedly changed the face and ultimately the politics of Prince William County. In 1945 he built 20 homes near Manassas Park and then in the late 1950s he literally began to rebuild Woodbridge.

He built single family homes, townhouses, apartments and shopping centers. He built and owned the first cable TV system in the county along with a water and sewer system. He was welcomed by the governing body of the county because he represented 'progress'.

New residents brought incomes, which brought commerce and eventually light and heavy industry. But the newcomers were not to be silent.

When services were lacking, as they were in the early 1960s, residents became vocal and demanded changes.

The problems associated with rapid population growth were most conspicuous in the delivery of educational services. Between 1960 and 1970 the county population grew from 50,000 to 111,000. In 1960 there were a total of 10 schools in the county. By 1970 there were 36 schools.

In one year alone, 1972, five new schools were completed. In spite of the determined efforts of the school board, schools were becoming vastly overcrowded and it probably was impossible for anybody to keep pace with a school-age population that had grown from a mere 4,000 in 1950 to 28,000 in 1970.

I began taking an interest in county politics upon separation from the Marine Corps in 1965. The Board of County Supervisors, at that time, numbered six.

Dr. Alfred J. Ferlazzo was a family physician who first came to the county in the 1930s. In the 1960s he purchased a controlling interest in the *Potomac News* and, along with editor Paul Muse, oversaw its maturity into the dominant newspaper in the county, surpassing the *Manassas Journal Messenger*. "Doc", a humanitarian to the core, possessed a passionate temper and was an enthusiastic champion of the poor and disenfranchised. Ferlazzo represented the Dumfries District.

In the mid 1960s the United States Supreme Court handed down an opinion which required the county to more equally re-apportion the population in each of the six magisterial districts. To help accomplish this and to lessen the likelihood of future tie votes, the Board of Supervisors created a seventh district and named it Neabsco.

It encompassed Marumsco Hills, Marumsco Woods, Marumsco Acres, Featherstone, Ordinal Drive, and Mr. Hylton's newest offspring, Dale City. This action necessitated the appointment of a seventh supervisor.

The circuit court appointed Mr. Francis Coffey a long-time resident, member of the Planning Commission, and developer of the rustic vacation home community of Country Club Lake (which is now known as Montclair). Coffey, built like a bulldog, was a staunch rural conservative and defender of property rights who advocated limited government. He lived on Cardinal Drive about one mile east of its intersection with Minnieville Road.

As my office was located near the courthouse, I began attending hearings in the supervisor's chambers.

One such hearing in 1967 was to gather public input concerning the possible establishment of a county police department to relieve the sheriff's department of law enforcement responsibilities.

The rapid population growth was necessitating the retention of additional law enforcement personnel, but the supervisors were becoming increasingly frustrated at the Virginia State Compensation Board's refusal to promptly approve and partially pay for, requested additions to the sheriff's manpower allotment.

Creation of a police department, while requiring complete funding by the county, would eliminate this source of frustration.

I was interested in the subject and wanted to know what my newly appointed representative thought about the proposal.

I cannot be certain, but I think that I decided to stand for election when I heard Coffey's statement: "I don't need any police department. I got all the protection I need—a German shepherd and a shotgun."

A Wise Delay

Potomac News, September 19, 1973. A2, Opinion page.

The cause of prudence was served when the Prince William School Board decided recently not to press for a $30 million school construction referendum until there is a new review and cost-updating of the proposed program.

The program, originally earmarked for a vote in this November's general election, appeared predicated on a county-wide conversion to year-round school, with a considerable saving in construction costs as a result. This meant the county's voters, in effect, would be voting on year-round school. The two months remaining before the November election would have been too short a period for a thorough public airing of the new concept, despite its apparent success and public acceptance in Dale City.

Furthermore, it was becoming obvious that galloping inflation, plus lightened construction requirements, were out-dating the $30 million figure even before the referendum date rolled around. The School Board was faced with the unhappy prospect of repeating recent history; costs out-raced one major bond program after its approval by the voters not many years ago, and some projects had to be carried over to a second bond issue. This generated criticism as well as voter confusion the second time around.

These points were brought to the School Board's attention by an expert in educational facilities planning who was summoned to Prince William by the new schools superintendent Dr. Milton Snyder. It was a wise move on the part of Dr. Snyder, who assumed the superintendency in July, as he will have to live with whatever program is finally brought before the voters. It should carry his stamp of approval.

The school officials now appear to be aiming for a referendum date in late winter or early spring. With some 2,000 additional students entering the school system each year in a seemingly inexorable procession, and a 1976 absolute deadline for public kindergarten growing ever closer, much more of a delay cannot be afforded. These same pressures make it all the more imperative that the school hierarchy produces a program that does not carry serious risk of rejection by the voters.

For the record: An editorial Friday attributed a proposed police commission to Supervisor Don Turner. Actually, the commission idea was proposed by County Board Chairman Scott Winfield, and Mr. Turner supported it.

Appendix B:
1974

Here We Go Again

Potomac News, January 17, 1974. Opinion Page, A6.

Here we go again. While responsible negotiations are apparently progressing toward a resolution of the long impasse over Osbourn Park High School's completion, the paranoia which too often permeates the conduct of county business at Manassas has produced a new outburst which we hope doesn't again throw the effort off track.

The culprits are the chairman of the county supervisors, Scott Winfield, and Supervisor Ralph Mauller, both of whom are so obsessed by a mistrust of the School Board and the school administration that it discolors almost every effort by the two boards to work together. A healthy level of disagreement, and of political maneuvering, is to be expected in relationships between two boards holding responsibilities which some times may seem at odds; however, in three years of railing at the School Board and school administration, Messers. Winfield and Mauller have produced little evidence that the school people are possessed by any greater degree of malevolence or frailty than can be found within the ranks of the Board of Supervisors itself.

The latest manifestations of this mistrust is the much-ado-about-nothing raised this week over an informal Dec. 20 memorandum from a School Board lawyer to Schools Supt. Milton Snyder and the School Board regarding efforts to finance Osbourn Park's completion. A copy of this memo came into the hands of Mr. Winfield, and Tuesday the two supervisors blew it totally out of proportion as a sinister plot "to unload" personal liability for the school completion on the supervisors.

What's more unfortunate, Clinton B. Mullen, the county's respected new executive, followed their alarm with a blockbuster of his own, declaring in a letter to Dr. Snyder that he felt he had been deliberately kept in the dark as a result of "a deep distrust" on the part of Dr. Snyder or the School Board lawyer. We hope Mr. Mullen was not stampeded into

this letter by Mr. Winfield's earlier explosive reaction. And we are concerned that, in the letter, Mr. Mullen said he would not support the School Board's plan to retain a construction manager to finish Osbourn Park on the grounds that he was being kept in the dark; we would have preferred to see Mr. Mullen argue the plan on its merits.

Let's consider memorandum passages the two supervisors appear to consider most omnibus. The memorandum was written by M. E. Gibson after he and Alfred Shilling, the county's bonding attorney, conversed in Richmond while dealing with the $2.1 million financing of Osbourn Park's completion through a Virginia Public School Authority bond issue. According to Mr. Gibson, the two discussed the need, among other things, for resolutions from the local county boards covering not only $1 million from a February bond sale, but $1.1 million which would be sought through a subsequent bond sale. In this respect, Mr. Gibson raised the problem of the School Board letting a contract when it does not have enough funds committed to satisfy the obligation; the School Board has no fund-raising powers of its own, and Mr. Gibson pointed out that school boardman did not want to risk being held personally responsible for paying the contractor if more funds did not later become available.

This was an entirely valid consideration, in as much as the supervisors do hold the fund-raising powers which would cover any eventuality, and they do hold the ultimate responsibility for financing Osbourn Park's completion. We can't understand why this restatement of reality would add any new concerns for Messers. Winfield and Mauller.

A second cause of perturbation came when Mr. Gibson discussed the possibility of the cost overrun on the project exceeding the estimates of $2.1 million. Suppose, Mr. Gibson conjectured, that a supervisor says the cost might end up $10 million. The School Board, he goes on to advise Dr. Snyder, could respond by saying it will complete the project as economically as possible—maybe for even less than a $1 million overrun.

This goes no further than anything that has been said publicly. In no way has the School Board absolutely guaranteed that a $2.1 infusion will completely do the job, although that is the board's considered opinion. It was obvious that Mr. Gibson used the $10 million figure as a casual example; few would rationally believe otherwise. Yet Mr. Mauller cites the figure in support of his own nightmares of a $10 million completion bill.

The remainder of the memorandum appears just as innocuous; we're sorry it was seized on the way it was by the two supervisors and are concerned by Mr. Mullen's reaction. Perhaps the memorandum indicated to Mr. Mullen that he was misled by the school people; his letter did not indicate this, but rather his resentment that he was not being kept totally informed.

To us it should be obvious that the memo constituted an innocuous continuation of a dialog of information, feelings and stratagems between Dr. Snyder and the board's lawyer, and changes nothing. It added no new consideration to the present effort, which should continue post-haste, to arrange for the completion of Osbourn Park in time for use next fall.

Assistant to Snyder Appointed

The Journal Messenger, July 3, 1974. A14.

Edward Thomas has been appointed administrative assistant to Prince William County School Superintendent Dr. Milton Snyder.

Thomas has been serving as the temporary administrative assistant for the past few months in addition to his duties as supervisor of middle schools.

His new appointment became effective Monday. The full time position is included in the new school district reorganization called for by Dr. Snyder.

Thomas first came to Prince William County in 1953 as principal of Bennett Elementary School in Manassas. In 1952 he assumed the principalship at Parkside Middle and Elementary School and in 1957 moved to the School Board Office as coordinator of the junior high school program.

Thomas received both his bachelor's and master's degrees from the University of Virginia. He has also taken graduate work with the University of North Carolina, George Washington University and Virginia Commonwealth University.

He is currently completing requirements for his doctorate degree from Virginia Polytechnic Institute and State University.

Four assistant principalships have also been assigned by the County School Board for the 1974-75 school years. These include Paul A. Banks, Kerrydale Elementary School; Aaron T. Jordan, Rippon Middle School; Ronald L. Keilhoitz, Fred M. Lynn Middle School; and Robert M. Stine, Woodbridge Middle School.

Banks began his teaching career in the county at Sinclair Elementary School where he taught fourth grade. He has taught summer school at Godwin Middle School and Gar-Field High School. During the past year he served as a fourth grade team leader at Sudley Elementary School.

He is a graduate of Bluefield State College, majoring in elementary education and social science. He has also attended the University of Virginia on a leadership seminar and served as a consultant to Fairfax County Schools on an interim evaluation committee.

He is completing his master's degree in educational administration and supervision at Virginia Tech. He and his wife, Rebecca, reside in Manassas where he is employed with IBM.

Jordan is presently teaching health and physical education at Gar-Field Senior High School. He formerly taught in Fauquier County and also worked in a community action program with VISTA.

He is a graduate of Saint Augustine College and has his master's degree from the University of Virginia.

Keilhoitz is returning to a position he held previously for two years. He is a former chairman of the music department at Rippon where he also assisted with the summer program.

He received his bachelor's from Murray State University and master's from Virginia Tech.

A former guidance counselor at Osbourn High School, Stine is currently serving as a counselor at Godwin Middle School.

Hawkins Re-elected School Board Head

The Journal Messenger, July 4, 1974. A1.

Ellis Hawkins was elected Wednesday to serve a second one year term as chairman of the Prince William County School Board.

Hawkins, who represents Occoquan District, was first named to the post a year ago, succeeding John Pattie of Dumfries District.

Thomas Beane, Coles District, was also re-elected vice chairman for a second year. His board term will expire during the next year.

The re-elections came at the board's regular meeting Wednesday which was also the meeting of the new fiscal year, according to the state code.

The new associate superintendent for school services, Mark Rothacker, was named clerk of the board upon the recommendation of School Superintendent Dr. Milton Snyder. Board members expressed some hesitation about naming an individual, new to the school district, to the post.

However. Dr. Snyder said that Rothacker would be working closely with him and he did not foresee any difficulty.

Beane noted that the state code requires that the board elect the clerk and "fix his compensation." Snyder pointed out that year ago a policy of no compensation for the clerk was adopted. Along with this was the provision that the clerk be one of the district's top administrative officials.

Herbert Saunders, while also serving as assistant superintendent of personnel, filled the clerk's position for the past year and did not receive any compensation for his additional duties.

Snyder was asked to check with the attorney on the legality of the board's... (newspaper clipping was cut off here).

'Something Different' Starts at G-F

Students take up optional year-round for variety of reasons

Potomac News, July 5, 1974. A5. Ann Holiday.

It was the quietest first day of school most teachers could remember, as well as a milestone for the Prince William County school system.

In the air-conditioned Gar-Field Senior High School on a warm July 1, optional year-round high school began its maiden run.

Most of the students were freshmen and sophomores who had elected one of the four year-round calendars either because their younger brothers and sisters were in 45-15 schools in Dale City or because they wanted a change from the traditional nine-month calendar.

"I wanted something different. I'm tired of the same old thing," explained Kim Smith, a ninth grader from Rippon Middle School, which is on a traditional school year.

"I wanted to try it and see what it's like," agreed her friend, Anita Guess, also a Rippon graduate. Anita wasn't sure she would like going to school in the summer, "but in winter it might be okay," she allowed.

There are actually five calendars in effect at Gar-Field. The orange calendar is out on vacation now. Red, blue and green are in school, and the purple nine-month calendar will begin Sept. 3. The choice was left completely to the students and their parents, unlike the Dale City elementary and middle schools, where calendar is assigned by neighborhood.

"1 would have gone on purple, hut everyone on my street took green," said John Waterstraat, a tenth grader who attended Godwin.

Mike Ruais, a 10th grader from Godwin, didn't choose year-round. "I was forced to by my mother," he explained. "She said I made better grades. I don't get bored with school."

Although he would rather be on a nine-month calendar, Mike said he believes all schools should be given a choice of going on year-round calendars.

Several others chose the year-round calendars at the insistence of their parents. Among them are Steve Wright, who listed as a disadvantage the difficulty in getting a summer job, and Laura Whelchel, who likes the three-week break every nine weeks. Both went to Godwin.

But Rossie Alston, student body president, chose the purple calendar partly because none of the classes he is taking, such as Latin IV, are offered on the year-round calender. Alston was at school Monday to participate in the opening day activities.

Erin Counts, a sophomore on the purple calendar, also dropped by the school to have lunch with some of his friends. He lives in Dale City, but his younger brother attends a private school on a nine-month calendar.

"From a personal standpoint, I don't like 45-15," commented Kurt Risser, a sophomore who attended Godwin. "I chose it because I can get a better education. I don't forget as easily." He also likes having a vacation after each grading period.

Dan Winslow, sophomore, chose the red calendar because "I like it."

That calendar has the entire month of December off, and Dan figures it will be easier to get a job at Christmas time.

"I thought it was a better deal," senior Chris Hoffman said, explaining why she had chosen the green calendar. "I can't stay in school nine months and learn anything. I need a break." Chris lives in Woodbridge.

Marcia Bent said she probably wouldn't have chosen a year-round calendar if it had been left up to her. However, her brothers and sisters are on the red calendar and it will allow her family to include her in their vacation plans.

Red is a pretty good calendar, she said, because

students get December and most of June out of school.

The optional aspect of the five school calendars is believed to be unique nationwide, Dr. David D. Myers, principal, told a news conference Monday at the school. He predicted that by August the students on the traditional calendar — about 70 percent of the student body — would be getting bored with vacation and would be giving year-round school second thoughts.

One of the major objects to year-round school among high school students has been summer jobs. However, according to a study conducted last fall, 80 percent of those who wanted summer jobs could not find them. Some firms have expressed a willingness to hire four students to rotate in one full-time position.

Schools Supt. Dr. Milton Snyder also predicted that work-study programs would become as much a part of the county's high schools as the traditional academic program.

The band program is going on during the summer, and it is anticipated that other extracurricular activities will be developed this summer.

Intramural athletic competition is expected to take shape, although there probably will be no year-round interscholastic athletics until other districts adopt year-round schools.

Myers described the year-round student body as a cross-section of the school population. He said he assumed the majority were from Dale City, although he had no figures to prove it. Nor did he have figures the first day of school as to how many students had chosen year-round school.

Some teachers said they were not sure how big their classes would be because they were not sure how many students would enter school late and how many were out on the orange calendar vacation.

Dr. Snyder hailed the first day of year-round high school as a milestone. It involved a cooperative program between the Prince William School Board, the State Board of Education, the community, students and staff, he explained.

"Community input is important," Snyder said. "Gar-Field is definitely unique in that respect."

Planning for the 117 different course offerings involved the Gar-Field staff actively for two full years, Myers said. Last year it was indicated the school was not quite ready for year-round high school, so a second year of work was launched.

Myers predicted the students would be deeply involved in their course work "right off the bat."

The five different calendars will take a special amount of planning on the part of the teachers, Myers noted. There might be as many as three different levels of students in the class at once, with some having been in school for several weeks, some only a few weeks, and others interrupted by vacations.

This dictates individualized instruction, he said. Many of the courses have already been following an individualized approach for the past year or two in anticipation of year-round school.

Ranger Replacement?

County leaders study Osbourn Park school

Potomac News, July 12, 1974. A3.

Construction at the Osbourn Park High School has slowed, and school officials are preparing for the possibility that someone other than Ranger Construction Company will have to complete the building.

Schools Supt. Dr. Milton Snyder briefly explained the situation to Prince William's supervisors in a joint session with the School Board Thursday night. School Board members promised to keep the supervisors closely informed.

The supervisors' reaction was subdued: Ralph Mauller asked quietly if Ranger Construction Co. was actively working on completing the building. School Boardman William Dunn answered that, although there are always a few people on the site, little progress is being made.

The supervisors asked if there is any possibility that the school would be finished by the August-September completion date. School Board members silently shook their heads "no."

The School Board, its architect and legal counsel will meet with Ranger's bonding company, Travelers Insurance, sometime during the week of July 22. The question is whether to call in the bond, get rid of Ranger and force the bonding company to finish the school.

Supervisors' Chairman Charles Colgan asked flatly, "do you intend to call in the bond?" Dunn replied that, at this point, the schoolmen would rather not comment. "That is a matter for executive session," Dunn added. School Board Chairman Ellis Hawkins assured the supervisors that the bond on the school guarantees that the bonding firm will complete the school; there is no money limit, Hawkins declared.

Snyder added that the School Board still has $1.7 million of the original construction fund on hand, plus money to equip the school when it is complete.

Supervisors revived some old grievances on the school, but neither surprise nor consternation over the new work slowdown was apparent. Supervisor Roy W. Doggett concluded, "Somebody must have screwed you all."

Snyder's First Year

School chief presses public involvement

Potomac News, July 26, 1974. A1. Lynne Grandstaff.

When Schools Supt. Dr. Milton Snyder sat down to assess his first year in Prince William, the issues were not Osbourn Park or the budget or vandalism. "My major concern is a personal one. With so many problems surrounding schools, we can't forget our reason for being here," Snyder declared. He talked about boys and girls, their parents and the school staff.

"Our reason for existing is to educate boys and girls to provide the best and most individualized program we can. It means that, in the end, we are not looking for a pupil-teacher ratio; we are trying to get to the point where we know what individual children are doing, what their hopes and aspirations are. Then, we can try to develop a program for them."

The emphasis, Snyder continued, must always be on boys and girls. For instance, Snyder said that the year-round school program at Gar-Field will not fail because only 500 or 600 students are taking year-round schedules. "We will win or lose depending on what students, parents and teachers think about it. Whether they're right or wrong, they're the ones involved in it," he maintained.

When Snyder arrived last year, he set three major goals for himself; looking at the year, he sees that he has done well.

The FIRST GOAL was to work toward a bond referendum. Although there is now no referendum, he feels that he accomplished his purpose. The idea was to study the issue, to make plans and to create a task force of citizens to assess the county's needs. The May referendum was dropped at the suggestion of the bond committee.

Progress toward the SECOND GOAL, communication, has been a few months behind Snyder's schedule. The intent was to develop long and short range plans for providing information and involving

people. A survey due for completion next month will speed that planning.

Snyder repeatedly reiterated the importance of the involvement of people in the business of the schools.

"The schools belong to the people. I don't own this district. We only work for the people of the district. We're almost here on borrowed time. This is one structure in a democracy which should be as close to the people as any. We have to develop a plan of community relations; we need to get people to participate. They come in now as a reaction to a crisis. Schools are famous for crisis planning. Let's get people involved."

Snyder stopped and thought a second; "That's not a political remark. Communications is the heart of the whole thing."

Snyder's THIRD MAJOR GOAL—getting the school system through the Standards of Quality requirements—has been completed. In Prince William, the most important aspect of the standards was the five year plan.

Snyder explained, "The planning process does not mean that only school planners like John Colson should gear up for the next five years. It means the whole community should be ready. The problem is that we are behind in certain areas; special education is one of these. Some people want to implement the entire five year plan in one year. That's difficult in a county that has financial problems."

TWO MORE major goals emerged in the course of the year.

Snyder had planned on reorganization of the administration as a secondary goal; it became a matter of prime concern. There are some new faces at the School Board offices, and some of the old faces are aligned with different positions.

The issue, however, is not individuals. Snyder

described the changes as "replanning, putting ourselves into a different structure so that we can get at the MAJOR GOAL, WHICH IS LEARNING. We're looking for a structure that gets to that issue in the most efficient way. We need to give teachers support and direction."

He added, "I didn't know this would be a prime goal; if I could have rewritten the goals, there would have been four."

The other surprise was kindergarten; Snyder wanted a kindergarten program, but he did not realize that parents and citizens were as ready for the program as they were. "The parents are the ones who really came in and supported and pushed this. We must also compliment the supervisors and the School Board in dealing with this major goal; they're the ones to be commended."

Snyder's goals are tailor-made for Prince William, but they are also aligned with educational movements throughout the country. Further, Snyder has developed his ideas about schools from 20 years in the education business. He also draws from his personal experiences in public school.

Snyder does not like to talk about himself. "It sounds phony. People will hear this and..." Snyder made a facial expression indicating the special nausea of people who feel conned by sentimentality.

Still, the one-room school in Idaho where Snyder spent the first eight years of his educational life has a strong impact on his ideas about education.

For instance, Snyder sees the involvement of the community as recapturing what is good from the past. "This is not a new idea. It is the one room school, the town hall meeting. Because of the size of school districts, we have lost the ability to function this way. I still think we can do it."

In Prince William, Snyder stands for change. However, he also sees value in tradition, "the predictable behavior of the way we've done it in the past. Both are right; the job is balancing the system of conflicts" (between tradition and motivation).

Similarly, individualization in teaching means a return to the advantages of the 100-student high school. "We didn't have a full program, but there was plenty of individual help. You got a lot of attention, maybe too much."

There have been many changes since Snyder took over a year ago. There will be more. Snyder is now working on his goals for the next year; he promises that they will be "more involved, more complete. We're going to base our evaluation on these plans."

Snyder's plans are not yet formulated, but one aspect is clear: they will be based on what is good for children.

The big issues are not the progress of construction at Osbourn Park or the general question of getting roofs over the heads of all the children who move into the county. New programs are not going to be implemented to make administrators happy or to fit schedules developed by the staff, Snyder asserted.

"I used to be for change for the sake of change. That's phony. The question is always 'is it sound?' What effect will new things have on learning?" Snyder pondered.

He declared, "Progress for the sake of progress is never the issue. No matter how many problems there are or how complex they are, the question is always the same. We must analyze everything from the standpoint of how it will affect the learning process, how it will affect boys and girls."

School Needs Put at $77 Million

Top Priorities Are Set

The Journal Messenger, September 5, 1974. A1. Kathi Keys, JM Education Editor.

Prince William County School District's construction needs have been put at nearly $77 million with the top priority items totaling over $44 million.

These are the figures developed by the citizens *ad hoc* bond committee and formally presented to the School Board on Wednesday.

The school district's needs are divided into four priority areas with the first the largest.

The top priority items have been identified as special education facilities, $2.6 million; kindergarten space (101 rooms), $5,231 million; three new elementary schools, $6.6 million; fire and safety remodeling, $422,000; elementary school heating, $1,123 million; Osbourn conversion to a middle school, $2,104 million; Saunders conversion to secondary school use, $1.76 million; and one new senior high school, $12.6 million, for a total of $32.44 million.

Added to this was $11,678,400 for inflation at a rate of 18 per cent each year for two years. This additional figure brings the total of the first priority area to $44,118,400.

School Superintendent Dr. Milton Snyder recommended Wednesday that a two-year bond referendum be approved for the first priority items.

He also requested that the School Board add to this amount, funds for a fourth elementary school, but delete the costs of elementary school heating improvements.

If Snyder's recommendations are approved by the School Board on Friday, this would increase the first priority area costs by roughly $1,464,720, including inflation, for a total of over $45.6 million.

In making his recommendation, Snyder suggested that the county's growth identifies four areas which need additional elementary school space, although he did not elaborate on specific locations.

He did, however, suggest that the School Board consider the transfer of the elementary school heating improvements from the bond referendum to the operational maintenance budget.

The committee's second priority items, totaling $11,997,000, include elementary library space, $2,013 million; middle school library space $1,748 million; art, music, and physical education space in elementary schools, $5,183 million; home economics, industrial arts, physical education and art space in middle …

(rest of sentence missing, cut off in photocopy.).

Ranger Suit to Arbitration

Potomac News, September 6, 1974. A1.

The score in the million dollar legal battle over Osbourn Park High School is now School Board one, Ranger zero.

Federal Judge Albert Bryant Thursday ruled that Ranger's complaints about the School Board should be considered in arbitration, per a clause in the School Board-Ranger contract. The $13.5 million in damages suit against the board will wait until the conclusion of arbitration.

The ruling was a victory for the School Board, which has already filed the papers to begin the arbitration process. The board favored moving the whole matter to arbitration because that process will be faster than a full court bearing and potential appeals.

Osbourn Park was to be finished last December. The board and Ranger negotiated a contract change which brought penalty-free completion dates to a staggered schedule beginning in August. No portions of the school have been finished; the school is not more than 75 percent complete. Work on the site is at a virtual standstill. If the School Board were to charge the $500 per day damages for lateness, the financial effect on Ranger would be considerable, since damages would be assessed mid-April.

Although the board clearly expects the arbitration ruling to enhance chances of an early completion of the school, there were no specifics available Thursday. Schools Supt. Dr. Milton Snyder said that more information may become available after the board deliberates in executive session today.

Ranger filed suit against the board on July 116; the suit charges breach of contract, conspiracy, libel and defamation of character. The suit asked tor damages on each of three counts.

The board's answer to the charges was a demand that the court stay all proceedings until after a panel from the American Arbitration Association had heard the case and made a decision.

In court Ranger attorney Donald Gavin argued that the matter did not belong in arbitration. He maintained that state rather than federal laws relating to arbitration were applicable to the case and would eliminate the case from the service arbitration.

The judge disagreed; he ruled that the federal law applies and added, that, even if state laws were applicable, there would be no legal difference.

Further, Gavin argued that a stipulation in revision supplanted the arbitration agreement in the standard contract. The contract revision called for Ranger and the board to appoint a third party expert to settle some disagreements which had arisen prior to the revision.

The judge disagreed, stating that the provisions of the original contract remain valid.

The situation now is that everything is in arbitration, including libel and conspiracy charges. The architect, Pentecost Wade and McLellon, is a party to the suit but cannot be a party to the arbitration. However, Judge Bryant is also staying the architect's portion of the suit until the arbitration is complete.

The arbitration will lake at least two months, possibly longer. The School Board would like the arbitration panel to declare Ranger in default on the project.

With the safety of an outside opinion backing it, the School Board could then kick Ranger off the job without fear that Ranger could subsequently win a court case against the board.

However, nothing is happening on the school site now; only a few Ranger men are at the job. Board attorney Lloyd Smith said there would be nothing to prevent the board from terminating Ranger while the arbitration is in progress.

$44 million Bond Package Eyed

Potomac News, September 6, 1974. A1. Lynne Grandstaff.

Prince William's School Board will decide today whether to send a $44.1 million two-year construction bond proposal to the Board of Supervisors for their approval.

The proposal, discussed at Wednesday's session, consists of only the first priority listing of the bond *ad hoc* committee.

Although the money need is high, the county will get only the tip of the iceberg of construction needs for $44,118,400.

The committee listed projects it felt necessary in four priority ratings; Schools Supt. Dr. Milton Snyder, in a different proposal, recommended that only the first priority items be included in the bond, since the committee's recommendations, in their entirety, would cost nearly $76.6 million.

Board Chairman Ellis Hawkins asked committee members if they could guarantee that passage of a $44 million bond issue would prevent double shifting in the next two years.

The answer was no. Committeeman Thomas St. Clair replied, "These are immediate needs, things we ought to have today, not two years from now."

The package being eyed by boardmen consists primarily of new construction. It calls for one new eastern Prince William high school ($12.6 million), three new elementary schools ($6.6 million), new kindergarten space at existing schools ($5.23 million), and new special education facilities ($2.6 million). Snyder's proposal calls for the construction of a fourth new elementary school in the two-year period.

Other portions of the committee package are: fire and safety remodeling ($422,000), conversion of Osbourn to a middle school ($2.1 million), conversion of Saunders ($1.7 million), and elementary school heating (1.12 million). Snyder recommended that the heating improvements be taken out of the bond fund and placed in future operating funds.

With the exception of eastern Prince William elementary school space, the bond does not reflect much growth: it is designed to handle the students who are already here. The two new high schools in eastern Prince William are already overloaded, and Saunders will probably be used to house a new high school student body next year, students will presumably stay at Saunders until a new building is finished.

Although there are spaces at some western Prince William elementary schools, the Manassas schools are badly overcrowded. Bennett, which was designed to hold 756 students, now houses 1,198 (including the annex, which has fire safety problems). Baldwin School, rated at a capacity of 554, has 717 students this year. Manassas needs an elementary school, even if no more families move into the area.

Kindergarten space, listed for 101 new classrooms across the county, is predicated on the current state law requiring a full-day kindergarten program by 1976-77. Again little growth is built into the plan; educators are looking for 3,000 students. There are now 2,795 kindergarteners in the new program with more youngsters coming in daily.

Special educational needs are based on the five-year plan for special education. They include $1.3 million to build the third phase of the Independent Hill School, and $1.3 million for space at schools around the county.

Although eastern Prince William elementary schools are slightly overcrowded, building needs there are predicated on growth. From discussions with major developers and the county's Planning Department, administrators expect 1,451 students from Dale City; 882 additional students from Lake Ridge; and 867 new students in Dumfries-Triangle during the next 2.5 years.

Boardmen discussed the plans in relation to expected growth. Although birth rates are declining and mortgage money is difficult to get, the county schools continue to add students. Hawking smiled. "I don't think you could shut off growth in Prince William County if you put a 10-mile-high fence around the county borders.

In the year since a bond program was first set for Prince William, many plans have at least temporarily been scrapped. Whopping 18-percent inflation figures ($11.68 million for 2-1/2 years) have gouged projects, from the list. New prices have been developed for construction costs, based on a current 14-percent inflation rate.

For financial reasons, most of the remodeling of existing schools has been dropped from the bond proposal.

In its second priority, the *ad hoc* committee listed providing library space for elementary and middle schools, adding art, music and physical education space for elementary schools and equalizing instructional spaces at middle schools. Those needs, plus administrative space, would have cost $16.3 million.

The committee's third priority items were converting Dean Middle School to an elementary school, acquiring a site for a seventh high school, and providing increased office and guidance space at existing middle schools. All that would cost $2.7 million. Finally, the committee recommended that all existing county schools be air-conditioned at a cost of $13.4 million.

All repair work originally slated for the bond package was dropped on principle; there is no point in paying for paint and ceiling tile over a 30-year period, everyone reasoned. All those projects which include heavy expenditures at some of the county's older schools, are slated for inclusion in upcoming operating budgets.

The board continues its deliberations at 4 p.m. today, and is expecting to vote on a bond proposal The School Board will meet jointly with the supervisors Monday night in preparation for Tuesday's supervisors' consideration of the bond proposal.

School Bond Hot Potato is Tossed in County's Lap

The Journal Messenger, September 9, 1974. A1. Randi Deiotte, JM Staff Writer.

A divided School Board will recommend to the supervisors tonight that a $45 million school bond referendum be put to Prince William County voters on Nov. 6.

The School Board thrashed out an initial proposal containing $33,275,000 worth of projects, plus an annual inflation factor of 18 per cent, at a special meeting Friday.

Manassas School Board member Robert Boyd voted against the proposed referendum after chastising the School Board for failing "to explore the possibility of other methods of financing additions, conversions and repairs to existing schools."

Coles School Board member Thomas 0. Beane abstained from voting after he was unable to justify costs for a new 2000-pupil high school. He said he supported the referendum concept, however.

Brentsville member T. Clay Wood did not attend the meeting, and the recommendation squeaked through by the required four-man majority.

Later, Superintendent Dr. Milton Snyder urged Boyd and Beane to reconsider their votes. "The most important thing is a unanimous vote," he stated. "In the end it would benefit boys and girls."

The projects include special education facilities estimated to cost $2.6 million. 101 kindergarten rooms at an estimated cost of $5.2 million, four new elementary schools—one each in Lake Ridge. Dale City, Dumfries-Triangle and Manassas—at an estimated cost of $2.2 million each, conversion of Saunders to a middle school at a projected cost of $1.76 million, conversion of Osbourn to accommodate either middle school students or a combination of middle and elementary students at a projected cost of $2.1 million, and construction of a new 2000 pupil high school in eastern Prince William County at an estimated cost of $12.6 million.

The School Board will recommend that elementary school heating plant improvements, at a cost of $1.1 million, be removed from the bond referendum and transferred to the general operating budget.

Also included in the proposal to the supervisors will be a modified fire and safety remodeling scheme. The School Board will recommend that construction of storage sheds for flammable equipment be moved to the operating budget at a cost of $242,000, while retaining $180,000 in the bond proposal for fire and safety remodeling and installation of standpipes in some schools.

The 19-member Citizens *ad hoc* Bond Committee agreed to the proposal modifications, according to Thomas Sinclair of Woodbridge, who attended the special School Board meeting Friday.

The School Board agonized over the amount of the bond proposal. Members were reluctant to trim any major items for fear that such a move would result in insufficient funds for the contemplated projects. "It looks like too much for the job that needs to be done," mused Gainesville member William Dunn. "But I'm very apprehensive of what to cut."

"If there is extra, it will not be misspent," Dunn promised. "It will not be utilized," he added.

"If those projects could be completed with less money, the bond would not be sold," assured chairman Ellis Hawkins.

Dr. Snyder resisted suggestions to cut the bond proposal. "I think that's phony. This is the truth. This is real. You may just do the projects for the first time and have some money left over," he admonished.

Dr. Snyder and Hawkins threatened year-round schools and double or triple shifting if the bond referendum does not pass.

School Board Dismisses Ranger From Mired Osbourn Park Job

The Journal Messenger, September 10, 1974. A1. Kathi Keys, JM Education Editor.

The Prince William County School Board dismissed Ranger Construction Company from the Osbourn Park Senior High School construction project, Monday.

The decision was reached when the School Board unanimously voted to terminate its agreement with the Atlanta, Georgia, firm because of default in the contact.

The School Board will, within seven days, terminate the contract and take over "full possession" of the site.

Ranger, along with its bonding company, Travelers Insurance, will be notified of the decision.

Construction of the $7.6 million high school has been underway since December 1971 with the project originally slated to be completed last December.

An amendment to the contract, agreed to in April, extended the completion date to April 15 this year along with a new schedule for finishing various sections of the building. The first section was to be completed by the middle of August and the last, by Sept. 30.

School Superintendent Dr. Milton Snyder was authorized to take the action necessary "to protect the interests and property of the School Board."

He will also be responsible for securing the site, making an inventory of all materials stored on the site, estimating the cost of completing the project and directing the bonding company to bring the bond into full force and effect.

This decision was reached after a nearly two-hour executive session on the Osbourn Park construction project, from 4 to 6 p.m. Monday. Meeting with the School Board and its top administration staff members were Lloyd Smith and an associate of Tremblay and Smith in Charlottesville, the board's attorneys, and A. Ray Pentecost, the school's architect.

At the conclusion of the session, Smith read the three suggested resolutions dealing with the contract's termination which were accepted by the school Board on a motion by William Dunn and a second by John Pattie.

No discussion took place during the School Board session, called for the purpose of Osbourn Park construction.

But there were a lot of questions from members of the Board of County Supervisors who were told the news about an hour and a half later at a joint session of the two boards.

Smith, in explaining the situation to the supervisors, noted that for the past 30 days Ranger has had a "token force" of 10 to 12 men on the job.

During this period, according to an amendment in the contract agreed to in April this year, most of the sections of the new school were to be completed.

But Smith pointed out, "We think the building is slightly over 75 per cent complete. We are going to proceed as rapidly as possible with the bonding company and a new contractor."

He noted, although stating that the architect would be better authority, that if a new contractor is obtained within the next 30 to 45 days, the building "would probably take six months to complete."

The Supervisors raised concern over the costs involved and effect the arbitration case will have on the School Board's decision.

School Board Chairman Ellis Hawkins pointed out that they have not yet determined what costs may be involved in completing the school. There is at least $1.8 million left to complete the project.

The supervisors questioned where additional funds would be obtained. The answer was that the financial situation would depend on the bonding company's decision to either concur or not agree with the School Board's decision.

There were also questions related to the arbitration case, raised by Dumfries District Supervisor Andrew Donnelly. Smith stated that if the board loses the case, "we pretty well lose the suit. But you won't have to pay any more money to Ranger, I'm fairly certain of that."

Other questions were raised by the three other supervisors present at the meeting, Chairman Charles Colgan of Gainesville District, Scott Winfield of Coles, and Don Turner of Neabsco District.

Turner noted, "I resent being called in at the last moment. My first reaction to the termination is 'hell, you can use your own money'."

Winfield's concerns related to the School Board "prejudging" the court's decision. "I'm afraid Ranger's lawyers will use it as a contempt of court."

Colgan also stressed communication between the two boards. Hawkins answered that it was "upsetting" to the School Board when a confidential letter, written by the school attorneys, was released to the press. "This is the reason for our judgment. If it is incorrect, I apologize."

Smith pointed out during the discussion that the agreement or change order reached in April "didn't change anything. We were lead to believe that the project would be accelerated. Maybe it was for 10 days to two weeks."

"Ranger's performance on the job was poor from the first couple months, then it improved. It is not grounds for terminating a contract because they are slow on the job," Smith said in reply to a question why the project was not terminated sooner.

"If we had done it earlier, it would have jeopardized the School Board's case and the performance bond," Smith added.

School Personnel Study Commissioned By Board

Potomac News, September 11, 1974. C6.

Prince William's School Board will commission an outside firm to do a job evaluation of all its classified personnel.

The supervisors recently completed a similar study for their own employees, but they neglected to have school personnel included.

The result is that pay scales for many county employees have been raised, while school workers with similar jobs did not benefit from the evaluation. When the School Board's study is complete, any recommended pay raises will take effect. The supervisors included $375,000 in this year's school budget for adjustments.

At Wednesday's board session. Associate Supt. Mark Rothacker explained that the job is too large to be done in house. He had received two proposals for the evaluation; one would cost $17,000 and the other would cost $23,000. Rothacker will receive a third bid; he will also investigate the possibility of having the firm which did the supervisors' study continue its efforts to include the school staff. The board is expected to name a firm at its next meeting.

Board members were unhappy that they were not included in the original study and suggested that the supervisors be asked to pay for it. There is no money for the study in the school budget; the only other possibility is to take the evaluation costs out of the $375,000 designated for salary increases.

The board will also undertake an evaluation of all administrative staff. Administrators in Prince William have never had either a pay scale or a specific means of evaluating job performance.

Schools Supt. Dr. Milton Snyder reported that the administrator's evaluation can be done in house. He will appoint a task force of administrators to look at salary adjustments.

School Admission Rules Reviewed By Leaders

Potomac News, September 11, 1974. A5.

The Prince William school administration will review a set of potential board policies for admission of students to the school system.

All the potential policies, promulgated by Schools Supt. Dr. Milton Snyder, would make it easier for children to be enrolled in the public schools in Prince William. The School Board looked at the policies last week and referred them to the staff for further study.

The policies include:

- Allowing 12th grade students to finish school in Prince William, regardless of where their parents may have moved.
- Allowing Quantico students to attend Prince William schools for special programs not offered at the base.
- Allowing youngsters who are younger than the state age limit to enter the public schools if they have completed an accepted kindergarten program, and have a high predication for first grade success.
- Allowing any child who has been in public school in another state to enroll in Prince William schools, regardless of the child's age.
- Allowing 12th grade students who do not live in the county to pay tuition based on their parents' ability to pay rather than on actual cost.

Boardmen had two concerns with the potential changes. First, they were interested in funding arrangements. No student who is younger than the state-approved attendance age can be counted in enrollment figures for state aid. The school system would have to foot the bill.

Apparently there would be no problem for 12th graders whose parents live elsewhere in Virginia; the state funding would follow the student, not the parents. Quantico students would not be a problem, either; federal impact aid would cover the county's costs.

The second problem is potential discrimination against some current county residents. Boardmen felt that, if transfers were allowed into the school system regardless of age or ability, it would be unfair to those people who have always lived in Prince William.

The staff will study both problems and return with recommendations.

The School Program

Potomac News, September 18, 1974. A6.

Schools Supt. Milton Snyder in whose hands Prince William County has entrusted its 39,000 public school children, is an experienced and dedicated school administrator. Therefore, when Dr. Snyder voices his fear that the school children "will be under-housed and deprived of a quality education because of inadequate facilities," it merits the most serious concern.

That fear is now being voiced by Dr. Snyder in connection with the alternatives to voter approval this fall of a $45 million bond issue for new school facilities. Dr. Snyder, fellow school administrators, and an *ad hoc* committee appear to agree that the $45 million program constitutes an immediate need—and then is only the surface of an iceberg of $77 million in actual new facility requirements.

Without the program. Dr. Snyder foresees a nightmare of renting makeshift space and bussing students every which way, plus double-shifting and-or mandatory year-round operations. Even splitting the program—perhaps submitting half to the voters now and additional segments later, as suggested in this space three weeks ago—would require double-shifting, which Dr. Snyder condemns as detrimental to a quality education, not to mention the further spiral in inflationary costs which a delay would entail.

Nevertheless, we find ourselves tempering our acceptance of these prospects, in their entirety, by past experience. We've been told year after year, that certain budget cuts would be destructive to quality education, only to see quality education continue to thrive: that past bond issues would meet certain needs which they did not; and that 45-15 year-round school would be expanded throughout the County and eventually cut space needs at least one-quarter. Now the word is that the space savings may be closer to 15 percent.

To lend new credibility to the bond program. Dr. Snyder, who is new to Prince William and not to blame for past misconceptions, moved positively to seek citizen input, through the *ad hoc* committee. And to avoid any short-changing on bond issue promises, the $45 million proposal anticipates the ravages of inflation, to the tune of over $11 million. While there have been questions concerning a $12.6-million-plus-inflation price tag on the one new high school in the program, Dr. Snyder's school plant services director, Paul Trautman, appears to have thoroughly researched today's cost expectations. We have little quarrel with his cost estimates.

But we do continue to suggest that the $43 million bite may be too big, in the light of unsettled growth patterns and a very unsettled economy. To move immediately with the most urgent problems, and hold the rest in one year's abeyance pending clarifications, may produce some temporary crowding. But we would hope it would not seriously impair the quality of education during this period of delay—keeping in mind that buildings alone don't make a school.

Elsewhere on this page is a space-needs analysis prepared by Dr. Troutman and he stresses that it is based on preliminary figures. For the most part, the youngsters represented by the numbers already are enrolled in county schools, and this is particularly the case with those who will be in high school by 1978, when all projects approved this year should be complete.

Clearly indicated is the critical need, in the county's eastern end, for the program's one new high school. Gar-Field and Woodbridge already are over capacity; they face severe overcrowding as 1978 approaches. The program proposes three east-end elementary schools; the chart would indicate that two (at Lake Ridge and Dale City) are unavoidable necessities for this fall. These elementaries would each cost $2.2 million, plus inflation.

In the western end, where an elementary school

also is proposed, one cannot resist moving the eye from the column indicating an elementary space need for 1,068 pupils to another indicating an excess of 976 student spaces in middle schools by 1978, plus an excess of 304 in high schools. Certainly the need for new elementary space is clear, particularly with the inadequacy of Bennett School. But a conversion of Dean Middle School, plus redrafting of school boundaries, might provide a good redistribution of Bennett's enrollment.

Beyond the new high and elementary school plants the proposed bond program contains a number of other projects, which again lend themselves to a limited time spacing, such as the construction of 101 new classrooms to handle kindergartens. There is a provision of $2.6 million for special education facilities; we would hate to see this construction delayed, and it might be a good candidate for direct funding out of current county revenues, rather than through the bond referendum. This would be in keeping with the advice of financial advisors who have repeatedly urged Prince William to finance at least a portion of its major capital outlay on a current basis.

Dr. Snyder, as he has stated, has carried out his obligation by indicating the needs to the citizens of the county, as he sees them. Now the Board of Supervisors must pass judgment not only on the validity of the proposed package but the prudence of committing the county to all of it at one time. The question seems to be how much, if any, can in good conscience be delayed.

1974 Bond Issue Space Needs Analysis

Location	1973-74 Capacity	Sept. 1974 Membership	1978 Projected Membership	1978 Space Needs	1978 Space Excess	Bond Proposed Space
EASTERN COUNTY (Includes year round)						
Elementary (K-5)	11,146	11,825	13,048	1,902		2,490
Middle (6 8)	6,494	5,690	6,510	16		0
Senior (9 12)	5,060	5,473	7,446	2,386		2,000
WESTERN COUNTY						
Elementary (K-5) (Old Bennett excluded)	7,024	7,488	8,092	1,068		1,120
Middle (6 8) (Includes Old Osbourn)	5,017	4,094	4,041		976	0
Senior (9-12) (Includes Osbourn Park)	5,600	4,438	5,296		304	0
TOTAL COUNTY						
Elementary (K-5)	18,170	19,313	21,140	2,970		3,610
Middle (6 8)	11,511	9,784	10,551		960	0
Senior (9 12)	10,660	9,911	12,742	2,082		2,000
Total (K-12)	**40,341**	**39,008**	**44,433**			

Snyder To Recommend School Business Study

The Journal Messenger, September 23, 1974, A4. Kathi Keys.

Prince William County's School Superintendent will recommend tonight that a comprehensive study be undertaken of the school district's business operations.

Dr. Milton Snyder will make his recommendation at the County School Board's special meeting which begins at 8 tonight.

If the board approves the study, it would include an examination, review, audit and investigation of all aspects of the school system's policies and procedures in the area of business operations.

The study's purpose would be to insure that adequate controls and proper methods are used to obtain the most practical and efficient use of funds and facilities in support of the education of the county's children.

Snyder urges close cooperation with the Board of County Supervisors, the business community and all county citizens in conducting the study.

The school district's areas which would be reviewed in the study include purchasing, contract, construction, accounts payable, payroll, data processing, maintenance, warehouse and property control as well as related support groups.

Snyder commented that any large organization has areas in which improvements can be made and an objective evaluation from sources outside the existing school structure will provide "valuable additional insight."

He is soliciting the cooperation and recommendations of the Supervisors and all county residents in helping identify problem areas.

Snyder requests that they immediately inform him of any situations which appear to be questionable, improper or inefficient in order that "prompt, corrective action may be initiated.

"This is essential for obtaining greater efficiencies in these times of limited resources and the erosion of the dollar through an inflationary spiral."

Snyder also added that the study has been under consideration for the past two weeks.

Superintendent's Seminar Appearances on Video Tape

The Journal Messenger, October 14, 1974. A13. Kathi Keys.

School-community participants are being urged to "move forward to create educational structures for boys and girls—a foundation needed for the 1970s and '80s."

This message is being given to all seminar participants by Prince William County School Superintendent Dr. Milton Snyder. Since the superintendent is unable to attend each session, a video-tape presentation was prepared for showing at each session's start.

Snyder relates the importance of each individual's participation in the seminar process and the need to "be open, honest and truthful."

Seminar participants are being asked to assess the school district's needs expressed at last school year's sessions and suggest new and additional ideas.

The results of the seminars, as was done last year, will be compiled by each school's planning council, composed of staff, parents and in some cases, students. This report will then be submitted to the school district's Division Planning Council for inclusion in the updated five-year plan.

Snyder stated, "The results of the seminars will become a basic document in setting goals" for the county school system.

The superintendent stressed the importance of community involvement since the "people know the schools best and the schools belong to the people. Some forget this."

Snyder pointed out that education is a responsibility of the state, which has, in turn, delegated its authority to each local school board.

"Your part is to identify needs" which will be presented to the school board. The superintendent's role in the process is to carry out the policy adopted by the board.

Ten school-community seminars remain to be held. The seminar schedule is as follows:

Oct. 15. Potomac View Elementary School and Woodbridge Senior High School,

Oct. 21. Triangle Elementary School; Rippon Elementary and Middle School.

Oct. 23. Occoquan Elementary School and Brentsville District Middle and Senior High School.

Oct. 24. Kilby Elementary School.

Oct. 30. Osbourn Senior High School.

Nov. 4. Stonewall Jackson Senior High School.

Snyder Lauds Year-Around School Policy

The Journal Messenger, November 8, 1974. A1. Kathi Keys, JM Education Editor.

Stressing the need for year-round school decisions "based on programs, and learning at the heart of the program, not space," Prince William County's school superintendent addressed an educator's group in Manassas Thursday night.

Dr. Milton Snyder spoke to 40 state, county and city school officials involved in various forms of year-round programs in Virginia. Prince William County's 45-15 plan, now in its fourth year of operation, is the oldest, continuous year-round program in the state.

The superintendent had high praise for the County School Board's adopted policy on year-round schools which involves not only school staff members but the community in the process.

The year-round policy, adopted last spring, includes procedures for the board, staff, individual schools and the public to follow in attempting to implement a year-round school program.

"I think Prince William County, after being first, is in better shape to deal with the demands or requests."

He called this procedure a "great deal different" than holding a county-wide bond referendum, which, if passed, would have mandated the year-round program throughout the county. Instead the decision is now placed in the hands of the community residents.

Snyder questioned mandating such programs and expressed a hope that the state will fund a portion of the high school year-round program for a second year.

Following Snyder's talk, Dr. Joe Roberts of the State Department of Education's Division of Educational Research and Statistics, agreed with the local superintendent, noting that year-round schools should be for the "betterment of education."

This is great — Stonewall dedicated

Potomac News, November 20, 1974.

Stonewall Jackson High School, completed in May, 1973, was dedicated Monday night.

Nearly 1,000 people attended the event and toured the new facility following the brief ceremonies.

Principal Robert Lewis emphasized that he wants to get the community again involved with the school. He said it is the "Spirit and tone from this day forward."

Lewis said the real dedication was in having parents tour the school. After comments in the auditorium, people were invited to tour the building before meeting again at the cafeteria for refreshments.

Dr. Milton L. Synder, Prince William's School superintendent commended the school for its being dedicated to students, parents and teachers. Snyder said he has seen several high school dedications that were "phony." He said by contrast there is "no better dedication than that to the total community."

Patty Prunty, a junior and chairman of the Student Needs Committee, observed that at the beginning of the school year the students "didn't even realize we didn't have a principal until Mr. Lewis arrived." She added that some educators take the attitude that children should be seen and not heard, but that is not the case with Lewis.

As parents toured the huge building, one set was overheard saying, "This is great."

No Open Bid Made For School Money

The Journal Messenger, Wednesday, November 27, 1974. A1. Randi Deiotte, JM County Editor.

The ticklish situation of who is going to pay how much for completing Osbourn Park High School failed to surface at Tuesday's supervisors' meeting.

Following a work session between the School Board and the supervisors Monday night, School Superintendent Dr. Milton L. Snyder was expected to ask the county board to work on a financial package to find more than $2 million in order to resume construction on Osbourn Park early in 1975.

Although Dr. Snyder showed up at the meeting as scheduled, he left without addressing the supervisors after conferences with several board members.

Some supervisors believe that the School Board has withheld information from them concerning a Travelers Insurance Company offer to complete the school. According to some supervisors, they want to "get all the facts" before taking any action to provide the excess funds needed to finish the project in time for September classes.

On Monday, Coles Supervisor C. Scott Winfield asked Dr. Snyder if the School Board had had any correspondence from the insurance firm since September when Travelers contended that Ranger Construction Company was an acceptable contractor.

Dr. Snyder answered that the insurance company had "changed its position" since September.

"Will you get the money from Travelers (to complete the school)?" asked board chairman Charles J. Colgan.

"That will be determined in court." Dr. Snyder replied.

"Did Travelers say it will not assume responsibility to complete the school?" asked Brentsville Supervisor Ralph A. Mauller.

Dr. Snyder said the School Board was "maintaining communications" with the insurance firm, which has issued a bond on Ranger guaranteeing completion of the school. The school superintendent added that the School Board had received "a rather elaborate communication" which was being analyzed.

"Either they're going to do it or Prince William County will do it and sue for it," declared Mauller.

"That's the issue," agreed Dr. Snyder.

Colgan told The Journal Messenger on Tuesday that the School Board received a letter from the insurance firm two days ago spelling out the precise conditions under which Travelers would pay for the school's completion.

The Offending Texts

The Journal Messenger, November 27, 1974. A5.

The approach of the Prince William County school system to the use of the controversial supplemental reading material known as the "Responding Series" is to be highly commended. Before making any of this material available for student use, the school district is going that extra mile by involving parents and civic groups in an evaluation of the "suitability of the textbooks for Prince William County youngsters."

The kid-gloves approach of the media in reporting the controversy over these books in other parts of the Commonwealth and in West Virginia has cloaked the entire dispute in an air of mystery. Wire service reports have been very circumspect in their references to the questionable reading matter while the electronic media might place their licenses in jeopardy if they quoted some of the language contained therein. Alluding to the material by name sheds no light on the points at issue for the public to form any opinion based on fact.

Early in November the syndicated Washington columnist Andrew Tully in his column, "Capital Fare," took the bull by the horns and reprinted some of the offending passages while apologizing to family newspapers for sending them such "scruffy" stuff. Tully's purpose was to let the nation know what the controversy was all about and why helpless parents have been so outraged. The quotes he used were supplied to him by an incensed parent.

County parents should be interested in some of the passages which aroused Mr. Tully's ire as much as that of the outraged parent. From one of the books intended for use by ninth grade students comes this gem. "She was a chunky kid, with a good tan and a sweet broad soft-looking can with those two crescents of white just under it, where the sun never seems to hit, at the backs of her legs." Another quote from the same book reads. "No you ain't, you… (missing word).

"Responding Five" for grade 11 students carries these choice words on page 318: "Ramrod up his bum. You whore cockney cullion" and a little further on. "You whining bitchboy, by God I'll run my knife to the hilt in you. You son of a whore, pigsticker." Tully doesn't argue the point as to whether this is literature or not. His contention is that literature of this kind is unsuited for "undeveloped and immature minds to read as part of their junior and senior high school education."

Tully says, "With few exceptions, even high school seniors are still children. They may know plenty of dirty words, and they may play sexual games, but the concept of education is to expose pupils to first-class ideas, not to nudge them into the gutter. Education should sharpen and polish a child's perception, so that later on he will have acquired the wit and the taste to place in perspective the untidy and obscene which intrude upon his daily goings and comings."

Most journalists and others associated with the writing crafts are likely to be somewhat leery of any move seeking blanket banishment of books. Too often there is tendency to be unselective in evaluation, condemning the good with the bad. The censorship of ideas with a meataxe approach can lead to suppression of thought in cases where obscenity is not a factor. However, keeping undesirable materials out of the hands of children is no more censorship than restricting juvenile admission to certain motion pictures.

The open approach chosen by the Prince William County schoolmen should result in a satisfactory resolution of the situation without exposure of county students to unsuitable material. The consensus should result in a solution in keeping with the moral tone of the community. Perhaps these revelations may make more parents interested in seeking active participation in the…(missing words).

Osbourne Park Decision Delayed Another Week

Potomac News, November 27, 1974. A1. Janet Pogue.

The monied fate of Osbourn Park High School in Manassas will stay up in the air one more week after the Prince William supervisors Tuesday delayed until (next) Tuesday a decision on appropriations to pay for the unfinished school.

The decision was a last minute one, urged on by Schools Supt. Dr. Milton Snyder, according to Board Chairman Charles J. Colgan.

The School Board was expected to request $2.24 million for completion of the school. The funds would be in addition to the $1.75 million which the School Board still has in the kitty from the original funds allocated for Osbourn Park.

Osbourn Park is currently about 75 percent complete, over a year behind in construction and the source of two law suits. One was filed by the school's contractors, Ranger Construction. The other is a retaliatory suit filed against Ranger by the School Board.

The prime interest is to get the school completed by September, so that this will be the last year Osbourn students attend school on double shifts.

In order to get the building finished, school officials feel that they must get work started again by January. Although the school is approximately 75 per cent complete, there is substantial amount of work which was improperly done. Taking it apart and redoing it will take time.

The other advantage to beginning construction as soon as possible is the general condition of the building industry. In the current economic slump, the School Board hopes to get a bargain: contractors need the work.

The tentative plan is for the schools superintendent and the county executive to work out the details of a financial plan, which will be presented to both boards for approval. As soon as it gets concept approval for the loan from the supervisors, the School Board can proceed toward getting work going again; the board does not have to wait for the specific financial plan to be completed.

Meanwhile, work on Euclid Avenue is nearly complete. School officials are preparing to award the contract for completion of the roof at the school.

The supervisors and the School Board met in joint session Monday night. Although only three supervisors attended (Chairman Charles Colgan, C. Scott Winfield and Ralph Mauller), they had plenty of questions.

School Plant Services Director Dr. Paul Trautman explained that, if the supervisors do not approve the $2.24 million loan, there may be other sources for the money.

The School Board could garner up to $750,000 from the state's Literary Fund. That fund is established in state law as a low-cost means of financing school construction. Loans from the Literary Fund are for 20 years at an interest rate of three per cent per year.

The remainder of the money, Trautman said, might come from another state fund. That money would be loaned to the county at whatever rate the state had to pay to borrow the money, plus a fee for administration.

The School Board and Schools Supt. Dr. Milton Snyder felt that the best approach to funding would be an agreement between the two boards which would allow the School Board to borrow the money from the county's general fund.

Most of the supervisors' questions related to the method by which construction would be completed.

The School Board, on the basis of technical advice, favors hiring a construction manager, rather than advertising for bids from a general contractor. There were several reasons for the choice; most of them related to the peculiar situation of finishing a school in which there are construction defects.

The School Board's general feeling is that a construction manager, who is paid a salary for his efforts and then hires subcontractors, can get the job done faster and cheaper than a general contractor.

Mauller did not believe it, although technical advisors had talked with the supervisors in a previous executive session. The other supervisors at Monday's meeting were apparently convinced that the School Board was right.

The big bear in the background is still Travelers Indemnity Co., the bonding agent for the high school. Under the terms of its contract, Travelers is required to guarantee enough money to complete the building. However, Travelers' making good its bond is dependent on the federal suit now pending.

If Ranger Construction Co. makes good its allegation that the School Board is the source of the problems with the school construction, then Travelers does not have to pay. If the School Board wins the mammoth $13.8 million damages case by proving that Ranger is the guilty party, then Travelers will have to foot the bill.

Although Travelers has been communicating regularly with the School Board, the firm has given no indication whether it will advance the funds to complete the school.

Decision On School Must Wait

The Journal Messenger, November 28, 1974. A1. Kathi Keys, JM Staff Writer.

A decision on use of Prince William County funds to help complete the delayed Osbourn Park project will apparently wait until Tuesday's meeting of the Board of County Supervisors.

No action was taken this week, supposedly because of the feeling of some county officials that the Supervisors would have rejected the proposal to come up with construction funds to finish the senior high school.

School Superintendent Dr. Milton Snyder told The Journal Messenger on Wednesday, "I urged them (the Supervisors) to give careful consideration to the proposal and to delay their decision until Tuesday so they have more time to study it."

But he stressed the importance of "some type of decision" being made Tuesday.

At stake during these deliberations between the Board of County Supervisors and the School Board is the completion of the county's fourth senior high school, a project originally dated to be completed 11 months ago. The facility is over 75 per cent complete and has already cost county taxpayers approximately $6 million.

Cost of completing the school has been estimated at $3.97 million with $1.93 million of the amount covered by available bond funds and the rest, another $2.04 million, needed from other sources.

Snyder has urged that the school be completed by next fall, a feat according to school officials, that cannot be accomplished unless a contractor gets on the job to finish the project early next year.

No major construction work has been done on the school for almost three months.

The supervisors are being asked by the School Board "to approve and guarantee obligations incurred by the School Board for the completion of Osbourn Park High School and/or incur such obligations as are necessary to raise funds for completion of Osbourn Park High School not to exceed $2.1 million."

If the School-Board is able to recover these funds, then the money would be returned to the supervisors for their disposal.

Snyder has also requested that the two boards "direct their respective executive officers to work together to develop the most advantageous financial package and recommend it to both boards for their respective approval."

Let's Start Doing

Potomac News, December 2, 1974. A6, Opinion Page.

Prince William County can no longer afford to continue compounding the mess left at Osbourn Park High School by Ranger Construction Co., the contractor which has been booted off the premises by the School Board.

The top priority of the Board of Supervisors when it meets tomorrow should be to authorize the School Board to pay up to $2.1 million, as requested, to complete the new high school in time for next September's school term.

Work on the project has been stalled too long by petty suspicions (such as who is trying to cover up for whom), by efforts to politicalize [sic] the tragedy, by legal maneuvering, and by too many hands trying to exercise authority, when one strong hand will do.

Well, all this is costing Prince William more money, as inflation continues to spiral the costs: and it is costing a lot of double-shifted students at the present Osbourn High School an opportunity for early use of the new educational facilities.

The time has come, according to the well-worn phrase, to fish or cut bait.

There certainly should be a full review of how the situation became a disaster, but the first job is to put the situation aright with the school's completion. We strongly recommend the three proposed action steps submitted to the supervisors by Division Supt. Milton L. Snyder—namely that the supervisors approve the incurrence by the School Board of up to $2.1 million in obligations to complete Osbourn Park; that County Executive Clinton Mullen and Mr. Snyder be directed to work up a financing package for submission to the two bodies; and that the School Board then take actions designed to both swiftly and economically complete the project.

The School Board already has indicated that, once given the go-ahead, it would retain a salaried construction manager to oversee the school's completion. This would be an alternative to submitting the project to open bidding, and in the peculiar circumstances existing, we see it as the least costly and most efficient route to follow.

Let's stop talking about Osbourn Park and start doing.

Supervisors Clear Way For Osbourn Completion

Potomac News, December 4, 1974. A1. Herald Grandstaff.

Prince William's supervisors, following a half-hour debate punctuated with shouting, on Tuesday cleared the way for construction to begin again on Osbourn Park High School.

By a 5-1 vote, the board guaranteed $2.1 million to complete the school, now one year late. By another 5-1 vote, the supervisors authorized County Executive Clinton B. Mullen and Schools Supt. Milton L. Snyder to develop the "most advantageous financial package" and recommend it to the supervisors and School Board for respective approval.

Supervisor Ralph Mauller, who fiercely opposed the commitment, was the lone opponent of the two resolutions; Roy W. Doggett was absent.

School Board experts estimate that it will cost $3.97 million to finance Osbourn Park's completion; $1.73 million remains in the school's construction fund.

Today's School Board agenda will include Osbourn Park. Apparently, a construction manager can be hired before the financial details are hammered out by Snyder and Mullen.

THE SCHOOL BOARD is tangled in a complicated federal suit with Ranger Construction Co., the contracting firm that the School Board booted off the Osbourn Park site on Sept. 10. Snyder indicated that "through litigation, some" of the additional costs for completing Osbourn Park "may ultimately be returned to the county."

Now, though, Osbourn Park should at least be completed by the beginning of the 1975-76 school year in order to take Osbourn students off double-shifting. Snyder warned the supervisors that "any further delays beyond the current week in producing an acceptable solution will delay the opening of the new school next year by as much time as it takes to arrive at a solution."

Snyder said later, "I commend the supervisors for having the foresight and strength to move ahead in order to finish this building for boys and girls."

By contrast, Mauller railed "The members of this board and the School Board ought to be held personally liable for any such amount of money that's expended to do some wild trip like this!"

DESPITE MANEUVERS by fellow boardmen and Chairman Charles J. Colgan to keep Mauller from reading a confidential Sept. 27 letter from contracting insurer Travelers Indemnity to the School Board, Mauller persisted through interruptions until he finally read one sentence of the three-page letter into the record:

"Therefore, should the School Board desire to proceed with any other contractor than Ranger," Mauller read, "it should immediately obtain proposals by formally advertised competitive procurement and expeditiously award a contract."

Mauller figuratively hung his hat on that phrase, re-read the sentence and argued several times that a contractor, instead of a construction manager, should be hired to complete Osbourn Park.

Colgan banged his gavel repeatedly for order, but Mauller persisted in his arguments and attempts to read confidential material into the record.

When Colgan called a five-minute recess to muzzle Mauller, Snyder, Assistant Supt. Paul Trautman, Supervisors C. Scott Winfield, Donald W. Turner, Andrew J. Donnelly and Colgan huddled with Mauller to explain the touchy situation—to no avail.

At another point, Turner, Winfield and Vernon D. Dawson left the chambers so there was no quorum in a futile attempt to quiet the ranting Mauller.

THE "CONFIDENTIAL" Sept. 27 letter from Travelers was the first of many and contained several possibilities for the School Board to contemplate. There are many more recent Travelers missives.

Concerning the confidential material. Snyder flatly warned, "The advice of our attorneys is that the individuals who violate the attorneys' recommendation (of confidentiality so not to jeopardize the court case) are to be held responsible for their actions."

Colgan later said it was a "mistake" for any supervisor to publicly bare material which might jeopardize the county's legal position.

When quizzed by the supervisors about communications received, Snyder only reported that much material has been sent the School Board /and the material is being carefully analyzed.

Turner, who sponsored the motions to insure that Osbourn Park construction get moving once again, said the school absolutely must be completed.

Mauller argued, "I think the citizens of this county have absolutely no obligation to put another dime into that school, according to the terms of that contract...When it (the school) is done, $2.1 million is probably gonna turn into $6 million, when they really find out how bad that school is and the condition of it."

MAULLER FUMED that the supervisors' guaranteeing completion of Osbourn Park was "one of the wildest schemes" he had ever heard of and that it was perpetrated "by someone" to get "Ranger and Travelers off the hook."

Donnelly asserted that Travelers has a "legal and moral obligation" to complete the school.

Mauller continued that if competitive construction bids were received, Travelers and Ranger should be notified that a contract should be awarded to the lowest "responsible" bidder—not just the lowest bidder. Then, with Mauller's plan, the school construction fund would be used up, and Travelers would be notified that it is to pick up the rest of the tab. If Travelers did not pay the bills, Mauller said, Travelers' assets should be attached "and get the taxpayers of Prince William County off the hook."

Mauller said the supervisors and schoolmen's plan for completion left "open-ended" possibilities for bills.

Turner pointed out that the supervisors are committing themselves to an absolute $2.1 million limit.

For a brief time, Winfield and Donnelly pondered whether the supervisors' action might jeopardize the School Board's legal position.

Colgan declared his intentions to vote for the motion to guarantee $2.1 million "because the legal counsel, which the School Board has hired and apparently is an excellent law firm, has recommended that this is the proper way to go. The architect also recommended it; the other counsel and the school administration recommended it. I'm going to depend on their expert judgment and hope that it's right."

Secrecy Cloaks Deal: Osbourn Park in Fog

Potomac News, December 4, 1974. 2A.

The volatile Osbourn Park High School situation exploded yesterday when Prince William County supervisors voted 5 to 1 to allow School Superintendent Dr. Milton L. Snyder and County Executive Clinton B. Mullen to find an additional $2.1 million to complete the high school by fall—a sum Prince William County taxpayers will have to repay with interest if Travelers Insurance Company doesn't make good on its bond for the school.

The furor was created by Brentsville Supervisor Ralph A. Mauller, who attacked the school administration, the School Board, and other supervisors for their position on the issue.

Mauller charged that the procedure the School Board intends to use to complete the school, which is nearly a year behind schedule, will negate Prince William County's ability to recover any of the $2.1 million from Travelers—thus socking the taxpayers with the entire bill.

Mauller threatened to reveal the contents of a "confidential" September communication from the insurance firm—a letter delineating the conditions under which the school should be completed. His threat created an uproar as supervisors hurriedly got up from their chairs and left the room to eliminate a quorum.

Board chairman Charles J. Colgan banged his gavel long and hard, declaring a recess. Board members converged on Mauller in an attempt to prevent him from reading the letter.

Dr Snyder, who had sat at ease throughout Mauller's speech, jumped to his feet and admonished Mauller that School Board attorneys had advised that an individual who breaks "confidence" will personally be held liable for any money which the county cannot recover because of public admittance of legal advice. Mauller read part of the confidential letter anyway.

Mauller and Coles Supervisor C. Scott Winfield grilled Dr. Snyder as to whether the School Board has received a recent letter from Travelers offering to complete the school.

Dr. Snyder replied vaguely, "We have received information. We are preparing a response. When we get close, we will let you know."

The school superintendent is reported to have done his politicking with the supervisors in the week since the board's Nov. 26 meeting when the Osbourn Park matter was scheduled for action but failed to materialize.

As supervisors raised points during discussion of the funding, other supervisors answered their questions, seemingly on all. Neabsco Supervisor Donald W. Turner reiterated several points the School Board has previously made by reading them off and County Executive Mullen silently mouthed encouragement to Dr. Snyder as Mauller shouted.

School officials have said they feel certain they can get the needed funds from two state sources in time to resume construction of the 2,500-pupil high school in late January.

Department Heads Go Extra Mile in Spending Cuts

Potomac News, December 18, 1974. A2.

Asked to trim back eight to 10 percent on their third quarter appropriations, county department heads went the extra mile and cut spending requests by 12.6 percent.

At the same time, however, the School Board gave notice to the Board of Supervisors that they could not trim their budget.

The Board of Supervisors had requested its department heads to cut back in the third quarter money requests in order to help balance this year's budget, hit hard by inflation.

Tuesday, the board received appropriation requests for $5,430,891, a total of $684,298 less than budgeted for the third quarter appropriations. In submitting the requests for supervisor approval, Finance Director G.C. Ball noted, "With very few exceptions, (I) found that the department heads made every effort to reduce appropriation requests to bare essentials."

The School Board's request was for $12,656,748, this figure not included in the one submitted by the county department heads.

Although the supervisors approved both appropriations. Supervisor C. Scott Winfield questioned $9,700 requested by the schools to the School Board for an administrative training program. He questioned whether such a program was really needed by the schools in these "critical times."

The school people, he said, were supposed to be administrators already.

Schools' Supt. Dr. Milton Snyder did not defend his request other than to note that his staff had to be receiving constant training in order to function better. He said the request was making its second appearance at the School Board that day, and that the School Board had indicated it would study the project closely.

However, the School Board Tuesday night did approve the request.

Supervisor Ralph Mauller cast the lone no vote in the acceptance of the School Board's appropriations request Supervisor Vernon Dawson was absent.

After approving the appropriations, the board was asked to okay supplemental budget requests for the school food service and the year-round school project at Gar-Field High School. Those-requests, for $225,000 and $115,000 respectively, are completely reimbursable from the State Education Department.

School Budget Shows $15 Million Jump

Potomac News, December 20, 1974. Front page. Lynne Grandstaff.

Preliminary figures for Prince William's 1975-76 school budget show that the price of education could increase by as much as $15 million next year.

In memo to the School Board, Schools Supt. Dr. Milton Snyder said that the budgets submitted by three major department heads show an increase of at least $7 million. These increases result from items such as free textbooks, more buses, conversion of Saunders and Osbourn, and the general inflationary spiral.

Not included in the $7 million increase are numerous major items for which the exact cost cannot yet be determined. For instance, the debt fund (money used to pay back interest and principal on school bonds) will increase by approximately $3 million.

In addition, there is no way to gauge additional expense in salaries until the teacher contract negotiations are complete. Therefore, when department heads calculated their budgets, salaries were counted at their current scale; no figures were included for paying additional personnel.

Including these factors, Snyder judged that the proposed budget increases could add as much as $15 million to the current budget of $50.95 million.

The budget materials submitted to the School Board have not been cut. Snyder obviously expects to make large deletions in the proposals submitted by his department heads, as he prepares his preliminary budget for formal submission to the School Board.

In his message to the School Board, Snyder explained:

"To keep our heads above water, there is no doubt that we will be forced to establish stringent priorities and make wholesale cuts in some areas. We should not, however, make indiscriminate cuts at the expense of our current employees, the safety and health programs affecting our school children, or our basic instructional program."

Alternatives Sought for Rental Textbooks

Potomac News, December 23, 1974. A11.

"We are not defending the textbook rental system," Prince Williams Schools Supt. Dr. Milton Snyder maintained.

"Parents are concerned about it, and so are we. We want more flexibility; we want teachers to feel free to use more supplementary materials. We don't want them to feel bound by a textbook."

Snyder would like to get rid of the textbook rental system, "but, so far, I have little support." Nonetheless, nearly $500,000 has been included in the rough draft of next year's school budget to provide free texts.

The parents of elementary students pay $11.75, while the parents of middle school students pay $13 per year, and high school parents pay $12.

Most of the money goes directly into textbook purchase. The remainder goes for art materials, instructional supplies, library books and current publications. In the high schools, fees paid by parents also go to physical education equipment, athletic uniforms, cosmetology materials and industrial art supplies.

The schools pay for all books and materials for indigent children. Each year, the school administrators get a list of children from the county Social Services department.

However, there are also parents who refuse to pay the book rental. Last year the parents of approximately 700 children refused to pay the fees.

Book rentals have not been raised for several years. Although the price of materials has outstripped the price parents pay, Snyder will not recommend any increase in cost to parents, "because parents have been hit with so many additional costs."

The result is that the schools now pay a large portion of the cost of texts, This year, parents paid $231,000 into the textbook fund; $390,000 worth of textbooks were bought.

Even so, Snyder said that there is not enough money to go around. Some textbooks are too old, but they are still being used. Snyder added that there may be insufficient texts, particularly for social studies and language arts classes.

There are numerous complaints about the rental system. Parents become concerned when they notice their youngsters are not bringing home a book each night. Snyder and textbook coordinator James Rote explained that much of what parents observe is not the result of a shortage of textbooks.

Since Prince William's schools no longer use a single textbook for many courses, a variety of books are available in the classroom. Students check books out overnight, but they do not necessarily bring home the same book all the time.

Another complaint comes from the parents of high school seniors who are taking only two courses. "We tell them that they are getting at least their money's worth in materials," Rote explained.

Although some complaints are not actually related to the textbook rental system, the administrators are not denying that there are, problems.

Snyder maintained, "Textbook rentals were established as an early plan to help start public education in many areas. Now, most public schools consider it their responsibility to furnish textbooks."

Schools Approve Training

Potomac News, December 27, 1974. B8.

Prince William's School Board last week approved spending $9,700 to conduct a leadership training program.

The board contracted with the Institute for Leadership Achievement to work with top-level administrators. School Supt. Dr. Milton Snyder will name an internal coordinator, who will be responsible for working with administrators on the leadership competencies.

Snyder explained that the training program for top administrators will be the first step in an overall training program for everyone from subject-area supervisors to principals. He added that the thrust of the training program is to help administrators make plans and carry them out.

"It will help them meet new concepts, new learning methods, new leadership styles, the best management and fiscal practices," Snyder explained.

Six Builders Okay to Bid School Job

The Journal Messenger, December 27, 1974. A1. Kathi Keys, JM Education Editor.

Six of the 16 construction management firms seeking the job of supervising the completion of Osbourn Park Senior High School have pre-qualified and have been requested to submit proposals.

The firms were selected by a group of school staff members and technical consultants on the basis of criteria identified by the Osbourn Park construction management advisory committee.

The six construction management firms will be required to submit proposals for supervision of the Osbourn Park completion in early January. According to Dr. Paul Trautman, director of school plant services, the exact date had not been decided as of Thursday.

The original schedule called for these proposals to be presented by Jan. 3, but due to the holidays, the firms may be given a few additional days in which to submit plans.

Once presented, the proposals will be given to the advisory committee for it to review, interview the firms and recommend three to five firms to the School Board. The board will then decide which construction management firm should be selected for the project. This decision is expected to be made by the middle of January.

The advisory committee includes School Superintendent Dr. Milton Snyder; County Executive Clinton Mullen; School Board Chairman Ellis Hawkins; Supervisor Chairman Charles Colgan; A. Ray Pentecost, from the school's architectural firm; Lloyd Smith, School Board attorney for Osbourn Park; Dr. C.W. McGuffey and Jim Bruce, school consultants; Trautman, and a representative from Travelers Insurance Company, the bonding company for the general contractor dismissed from the project.

The criteria used to select the six construction management firms contains 10 items. Two of these identified by the advisory committee as the "most important." These two are that the firms "have provided construction management services for three or more years" and "have demonstrated the capability of meeting a time deadline for comparable-sized construction projects of similar magnitude and complexity."

The next most important item according to the pre-qualification criteria is, "The person responsible for this project shall have not less than 10 years combined experience in construction management and general contracting at the management level.

"At least two years of this combined 10 years experience shall be as a construction manager. The construction experience could be either as an architect, engineer, or a construction manager involved in the construction phase of building construction projects."

The construction management firm must also "have on its staff or available as consultants a full range of professionals to include the following: management engineer, architect, mechanical engineer, structural engineer, civil engineer, cost estimator, CPM engineer, systems analysts, construction inspector and cost control accountant."

"At least one of the principals of the firm shall have construction management experience of not less than three years."

The other criteria include:

1. "Have successfully completed one or more projects of $8 million or more as a construction manager."
2. "Have at least one construction management project in progress."
3. "The firm shall be fiscally capable of supporting the services it provides and have liability insurance or a performance bond for this project in the amount of $300.000."
4. "Preference will be given to any firm having experience in the management of a project declared in default."

5. "Preference will be given to construction experience with a school or public construction of a nature similar to schools."

Following the School Board's decision Dec. 4 to proceed with securing a construction management firm to supervise the completion of Osbourn park, firms were invited to submit pre-qualification material.

The information covered the firm's experience and capabilities, the projects the company is currently involved in, a statement on whether the firm has ever been involved in completing a project in default, a listing of the total professional staff, and information concerning the financial strength of the company.

Firms were given from Dec. 5 to 16 to submit this information with the 16 construction management firms replying. It took the school district a week to select the companies which pre-qualified for submitting proposals.

Kindergarten, Osbourn Dominated News

Potomac News, December 30, 1974. A2. Lynne Grandstaff.

"Overall, this is a better school system than it was a year ago," School Board member Thomas Beane assessed the past year.

"There were two big things: kindergarten and Osbourn Park. One we accomplished, and one we didn't," boardman William Dunn added.

As School Board members and Schools Supt. Dr. Milton Snyder contemplated the past year, their thoughts were nearly identical.

"We have some problems, but we coped with many of them," Board Chairman Ellis Hawkins observed. "I think we've come a long way with things in general. We have a handle on Osbourn Park; I'm convinced we will move onward with it. We'll have it ready for next September." Osbourn Park, the 75-percent-complete, year-late high school building, topped everyone's list of unfinished business. Topping everyone's list of accomplishments was kindergarten.

Second on the list was improved cooperation with the Board of Supervisors. Regis Lacey maintained, "There has been a big change in both boards. Both are trying; there is an honest effort to get along. They raise the money, and we spend most of it. Therefore, it is essential that we have an understanding. We don't have to agree, but there must be understanding."

Lacey added a related improvement; he feels citizens have become increasingly willing to call School Board members with their concerns and interests.

"I get a lot of calls from people who are concerned, and not all of them live in Neabsco District. I think it's good when they feel they can call us, even on little things. They're the ones who are footing the bill," he commented.

Boardmen and Snyder had a lengthy list of improvements in the instructional program. "We got the skill development program going in reading and math. We're going to zero in on skill development," Snyder said.

Snyder also mentioned the new alternatives in education which became available for students this year. Under the new programs, students may earn high school credits for a variety of work-study activities. Advanced students may earn credits in short periods of time if they have completed all the work required in a course.

Snyder and the boardmen also talked of improvements in the schools' special education program. The school system is providing more opportunities in special education than ever before, and the movement toward increased services will continue.

There are other areas of improvement. "We started the 45-15 program at the high school level," John Pattie observed.

Beane added, "The attempt at Gar-Field is bringing new thoughts to year-round school concepts."

Beane also observed that class sizes have been reduced, and course offerings have been expanded, in addition, he maintained that the board has made headway in the field of conserving natural resources.

"We are proud of the award given this county by the soil conservation group," Beane said.

Besides the instructional areas, boardmen were proud of in-house accomplishments.

"The budget has been tightened up," Lacey maintained. "We're operating on a tight budget. I don't personally think that has ever been done in the past." Lacey and others commended the work and leadership of their superintendent, Dunn maintained that the reorganization of the staff was a big achievement: "I'm very pleased with the reorganization. Only time will show the fruits of his (Snyder's) labors."

On the other hand, Snyder felt that he spent most of his efforts on reorganization and school plant services: he would have liked to work more on learning behavior. Nonetheless, he concluded, "1 think were doing a great job in certain areas."

Time of Look-Ahead, Fiscal Outlook Worries County School Officials

Potomac News, December 30, 1974. A2. Lynne Grandstaff.

Financial fears and educational aspirations mark Prince William school officials' thoughts about the coming year.

"Even when I think about maintaining the kind of program we have already developed, it scares me." School Board Chairman Ellis Hawkins declared. "I know how tight things are, and I don't know what we're going to do."

"We've got an awfully big job staring us in the face over the next 12 months. We are definitely not going to have many of the things I would like to see," Hawkins maintained.

Other board members seconded Hawkins' concern about finances. "We will have to pull in our belt and make it through another year," Boardman Regis Lacey declared.

Lacey added, "There are a lot of eyes on Prince William; we're one of the fastest growing counties in the country. People are going to look at us more in relation to inflation to see how were combating it. I don't know — the people cannot afford a perfect budget."

The related problem is growth, "a critical issue that will not go away," Schools Supt. Dr. Milton Snyder maintained.

Snyder has estimated between 1,200 and 1,300 additional students next year. For this year, "our enrollment is right on target with the predictions."

Asked about a bond referendum in 1975. Hawkins was pessimistic: "I don't think, with the frame of mind people are in, that a bond referendum of any kind will pass. We're going to have to go to alternatives. We have the children; we have the growth. Children have to be educated, and we have to put them somewhere."

Although officials are leery of financial problems, they also have a wide variety of aspirations for the new year.

Topping most people's list of priorities for the coming year is the completion of Osbourn Park High School. "We've got to get that school done," Boardman Thomas Beane declared. "That's the first priority."

Most officials are also hoping for a closer relationship between the School Board and the Board of Supervisors. "We need more progress toward better relations," Boardman John Pattie explained. "We have had some improvement. It needs to be a two-way street."

Also frequently mentioned was the completion of the year-round school evaluation. Snyder explained. "I think we have a real responsibility to evaluate continuously. We are in a position now where it would be difficult to stop year-round school, but we must know."

Lacey is pushing for an early decision on continuing the year-round program at Gar-Field High School. "I don't know my true feeling yet. My feeling now is that people are willing to pay additional money to stay on year-round school at Gar-Field."

These are other hopes for the new year. Snyder is looking for "mass involvement of the total community. The big thing is people wanting to be involved and our providing a way for them to be involved." Snyder has major instructional goals—continuing the skill development program, working on career and vocational education, examining early childhood education, increasing opportunities in alternative education. "Our major goal is in learning behavior," he explained.

Lacey is looking forward to the public schools taking over the operation of the Didlake and Muriel Humphries Schools. "It is going to be a good year for special education," he declared.

Both Lacey and Pattie place prime importance on providing information for citizens. "We need a public information officer to handle everything that is happening. That is not something the superintendent should have to do," Lacey said.

Snyder and Lacey are concerned about improving fiscal management and accountability. "That continues to be a major goal; I see major changes in planning, controlling and accounting," Snyder maintained.

Beane has another concern: "We need to make sure that we do not allow censorship to take over in the schools. I'm not necessarily in favor of having everything in the schools, but we are running the risk of getting a group of self-appointed censors."

Snyder added, "I really believe in the comprehensive type of education. In a comprehensive school, all types work together."

From instructional goals to financial problems, everyone agreed that people will have to work together in the coming year. Hawkins maintained, "It's going to take a lot of searching to find the right way to go."

Appendix C:
1975

Presentation to Prince William County Principals

by Milton L. Snyder, Ph.D., 1975.

I welcome you today to the beginning of an undertaking that offers you unique opportunities in community leadership and educational development.

You are the first group of principals in Prince William County to undertake a study of year-round education on its merits as an educational program, without the pressure of overcrowding in your schools, and without the need for an immediate decision.

The possibilities are exciting. You have the time to examine with your community and staff the alternatives by which you can best meet the needs of your students, and to do that in an atmosphere relatively free of anxiety about space needs.

As principals, you are the focal points in this study. Your parents look to you as a source of accurate information about educational programs. And, as the educational leader concerned with the best interests of their children. The school board looks to you as the source of valuable information from your school community as they seek to make sound decisions. It is important that you be highly visible to your parents and staff as the leader in this study and that you actively facilitate the free exchange of information between the community and the board.

We are interested in an orderly process of involving people.

This system operates on the premise that people should be involved and informed in the decisions that affect them. Quite simply, people don't like to be surprised. They want to know the alternatives available, the advantages and disadvantages of each, and they want to have an opportunity to give input in their own areas of expertise. If they have been informed and involved in the process, they are far more likely to commit themselves to the outcome.

It is your responsibility to provide opportunities for these exchanges to occur. We welcome discussion, exploration and debate, because the best decisions result from the free flow of information, opinions and feelings.

Once the decision is made, we are all committed to its implementation and so it is important that we adhere to an orderly process leading to the decision.

Board policy is clear on the procedures to be followed, and the policy is a good one.

First, you and your School Planning Council will establish the processes for the study and collect information that will be needed by your community. Your community may have unique needs for information that only you can anticipate.

Next, you will involve parent leaders in studying available information and presenting it to the community. This step in raising community awareness is critical, because your goal is to reach your community with the basic information of the study by the time the formal survey is conducted by an outside agency.

Based on the data supplied by the outside agency and the information collected in your schools, the Board will reach a decision, either to implement year-round school, to drop the study, or to continue it at a later time.

Remember that the work you do with your staff and community will ultimately determine the quality of information available to the Board.

Our aim is to reach the best possible decision for the children of Prince William County. I commend you in your efforts as you begin your study.

Back to Basics

Potomac News, March 1977.

A new year, whether it be fiscal, calendar or school, always presents an opportunity and a challenge for those who are willing to expend the extra effort to seek the opportunity and to accept the challenge. The direction for seizing the opportunity and meeting the challenge in the Prince William County schools was presented this week to the county's teachers in a welcoming address by Dr. Milton L. Snyder, superintendent of schools. His straightforward approach to a program to place greater emphasis on fundamentals comes like a breath of fresh air to many of us who have expressed a good deal of concern about the products being turned out by the public schools. Dr. Snyder has decided to stress a back-to-basics program to reverse the drift toward rejection of specific knowledge in favor of generalities reputed to represent some form of development of the whole person.

The task which awaits Dr. Snyder and his staff is no easy one. There are aspects of the educational process which call for inspiration and stimulation of the individual student. There is a need to guide children to think in terms of concepts, to form value judgments and to learn to cope with life in a complex society. Basic to all these worthy objectives is the need for children to be provided with the fundamental tools by which these goals will be reached. In simple terms, this calls for the ability to read, write and spell correctly while comprehending what is being read. It also means the ability to perform the basic mathematical skills on which our society depends for its everyday functioning. Without these abilities the most innovative educational programs are nothing but a waste of time and effort.

Half measures have been eroding our educational system at all levels for a number of years. Standards have been lowered in the colleges with a corresponding domino effect which has worked its way down into the secondary and primary grades.

An educational permissiveness has resulted in professors of journalism telling college students that spelling and grammar are no longer important. The basic tool of education, our language, has deteriorated because of such loose attitudes and the incorporation of the filth and slang of the gutter into everyday conversation. When high school graduates cannot express themselves in the simplest of terms and are unable to do the simple addition and subtraction necessary to balance a checkbook, something is missing in the educational process.

The new thrust to be given to the development of fundamental skills in the Prince William County schools should be accompanied by the subtle development of character through example and inspiration from the teaching staff. Character development must be interwoven with the teaching process in an unobtrusive manner. As in the television commercial, in which the supposed nutritional cereal turns off the two small boys, courses publicly stamped as character builders will build nothing but resentment. The foundations of character in the church, home and school must be laid by right living and the good example of parents and teachers. This may require a bit of inspiration if it is to take root.

All of us will be watching our county schools closely during the next year as Dr. Snyder and his legions pursue the monumental task they have set for themselves. As we have previously pointed out, quality of education, like many other things, must be judged by the end results. We will be awaiting these results anxiously, not only in form of what scores the educators may devise, but also in that more important criterion, the ability of the students to do things right as they cope with life. The challenge is tremendous and we wish the teachers and administrators of the county schools the greatest success in meeting it.

Snyder: Osbourn Park in the Fall

The Journal Messenger, January 10, 1975. Front page. Kathi Keys, Education Editor.

Osbourn Senior High School students, faculty members and parents were informed Thursday. "We're going to that school (Osbourn Park) in the fall."

This statement was made by Prince William County School Superintendent Dr. Milton Snyder during a meeting with 22 Osbourn patrons. The session was held to inform Osbourn representatives of the progress of the Osbourn Park Senior High School project originally scheduled to be completed over a year ago.

Snyder called the next five days "critical" for completing the school. Proposals from the six construction management firms which prequalified, were due Thursday.

These firms will be interviewed by the construction management advisory committee Monday and the School Board will hold a special meeting Tuesday night to select a firm for the Osbourn Park project.

Snyder explained that the construction management firm, selected by the School Board, will have the responsibility of supervising Osbourn Park's completion as well as working with the subcontractors selected to finish the project.

This firm will be paid a fee for its job and also work with the school architect, Pentecost, Wade and McLellon of Norfolk. The construction manager will also report directly to the School Board and school staff.

Snyder remarked that Osbourn's completion is dependent on two areas, construction and negotiations. The first includes roofing the school, for which a bid has been let. Work has begun. The second item affecting construction is the selection of a construction management firm.

The second area, negotiations, is "on going," according to Snyder. The School Board's attorneys are continuing negotiations with Travelers Insurance Company, the bonding company for the dismissed general contractor, Ranger Construction Company.

Snyder also informed the group that the state treasurer has included Prince William County in the 14 to 15 school districts for which bonds will be sold in February. The amount approved for the county is $1.1 million of a $2.1 million request. If necessary, the additional $1 million will be put on the September bond list for the county.

Once bids are made for the state bonds, the county must approve the interest rate and if accepted, then the funds will be turned over to the Osbourn Park project. These funds are provided through the Virginia Public School Authority.

Questions raised at Thursday's hour-long meeting related to the Osbourn Park building's safety and the use of equipment earmarked for the new structure.

Snyder stated that, according to the architect and a national roofing expert, "the building is structurally sound."

He also said that much of the equipment for the new building is presently being stored.

Osbourn principal James Bailey said 85 percent of the $500,000 appropriated, from bond funds to buy the new school's equipment, has been spent with the items either being used at Osbourn or stored. The remaining 15 percent, to buy such items as wastebaskets and pencil sharpeners will be expended later.

Bailey said Osbourn is unable to use some of the new equipment because of lack of space, but 50 to 60 percent of the electronics equipment is now being used, as well as some science items and 90 percent of the power transportation supplies. Since auto mechanics is being taught in a trailer, the school does not have space to use the new equipment.

Another parental concern was that tables, marked Osbourn Park, were being used at other senior high schools. Bailey explained that such items, as table tops, were simultaneously ordered for the three high schools being built at the same time. Osbourn Park, Stonewall Jackson and Woodbridge.

The items were divided among the three schools with some things, marked with Osbourn Park, going to other locations. But Bailey said the new school will still receive its allocated items.

In addition to the discussion. Osbourn patrons were given copies of a statement Snyder made Tuesday concerning the project's status and a School Board release supporting the proposed grand jury investigation.

Snyder opposes new contract with Ranger

Potomac News, January 10, 1975. Front page. Lynne Grandstaff.

"In view of Ranger's history of performance here and elsewhere, I still cannot recommend a new contract with Ranger." Schools Supt. Dr. Milton Snyder declared in a written statement to the School Board Wednesday.

Snyder's recommendation came as the School Board nears the point of decision on how Osbourn Park High School is to be completed.

In his statement, Snyder briefly reviewed the history of the School Board's association with Ranger Construction Co., the original contractor on the year-late Osbourn Park High School. He also outlined the communications with Travelers Indemnity Co., the insurance company holding the bond for the school.

Snyder maintained, "In essence, Travelers has so far indicated no intention to step in and complete Osbourn Park under the existing performance bond. Travelers says that action on the bond will be tied up in litigation between Ranger and the architect, even if we do negotiate an agreement."

Of Ranger, Snyder declared: "There is no evidence available to indicate that a new contract between the Board of Education and Ranger will produce a completed project. All of the evidence is to the contrary."

Although Snyder is strongly opposed to bringing Ranger back to the Osbourn Park job, he said he feels "the option is open" for Travelers to either elect to remedy or to perform under our original contract with Ranger. Otherwise, we have no choice but to complete the project and litigate the case."

The School Board may reach a decision next Tuesday night at its special meeting. There are two options: the board may either accept a settlement with Travelers or it may elect to hire a construction management firm and complete the project itself.

Negotiations with representatives of Ranger and Travelers are continuing through this week. If there is a new proposal to suggest to the School Board, it should be complete by Tuesday.

Meanwhile, the committee which has been working to find a construction management firm will hold final interviews all day Monday. Their recommendation will also be ready Tuesday night.

There are two apparent advantages of settling with Travelers: the multi-million damages suit brought by Ranger against the School Board would be dropped, and Travelers would pick up the estimated $2.1 million cost overruns on the building.

At the special School Board meeting earlier this week, the School Board was concerned that the building would not be completed by the beginning of the school year and that there would be no assurance that Ranger would perform better than the last time. Travelers attorney Paul Walstad said Monday night that both points would be the subject of this week's negotiations.

The School Board heard a report on those negotiations at Wednesday's session. There was no public word on the progress.

Who is paying? Our Readers Speak

Potomac News, January 22, 1975. Opinion page, A6.

To the Editor:

I am submitting a copy of this letter to the Journal Messenger and the Potomac News as the only action that I, as one citizen can take, at this point in time.

I have been completely disgusted by what I have observed as coming from the attorneys for Traveler-Ranger. I would have far more explicit comments regarding the arguments Traveler-Ranger has put forth but having no legal advice on this, and seeing the vast number of suits this company has engaged in, I shall defer at this time any further comment, other than to say to you, please don't let Ranger get within a hundred miles of that school. (I do hope I can't be sued for this thought.)

Lest anyone question my motives concerning this letter, let me assure them I am in no way, shape or form, connected with anyone on the school board or the staff, unless having a son as a freshman at Osbourn would so qualify me.

I have sat through many meetings of this board, one last Thursday night until 12:30 a.m. I have seen the board, Dr. Snyder and the staff, struggle with one objective; to get Osbourn Park open for the fall semester, to get the school open in the least costly manner, and to be assured of the safety of the building. With the maneuvering of Traveler-Ranger attorneys, and some of the local politicians with their own particular ax to grind, it seems they have apparently lost sight of the question as to who is paying the price for all of this. And that is the 1,750 students attending Osbourn.

Because the board, Dr. Snyder and the staff, are fully cognizant of who is paying the price, they have worked valiantly toward alleviation of this situation. Therefore I wish to publicly extend to you my heart felt and deepest gratitude for your efforts.

Nancy Breeden, Manassas, VA

White males hold most top school posts

Potomac News, March 5, 1975. B6. Lynne Grandstaff.

Of 142 supervisory and administrative staff in the Prince William schools, there are three black women, 10 black men and 20 white women, the rest are all white men. The figures were supplied by school officials.

However, well over half the regular school teachers in Prince William are women. In the elementary schools, there are 635 women teachers and 58 men. The middle schools have 295 women teachers and 167 men. At the high school level, there are 272 women teachers and 242 men. Of those, approximately 90 are of minority races.

There is one black woman employed as a visiting teacher and four white women who work as school psychologists.

Most of the women and blacks in the school administration are principals or assistant principals. Of 29 elementary school principals, there are seven white women and one black man. There are neither women nor minorities among middle or high school principals. There are two black women serving as assistant principals, as well as seven black men and eight white women. Overall, of 91 principals and assistant principals. 24 are women or minority representatives.

The most prestigious position held by a black or a women is human relations specialist. Dr. Walter Dean serves directly under the schools superintendent in that capacity; Dean was hired recently for the new position.

The supervisory positions held by blacks are Title I supervisor, reading supervisor, elementary social studies supervisor.

There are three women working as elementary education supervisors. The food services supervisor is a woman, as is one middle school supervisor. The Title I (the federally funded program for the culturally disadvantaged) supervisor is a black woman.

At last week's School Board meeting. Schools Supt. Dr. Milton Snyder included an information item concerning equal employment opportunity. The board was not asked to act on the proposal. Basically, the plan calls for all current staff to comply with both the letter and the spirit of the federal Equal Employment Opportunity Act in hiring and promoting practices.

The memo states: "Supervisory personnel must recognize that the assumption of their responsibility for making constructive contributions to the goal of equal opportunity is a condition of their employment."

In addition, the memo proposes an affirmative action program in relation to hiring and upgrading minority and women employees.

The proposals include:

- Analyzing the present work force to identify jobs, departments and schools where minorities and women are underutilized.
- Setting specific, measurable goals for hiring and promotion, with target dates. All supervisory and administrative personnel would then be held accountable for meeting the goals.
- Re-evaluating job descriptions and hiring criteria to assure that they meet actual job needs. Current personnel would then be responsible for finding minorities and women who qualify, or who can become qualified, for positions.
- Focusing on getting minorities and women into positions or training opportunities which will allow them greater opportunities for advancement.
- Monitoring the plan to make sure it is working.

What's in a Name? A Board Night's Work

The Journal Messenger, March 6, 1975. Front page. Kathi Keys, JM Education Editor.

Names may now be placed on such Prince William County School facilities as auditoriums, field houses or gymnasiums, stadiums and libraries.

This decision was reached Wednesday by the Prince William County School Board in a 4-2 vote, with one member abstaining.

The board policy previously restricted appellations to school buildings, although the senior high schools have been allowed in the past to denominate stadiums.

The addition of building parts to the school naming policy means that nominations must come from a committee composed of board members, professional staff, students and citizens of the school's community. The final denomination rests with the school board.

The policy change was prompted by a request from Woodbridge Senior High School to name the new school's gymnasium. Since the policy only covered the naming of buildings, the School Board referred the matter to its staff for a review of policy.

The staff report was presented Wednesday to the board in the form of an administrative interpretation of the policy.

School Superintendent Dr. Milton Snyder said the existing policy could be interpreted to cover a "major component of a building or buildings on a given school site, provided such components are distinctly used for community affairs, for extended school days, or have been provided because of a substantial gift from a patron and it is deemed in the best interest of the school board to assign such additional name or names to a given school building component on a school site."

He suggested that names could be assigned to auditoriums, field houses, stadiums and libraries.

A lengthy discussion look place on whether names should be given to the parts of a school facility and if the final decision should rest with the board.

Regis Lacey of Neabsco District introduced a motion, seconded by T. Clay Wood of Brentsville District, that the policy remain intact.

Snyder took exception to this as he asked that his recommendation be shown along with the motion. "I don't see your purpose. It's a way you could even make friends with the people in a community."

Wood withdrew his second to the motion which died for lack of another second.

William Dunn of Gainesville District introduced a second motion stating that the board follow the policy, as recommended by the staff, and add auditoriums, field houses, stadiums and libraries. This was seconded by John Pattie of Dumfries District.

The vote showed Chairman Ellis Hawkins of Occoquan District, Thomas Beane of Coles District, Dunn and Pattie in favor of the change; Robert Boyd of Manassas District and Lacey against the motion, and Wood abstaining.

The board named the committee responsible for making nominations for the Woodbridge gymnasium. Included were Hawkins as the board representative; faculty members, Thomas Beavers, Douglas Dean, Austin Parker, Marjorie Florence, Phillip Farley and Hugh Browning; and Eugene Lee, supervisor of health and physical education.

Other committee members include Woodbridge patrons, Charles White Sr., Mary Valentini, Steve Cantu and Charles Fields, and students, Joe Manderfield, Karen Oliver, Jay Trehy, Pam Bureess and Fritz Veasey.

School Budget Work Scheduled by Board

The Journal Messenger, March 7, 1975. 3A. Kathi Keys.

The Prince William County School Board has scheduled a budget work session for Wednesday at 4 p.m. to continue its review of the preliminary 1975-76 school budget.

The board began its line-by-line review of the budget Wednesday during a two-hour work session which came at the conclusion of a day of regular school business.

The preliminary budget amounts to $56,619,954, a $4.8 million increase over this year. This does not include additional professional and classified personnel, salary increases for present personnel or the increased costs of employee benefits, since negotiations are continuing between the board and the Prince William Education Association.

School Superintendent Dr. Milton Snyder has scheduled four meetings to speak to members of the School Planning Councils and parent organizations on the preliminary 1975-76 school budget.

Two meetings were scheduled Thursday, at Woodbridge Senior High School and Gar-Field Senior High School for Woodbridge area parents. The third meeting was to take place today at Osbourn Senior High School and the last, Monday afternoon at Stonewall Jackson Senior High School.

Other matters coming before the school board Wednesday included:

Learning Disabled Program—The board, by a 5-0 vote, with two members abstaining, agreed to implement a program for middle school students who have been identified as learning disabled, provided funds are available. There are presently no school funds available for the program, estimated to cost $116,355, and a supplemental appropriation will be necessary.

Special Education Plan—the board unanimously approved the five-year special education plan and asked for a clarification from the State Department of Education on the state funding of the special education programs, required by the state.

Vocational Foundation—The board gave final approval to the formation of vocational foundation, similar to one which exists in Fairfax County. The foundation's purpose is to provide practical vocational training for high school students in such areas as the building trades.

Fourth Quarter Appropriation—The board requested the supervisors to allocate the fourth quarter appropriation of the 1974-75 school budget. This amounts to $11,329,687.

Alternate Education—Sam Cox presented a report on the progress of the alternative educational programs which have been implemented during the 1974-75 this school year. Fifty-two students are presently enrolled in the individualized program.

Schools call hiring freeze

Potomac News, March 12, 1975. Front page.

Prince William's schools will institute an across-the-board hiring freeze on all personnel.

The school problem is not with the current year's budget; the problem is hiring people to finish the current year and continue in the school system for next year. With a large budget cut, their positions could be abolished, even though the board had contracted to pay them.

In his message to the School Board Wednesday. Schools Supt. Dr. Milton Snyder said the hiring freeze was essential in light of expected cuts in the 1975-76 school budget. Snyder said, "Although undesirable from the standpoint of personnel needs, it would be difficult to conceive of a sizable cut without a reduction of personnel, since the pay of people accounts for the major part of our budget."

The School Board gave only informal assent to the proposal. Snyder did not feel a formal vote was necessary, and the board's consent was unanimous.

Snyder excluded what he called emergency situations, he said each of those would be individually evaluated. Snyder said any personnel problem which impacts the learning process would be an emergency. Apparently, no one is precisely sure how teacher vacancies between now and the end of the year will be handled, but classes will not be dispersed if the teacher does not finish the school year.

School Board Slaps Freeze On Personnel

The Journal Messenger, March 13, 1975. Front page. Joan Mower, JM Staff Writer.

Efforts to pare the proposed $56 million school budget will directly affect the educational programs offered in the schools. School Superintendent Dr. Milton Snyder told the school board Wednesday.

"It's tragic," said the impassioned Snyder. "You must touch the instructional program, but classrooms will remain the priority item," he added.

Taking a dramatic step to keep to a skeleton budget. Snyder asked for an immediate freeze on hiring school personnel. The freeze would cover instructional, administrative and classified employees. The school board backed Snyder's request, without a formal resolution.

In practical terms, the freeze would mean an end to hiring even when a position opens. Gainesville Board member William Dunn asked Snyder what would happen if a classroom teacher left the county.

"We'd probably make do with substitutes," replied Snyder.

Board members bandied around the idea of redirecting part of the school board's central staff back to the classrooms. "We'd probably cut the central office staff by about 14 to 15 people and put them on the teaching staff," said Board Chairman Ellis Hawkins in a telephone interview today. The board is awaiting a job classification study before acting.

The $56 million budget excludes pay hikes for the school staff. Negotiations between the school board and the Prince William Education Association (PWEA) are continuing.

The revised school budget must be presented to the Board of County Supervisors by April 1 and the budget will determine whether or not the county can expect a tax increase.

County Executive Clinton Mullen has instructed the school board to "hold the line" on the budget. Mullen's county budget, given to the supervisors Tuesday, calls for a two to three per cent increase over 1975 and alone will not necessitate a tax raise.

A disagreement arose between Hawkins and Neabsco board member Regis Lacey on how much the budget should be cut before final presentation April 1.

Hawkins advocated keeping budget increases at 10 percent over last year, excluding debt service and special education funds. The total 1974-75 school budget was $51.8 million.

Following Hawkins line of reasoning, the school budget would be projected at about $55 million. If special education costs to handle the takeover of Muriel Humphrey and Didlake School, facilities for the retarded, are added in, the projected budget would near $56 million, said Hawkins.

Hawkins' calculations call for roughly $4 million for staff salary increases and $8.1 million for debt service.

"There is only so much money you can hope for… times are tough," said Hawkins.

Lacey, argued on a different tack, suggesting the school board look at "educational programs rather than money." He said the supervisors hold the final purse strings and they will decide how much the budget is cut.

"We have to present the best programs in the county rather than trying to outguess the supervisors," said Lacey. Using hypothetical examples. Lacey said, "If you go with a 10 percent increase, they (the supervisors) will cut you to five percent, if you go with a 25 percent increase, they'll cut you to 15 percent. "We should go to them and say, 'this is the program we want' ."

The special education fund remains a sore point with the school board. To take over Muriel Humphrey and Didlake Schools, the school board allocated a $769,643 for 1975-76.

Some board members say the responsibility for the schools was shoved on the school board by the supervisors.

Hawkins said today he hopes the supervisors

will provide a special allotment for schools from the county-budget.

The Tuesday budget-cutting session dealt with reductions in the school's capital-outlay fund.

On instructions from the school board, Snyder said the staff has slashed the proposed fund $2 million to $1 million.

"You've cut everything we asked." Dunn said to Snyder.

In another matter, Mullen appeared before the board to get input on his proposed "central construction management office." The construction office would oversee administration for new county facilities. Mullen suggested the school board join forces with the county in running the construction management office.

The board liked the idea, but sought legal advise before firmly accepting the offer. By state law, the board is responsible for its own construction.

Classroom given priority

School board seeks 10% budget hike; will trim some areas

Potomac News, March 14, 1975. Front page. Lynne Grandstaff.

Prince William's School Board on Wednesday informally directed Schools Supt. Dr. Milton Snyder to return next week with a school budget which is 10 percent higher than the current spending level. Because of uncontrollable cost increases and increasing enrollments, a 10 percent increase means a decrease in services for Prince William students.

With part of the cutting done, Snyder told the hoard, "You must touch the instructional program to make it through 1975-76. It is going to affect everyone, although we will set education in the classroom as a priority." One potential victim will be the transfer of the Muriel Humphrey and Didlake schools to the public schools.

The budget reduction is, at least in part, a reaction to the supervisors' call for a hold-the-line budget. Board Chairman Ellis Hawkins said a no-increase budget is "entirely out of the question. There has to be some increase."

Hawkins, who made the reduction proposal, explained, "In my time on this board, I have never had to deal with times as tight as these. The federal government is looking at a tax cut; if we take the money back in county taxes, not much has been accomplished."

Hawkins excluded the $2.8 million increase in the debt service from his call for a 10-percent budget increase. He said he is envisioning an increase of approximately $4.5 million in the school operating budget, plus the debt service increase.

The previously proposed $56 million school budget shows a $4.06 million increase in the operating budget, but it has no money for either personnel additions or salary increases. Salary increases alone, most of which are part of the negotiated teacher contract, have been estimated at between $2.5 million and $3 million.

Therefore, the directive to get the entire operating budget to a $4.5 million increase means that most current budget increases will have to be scrapped, along with some longstanding budget items. Also, the board directed that no additional staff positions will be included. These range from bus drivers and secretaries to teachers and central office staff.

With an expected increase of approximately 1,500 students, there will be increases in pupil-teacher ratios in some county schools, as well as potentially longer bus rides for some students.

Both Hawkins and Snyder are also talking about reductions in the central office staff. Probably, some instructional supervisory people will be teaching classes next year.

Hawkins does not believe that the budget reduction will mean releasing current teachers. Snyder said he will develop a number of alternatives on staffing, the board will presumably get to choose among them.

The other major problem area is special education. In its original budget, the School Board carried special education program improvements and the transfer of the Muriel Humphrey and Didlake schools to the public school system as separate items costing approximately $1.2 million.

Now, Hawkins is saying those programs may have to be scrapped, unless the Board of Supervisors chooses to provide separate funding for them. He said, "Without additional funding, we cannot hope to achieve what the Board of Supervisors is asking us to do."

Other boardmen may be less willing to part with the special education programs. Both Regis Lacey and Robert Boyd said at Wednesday's board meeting that they were opposed to backing away from special education commitments.

There will be other reductions. All money for equipment replacement has been cut, along with all money for new vehicles, including school buses. Construction and maintenance money has been trimmed to a contingency fund. Administrators hope to make it through the year.

The maintenance cut may cause problems. Three schools are now operating on only one of its three boilers. The boardmen agreed that, if the third boiler blows, the School Board would have to go to the supervisors for extra money. The problems at Parkside and Saunders Middle are as bad as at Stonewall Middle, Snyder said.

Hawkins believes that his proposed budget reduction would get the county schools through the year and "not hurt the program tremendously. If I didn't think that, I wouldn't propose it. But a lot of things aren't going to be there, which people have gotten used to."

Racial imbalance in schools?

Court order takes Prince William officials by surprise

The Journal Messenger, March 19, 1975. 3A. Lynne Grandstaff.

"I'm almost certain we're not in violation," Schools Supt. Dr. Milton Snyder said this weekend concerning the pending HEW investigation of racial imbalance in Prince William's schools.

On Friday, Federal District Court Judge John Pratt ordered the Health, Education and Welfare (HEW) Department to challenge racial imbalance in 125 school districts in 16 southern and border states. Prince William was on the list, along with Fairfax and Montgomery counties.

Judge Pratt's definition of imbalance, according to published sources, is any school with a minority enrollment more than 20 percent above the district's average of minority students.

In Prince William, there were 2,535 black students among the 39,455 students reported to HEW in October. The average is 6.4 per cent, but no Prince William school has more than 20.6 per cent black students.

Antioch, which houses the kindergarten and first grade students from Gainesville Elementary, has the 20.6 percent black enrollment. Gainesville was the only county school which did not report its racial composition figures to HEW this fall.

Other schools with relatively high black enrollments include Dumfries Elementary (16.8 percent), Tyler Elementary (16.6 percent) and Triangle Elementary (16.5 percent) Coles Elementary has no black students, and Loch Lomond and Sudley Elementary schools have less than one percent black enrollment.

From published sources, it is apparent that officials in Fairfax and Montgomery counties knew they had schools with minority enrollments exceeding Judge Pratt's guideline, which was set in 1973.

In Prince William, officials were taken completely by surprise. School information officer William Helton told The Potomac News, "All I know about it is what other reporters have told me. All I know is from the wire service reports. We have been so busy with reporters on the phone, we haven't had time to get a copy of the judge's order from the court. It came as a complete surprise."

Snyder said. "According to our information, we're puzzled by the judge's order. Naturally, we're going to have to study it, but I'm almost positive there must be some mistake."

The racial balance information given to the Potomac News came from carbon copies of the reports sent to HEW. Besides black students, the reports include the number of American Indians, Asian Americans and Spanish-surnamed Americans. Prince William, overall, has 138 American Indians, 313 Asian Americans and 336 Spanish-surnamed Americans. They are spread among the county's schools. Overall, the minority population in Prince William's schools in 8.4 percent.

If there is a problem at Gainesville-Antioch, there should he little difficulty correcting it. Gainesville is overcrowded; a large boundary change with Tyler has already been planned for next year. Judge Pratt's order directs HEW to bring wayward schools districts into line in seven months.

A potential clarification may be on the way. School Board Chairman Ellis Hawkins arrived home Saturday to find that a packet of registered mail had been returned to the post office.

"As far as I know, we've been following the guideline," Hawkins said, "but that may be HEWS information which the mailman tried to deliver. Now, I have to wait until Monday morning to find out what it is."

Turner Calls Recess In Board-School Fuss

The Journal Messenger, March 19, 1975. 3A.

Neabsco Supervisor Donald W. Turner, standing in as chairman for C. Scott Winfield who was ill Tuesday, kept a tight rein on the board meeting and called a halt to the proceedings when Brentsville Supervisor Ralph A. Mauller began yelling at the county's superintendent of schools.

School Superintendent Dr. Milton L. Snyder was before the board to answer questions about the progress of Osbourn Park High School and the financing of the multi-million project which was to be completed nearly 15 months ago.

Snyder was evasive on the advice of school board attorneys, he said, and refused to answer Mauller's insistent questions about whether the school board has a contract with Ranger Construction Company.

When Mauller paused for breath, Turner recognized Gainesville Supervisor Charles J. Colgan, who could not get in a word when Mauller started on Snyder again.

"It you do not have a little respect for a member of this board, then I am going to adjourn this meeting and you can talk in the hall," Turner threatened.

Colgan protested Mauller's tirade, saying the Brentsville supervisor should have a "little respect and dignity for the superintendent of schools... and not talk to him like (he were) some kind of criminal."

Mauller turned on Colgan, shouting, "You and your damned people are trying to get another million out of them (taxpayers)" to complete Osbourn Park.

At that, Turner refused to allow the meeting to continue and called a recess.

Snyder recommends allowing readings

Potomac News, Friday, April 4, 1975. A2.

Schools Supt. Dr. Milton Snyder recommended Wednesday that students be permitted to have religious readings on extracurricular time in Prince William's schools.

Snyder also recommended that the School Board contemplate the proposal before acting on it.

Snyder said, "I've been concerned for several years about criticism of the public schools because of the Supreme Court ruling. People have criticized public schools about students' not being able to talk about the Bible or study religion. I think students may study and talk about these things."

Snyder's proposal is that religious reading groups may be established in the schools under the guidance of the principal in the same way as any other extracurricular activity. The proposal would allow students to gather for religious study before and after school or at their lunch period. Study halls would not be included.

Snyder said, "Without advice, school principals are on their own and may need some help. The board should help in reviewing this and see if it wants to go this far."

Snyder's proposal follows an opinion from the School Board attorney that allowing religious readings in extracurricular time would not violate the Supreme Court decision concerning religion in the public schools. To be legal, the board must allow any kind of religious group to meet and study in the schools.

However, attorney R.O. Kellam advised against starting religious reading groups. He said there would be a legal problem if the board (or the principal) refused to allow any kind of religious group to meet in the school if it allowed orthodox religious groups to hold reading or study sessions.

His opinion said, "Looking at the matter from the 'Establishment' point of view (of which I am a part), I find that our orthodoxies generally have plenty of space in their places of worship for reading of 'the word.' Some of the cults which I consider kookie do not. If we extend a convenience to the established religions, we must also provide a spawning ground for the kooks."

Snyder also told the board that the staff is studying school policies about flags and saluting them. At a future meeting, he will ask the board "to review our policies on patriotism."

Uneasy Lies the Head

The Journal Messenger, Vol. 107 No. 18, April 24, 1975.

"Uneasy lies the head that wears a crown." This quotation from Shakespeare's "Henry IV" is usually applied to those in positions of great responsibility. One such person on the local scene is Dr. Milton Snyder, superintendent of schools for Prince William County. While Dr. Snyder wears no crown, his position as chief administrative officer of a school system serving more than 35,000 students makes him a prime target for all those who have the least dissatisfaction with any phase of the operation of the county's schools.

While not necessarily agreeing with all of Dr. Snyder's positions or philosophies, we do not believe that he should be made a whipping boy by everyone whose individual desires are not being fulfilled by the school system. The recent hard times which have befallen the county are one example of the situations which result in abuse being heaped upon the superintendent from all quarters.

Those who consider the school budget and the taxes it generates to be too high put the blame on Dr. Snyder. The teachers label Dr. Snyder as the villain because of the cuts he is forced to make in trimming the budget to fit the requirements of the Board of County Supervisors. Those whose special programs have become victims of the budget add their darts and brickbats to those already aimed at him from all sides.

The recent hassle over the completion of Osbourn Park High School was another instance in which Dr. Snyder was caught in the middle. Coming into the county after this project was well under way, he was called upon to straighten out messes which were not of his making. Political overtones connected with the controversy did nothing to make his job any easier. The groundwork for many of the problems was laid by a former School Board and a former Board of Supervisors working with administrators who were no longer on the scene. As the current head of the school system. Dr. Snyder caught the flak.

In the current controversy over the school budget and the curtailment of educational services. Dr. Snyder is caught between a rock and a hard place. A large bloc of parents and teachers are making demands which are next to impossible to meet in view of the irrevocable restriction which the county supervisors have placed on the tax rate, the principal source of county revenue. Whether he likes it or not, the school superintendent must operate within this framework in trying to make the best of a bad situation. Acting under orders to do all the trimming from the school budget to meet the $3.62 tax rate. Dr. Snyder has no alternatives open.

In spite of all the unwarranted abuse which has been directed at him. Dr. Snyder has managed to maintain his composure in the face of situations which would try the patience of a saint. Required by the nature of his job to be a business tycoon, a construction expert and an educational savant, the superintendent is expected to combine all these diverse elements and keep everyone happy at the same time. It should be obvious to anyone with a modicum of common sense that this is, at best, an impossible task. Dr. Snyder has done remarkably well in view of the circumstances with which he has been faced.

To his credit, Dr Snyder has displayed an openness and accessibility which would be hard to match in any administrator working under like conditions. His policies of citizen involvement through school seminars and his approach to the recent book controversy demonstrate his willingness and ability to work with the citizenry. Many of the changes he has planned for the streamlining of the school system for greater efficiency are just coming to fruition. When one totals up the balance sheet in a fair manner, the realization should come that we have an unusual man trying to do an impossible job against overwhelming odds. Think twice before you cast that next stone.

Board Takes Responsibility

Snyder Backed on School Budget

The Journal Messenger, May 8, 1975. A1. Joan Mower, JM Staff Writer.

The members of the Prince William County School Board publicly defended the proposed $55 million school budget Wednesday, and backed up the actions of Dr. Milton Snyder, superintendent of schools.

Snyder had faced a grilling on the budget by the Board of County Supervisors Tuesday. Several supervisors had accused Snyder of dissimulating on the budget proposals.

"I want every one to know that the proposed budget is the school board's budget. It is not Dr. Snyder's budget," said chairman Ellis Hawkins.

Hawkins charged the supervisors were assuming the $55 million budget was Snyder's personal outline of expenditures. In fact, Snyder had presented the school board with a much larger budget (missing text). The school board chopped the original proposal (missing text) $55 million budget.

The other school board members echoed Hawkins sentiments. They took responsibility for the budget.

Wayne Moore, the school board's financial advisor, told why the board expects a surplus of about $900,000 left over from the 1974-1975 budget. The anticipated surplus irked some supervisors Tuesday. The supervisors reasoned the school board consistently over-estimates expenses to come up with operating surpluses.

About $700,000 derives from federal impact aid, said Moore. The school board cannot count on the impact aid in balancing the budget because the aid varies from year to year.

The federal impact aid goes to the county coffers, said Moore. The county does not use the money for additional school programs, he added.

"I would quarrel with the supervisors for not putting the impact aid into programs," said Snyder.

According to Moore, he and his predecessor had "never over-estimated revenue from outside sources."

Another $200,000 surplus in 1974-1975 is the result of school belt-tightening. Snyder put the brakes on spending this year by implementing freezes on hiring and purchasing he said.

Regis Lacey opined the cash surplus in 1974-1975 demonstrates "good fiscal control on our part."

In a rare moment of ire, Hawkins predicted the supervisors would look at the school's excess funds and say, "Why the hell didn't you save more?"

School board members vowed to attend the supervisors' hearing on the $3.62 tax rate today. The tax rate is expected to be set this afternoon.

In other business, the school board considered:

Classified Personnel: The board approved expenditures (missing text) for a (missing text) workers from January (missing text) employees raises last year. The supervisors doled $130,000 out of the fund for the six month raise.

Tax bills to go out at $3.62 rate

Potomac News, May 14, 1975. A1. Janet Pogue.

Real estate tax bills with a $3.62 per [sic] $100 rate will go into the mail this week, but neither the School Board nor the county knows how much money they will have on which to operate in the new fiscal year.

Prince William supervisors Tuesday approved the long-awaited and expected $3.62 rate to fund a total school-county budget of $75.3 million. They could not agree on the school budget; however, the motion approving the $3.62 rate directed school administrators to cover the hiring of 50 new teachers and the funding of a special education program and transfer of Muriel Humphrey and Didlake Schools into the county's school system.

Also included in the motion, made by Supervisor Charles J. Colgan and seconded by Supervisor Donald Turner, was a directive to the school personnel that they come up with another plan for cutting out $2.5 million from the budget. The $2.5 million cut was imposed by the supervisors when they first agreed to advertise a $3.62 tax rate, prior to the public hearings and prior to Tuesday's adoption of the rate.

Basically what the supervisors are requesting is that the School Board try to make as many cuts in the budget as they can without affecting the instructional level, i.e., the pupil-teacher ratio and the number of teachers. To do so, the supervisors are asking the School Board to make as much of the $2.5 million in cuts in areas outside the teaching fund where the School Board had originally proposed $920,000 be trimmed by eliminating 92 teachers.

Until they hear from the School Board again, then, the county and schools do not know how much they will have on which to operate next year.

The 5-1 vote assures that 50 new teachers—or $500,000—will be included in the budget. Another $475,000 will be used to fund the learning disabilities program and a total of $571,000 for the transfer of the two schools for the retarded.

Supervisor Ralph Mauller was the lone holdout in attendance who voted against the motion. However, Supervisor Roy Doggett, in the board session during the early part of the budget talk, stated before he left that he wouldn't go higher than a $3.40 rate.

Two motions were defeated before Colgan finally authored the successful wording. Mauller made a motion for a $3.40 rate, with he and Doggett voting against the board majority.

Board Chairman C. Scott Winfield gave up the gavel and made a motion to adopt a $3.62 tax rate with the stipulation that $1.6 million of the $2.5 million cut from the school budget be added back in. That motion was tied in a 3-3 split, with Mauller abstaining.

Although the $3.62 tax rate was set, it may not be the same rate the county residents will be charged with in December. If the School Board can come up with a budget closely aligned with the $2.5 million cut, and if the county budget can be trimmed in some area as Colgan had earlier suggested, the board may vote to lower the tax rate prior to the December billing. The supervisors may at any time vote to lower the tax rate.

Some supervisors strongly criticized the administrators who prepared this year's school budget, suggesting that the School Board "take another look at their management team."

Winfield said he was very unhappy with the answers he had received from Schools' Supt. Dr. Milton Snyder and his regime. Supervisors Andrew Donnelly and Dawson also said they did not feel their questions were answered.

Following the $2.5 million cut imposed on the school budget by the supervisors, the administrators cut out $43,495 in supplies—including $13,780 in instructional non-vocational supplies.

Capital outlay cuts amounted to $751,000,

including a sacrifice of $175,000 for new buses.

Dawson also said that several board members had been told that the administration—presumably from Dr. Snyder's office—had ordered school personnel to muster their forces at the two public hearings on the budget.

Winfield said he would "be willing to vote to supply the $60,000 to buy out Snyder's contract."

A spokesman for Dr. Snyder said he was "not aware of any organized, centralized drive or to put words in their mouths." The spokesman said that principals were called in after the budget cut but prior to the release of information on what effect the cut would have on the school system. They were not urged to marshal their forces, however, the spokesman said.

Monday night, during the third work session with school people, the Board of Supervisors weren't ready to talk final budget figures. They were more interested in getting answers to questions that have plagued them since the school budget talks began.

The school administrators came fully prepared to document pupil-teacher classroom ratios and explain where they had made the $2.5 million cuts the supervisors had first imposed on the requested school budget. Mauller, however, kept up a barrage of attacks on the administrators' pupil-teacher ratios, arguing that they were intentionally misleading to paint a blacker picture of the classroom situation.

At Stonewall Jackson High School, for instance, the school people determined through a step-by-step analysis of each department, the number of classes and the number of teachers instructing in those areas, that the average pupil-teacher ratio was 20.6:1.

Mauller said no. He came up with a figure of 24.5:1 by taking the number of class periods and dividing them by the total number of students enrolled in those areas. By his analysis. Stonewall Jackson has 17.4 too many teachers; the School Board in its requested budget asked for six additional positions, although all of them may not be full-time teachers.

The school leaders also had figures on Osbourn and Brentsville senior high schools, all middle schools and all elementary schools. In addition, they said they would have the information on Woodbridge and Gar-Field high schools in the next day or so. According to the school peoples' data, Brentsville has a ratio of 15.46:1 and Osbourn a ratio of 20.25:1.

The supervisors questioned Schools Supt. Dr. Milton Snyder why, if the schools were presently below the state and Southern accreditation standards, the schools could not absorb the additional 1500 students expected this year.

Dr. Snyder said that although Prince William schools on the average were lower than state standards, the schools were above the state average of pupil-teacher ratios. Overall, the average of all counties in Virginia is 18.08:1 in secondary and 22.5 in elementary. Prince William's average is 17.32 in secondary and 23.97 in elementary.

Winfield quizzed Snyder on rearranging the present number of high and middle school teachers to ease the work load in elementary schools, where the worst ratio exists. Dr. Snyder said that transferring high and middle school teachers to elementary levels did not work out.

In addition to explaining the teaching ratios, school administrators documented their cuts in capital outlay and supplies areas.

Dr. Carl Riehm, associate superintendent for instruction, said that with the present cuts imposed on the school budget. "This is the worst year instruction-wise as far as instructional materials in the six years I have been here."

Citizens back Snyder

Potomac News, May 23, 1975. B10.

A small group of citizens from across Prince William stood at the School Board meeting Tuesday to endorse Schools Supt. Dr.. Milton.

The citizens reacted to public comments by members of the Board of Supervisors that Snyder ought to be replaced. The citizens at Tuesday's School Board session backed Snyder for his efforts in education and in community involvement in the educational process.

Vi Yount of Manassas explained, "In the two years I have worked with Dr. Snyder, I have never found anything but cooperation and concern. I urge you (the School Board) to ignore the remarks of the Board of Supervisors and continue to give your full support to Dr. Snyder."

Bill Slack of Lake Ridge pointed to Snyder's implementation of kindergarten, increased information for the community, improved programs in special education and the general improvement in the procedures for education. "I want to congratulate the School Board for its wise decision to hire this superintendent. Thank you. Dr. Snyder, for your efforts and enthusiasm. Stay with us, and help us build a comprehensive educational program," he urged.

David Jones of Catharpin said that, if the supervisors who talked of replacing Snyder spoke as public officials, "they should be formally informed that the responsibility for hiring rests with the School Board. If they spoke as private individuals, that is fine. But I am a citizen, too. My insight is at least equal to theirs. In any opinion, we are fortunate to have such a superintendent. If anyone needs replacing, it is the Board of Supervisors," Jones said.

Nancy Breedan of Manassas said, "I have long wanted to express my admiration to one of the most dedicated, capable men I have met. He is always sensitive to the needs of children. He has done more in two years to involve the community than was done in the previous 20 years."

Boardman William Dunn read a prepared statement, reaffirming his support for Snyder's superintendency. Dunn said, "These people who criticize Dr. Snyder's efforts today did the same for our previous two superintendents. Therefore, I can only conclude that it is not Dr. Snyder, but our public educational system, which they are against. These people, who I feel would come close to destroying our school system if they had the authority, are chipping away by the their continuous criticism of our superintendent, our staff and our teachers, as well as program funds."

Board Chairman Ellis Hawkins said he did not intend to make a statement. However, he said, "I became as upset as I have ever been over the remarks made by various supervisors. I for one want to make it clear to Mr. Winfield and the supervisors that hiring and firing responsibility rests with this School Board. It will remain that way as long as I here."

School board defeats budget change

Potomac News, June 16, 1975. A3.

Prince William's School Board Thursday defeated an attempt to change its school budget presentation to the Board of Supervisors. The vote ended in a tie.

Emily Rosenberg, the new School Board member, arrived at the board session with a proposal: She would try to present the original, April 1, school budget to the supervisors in an effort to increase school funding for the coming fiscal year. With the inclusion of the two supplemental special education budgets, the cost would be $58.38 million. However, her plan was tied to a School Board commitment to conduct an audit of the financial practices of the board's management.

None of the board members objected to either Mrs. Rosenberg's presenting the original, uncut budget or to the management audit.

However, George Mullen voted against the resolution because he said he was concerned about the board's presenting numerous budget proposals to the supervisors. In addition, he stated that the supervisors did not have enough money coming in under the $3.62 tax rate to fund the full budget.

The supervisors' tax rate was based on the idea that $2.56 million would be cut from the school budget. The School Board recently voted for a compromise budget, which includes a $1.5 million cut in the original budget.

Mrs. Rosenberg replied that it is the supervisors' responsibility to find the money. Further, she said that, when she broached the subject with Supervisors Charles Colgan, Scott Winfield and Ralph Mauller, they "indicated that it would meet with favorable consideration."

School Boardman William Dunn said he was not opposed to a management audit; he questioned whether the supervisors had sufficient money to fund the audit. "I would rather put another 2.5 buses on the road than pay for another study," he said as he voted against the resolution.

T. Clay Wood also opposed the Rosenberg idea. He said the School Board has not yet formally presented the compromise budget. He felt that going back to the supervisors with the original budget would simply delay the budget approval process.

Schools Supt. Dr. Milton Snyder recommended that the board adopt the Rosenberg plan. He said, "The audit ties right in with one of my management goals for this year. However, it is still a matter of money. The county executive and the Board of Supervisors have repeatedly indicated to us how little money they have."

School staff research concerning an audit indicated that between $20,000 and $40,000 would be needed; the money would have to come from the supervisors. Board Chairman Ellis Hawkins said he would do anything to restore funds to the school budget. John Pattie apparently agreed, although he did not comment. Both voted with Mrs. Rosenberg in favor of the idea.

Fellow boardmen encouraged Mrs. Rosenberg to personally back the original school budget, in spite of the board vote on the combined proposal. She refused: "I don't have enough information about this budget to be able to back it. It isn't anyone's fault, but there is nothing to compare it to." Mrs. Rosenberg was not a member of the School Board when the budget was approved.

Dunn replied a bit incredulously, "But Mrs. Rosenberg, this audit could not possibly be made until after the budget is approved. How could you possible know more about it because of an audit which has not taken place?"

Mrs. Rosenberg answered, "I will not support the budget without the audit. At least, it would provide us more information in coming years." At the last School Board meeting, Mrs. Rosenberg complained long and loudly that she had been unable to get some information she requested from the school staff.

Happy Results

Potomac News, June 16, 1975. A6, Opinion Page, editorial.

Prince William Schools Supt. Milton Snyder and the School Board majority which supported him appear on the way to vindication over the approach taken to complete the long-delayed Osbourn Park High School after the original contractor, Ranger Construction Co., was kicked off the project.

Last week personnel at the present Osbourn High School, where students have had to attend classes on split shifts pending completion of the new school, were happily packing for the move to the new plant. At the construction site, where work is being supervised for the School Board by a construction manager, rather than a contractor, the word is that things are moving right on schedule. Barring any unforeseen catastrophe, the plant should be ready for occupancy in late August, in time for the fall term.

Financially, there is also optimistic news. Dr. Paul Trautman, school plant services director, says costs are being kept within the $2.1 million contract overrun anticipated when work on Osbourn Park was resumed—in fact, there's a chance the final figure will fall below that total. The School Board is expected to seek reimbursement from Travelers Indemnity Co., which had bonded Ranger—but the legal complexities are such that few can predict the final settlement.

That things are moving so smoothly is in sharp contrast to the trauma surrounding the Osbourn Park affair just a few months ago. Dr. Snyder, backed by a School Board majority, had come to the conclusion that the way to finish Osbourn Park after Ranger was declared in default, with 25 per cent of the school unfinished, was to hire a construction manager to put together the various untied ends. He found himself under very heavy pressure from Travelers to return Ranger to the job—a move Dr. Snyder was convinced would never produce a completed job.

A minority block on the Board of Supervisors, with their own line of communication to Travelers, kept the pot boiling. There were predictions of a $10 million cost overrun, as well as a couple of unfounded "legal opinions" pronounced by one boardman regarding the project's financing. In the midst of Dr. Snyder's efforts to expedite Osbourn Park's completion, the same boardman, Ralph Mauller, maneuvered a request for a grand jury investigation, announcing he had "a bundle of stuff" to present. It turns out he didn't, and the jury probe fizzled.

After overcoming repeated hurdles thrown in its path, the Snyder plan was able to proceed—and the results have been happy thus far.

The Osbourn Park project has been an unhappy affair, but would have taken only the most enlightened hindsight to avoid. The shame is that when efforts were made to resolve the problem as speedily and economically as possible, the distrust with which some members of the Board of Supervisors hold the school administration and School Board is of such a magnitude that it produced only unnecessary turmoil and further delays.

Good Relationship

Potomac News, August 4, 1975. A-4, Opinion Page, Editorial.

Despite changes in the composition of the Prince William School Board and attendant changes in philosophy of its members. School Supt. Milton Snyder continues to receive his board's support on important matters.

Recently the School Board approved Snyder's priority reorganization proposals. Without this kind of support (which County Executive Clinton Mullen has not been able to muster with the Board of Supervisors), Snyder would in effect cease to be the administrator of the school system and the School Board would take over that role.

But Snyder got his reorganization, and while the changes it makes are internal, they should strengthen the entire school system.

The changes are aimed at three basic areas, the School Board's method of functioning, fiscal services—particularly the budget process—and separating out instructional support services.

Changes for the School Board will mean two "action" sessions each month and two "study-report" sessions at which the board will get in-depth staff reports. The idea is to both streamline the action sessions and to keep the board informed about school matters. There are to be some other changes, too, affecting the board agendas and resolutions suggested by the administration.

Snyder plans to rename fiscal services and call it fiscal planning, management and control. He would broaden the unit's responsibilities and has suggested that the staff and the citizens be more involved in the budget-making process.

A separate instructional support services unit is to be developed with its director reporting to Snyder. This unit would cover such people as those involved in guidance, the school psychologist, visiting teachers, truancy people—those involved in helping to get the child ready for instruction. This should mean that these areas will get more emphasis.

One of the nine proposals which make up Snyder's reorganization is for the establishment of a formal School Board–County Board of Supervisors liaison committee to improve communications and relationships between the two bodies. In the past, the two boards have frequently opposed one another, often because of a failure to communicate.

Another proposal would establish seminars so school board members may study educational developments throughout the United States, which are of interest in Prince William.

This is the second year in succession it which Snyder has received approval for reorganization. Last year the reorganization resulted in big changes in personnel. Many of the faces that had been at the top in school administration for years are now gone and new people are in positions of responsibility.

We do not see this year's reorganization as being so drastic as last year's phase one. But it should refine the base already established and allow Snyder to move his organization along toward long term goals.

The School Board is by no means a rubber stamp of Snyder's opinions, nor should it be. But we are glad to see that the relationship between the school board and its administrator is one which mutually supportive on important matters.

Reorganization: Past, Present and Future

Seminar to Study the Management Team Concept at Prince William County Public Schools, Virginia

A Presentation by Dr. Milton L. Snyder, held at Woodbridge Senior High School, August 13, 1975.

In any type of organization — school systems included — the term "reorganization" conjures up the vision of a demon.

To many people, reorganization means unwanted change, or worse — job insecurity. It's an uncomfortable term, loaded with negative connotations.

In some places at some times, there is no doubt that reorganization was used for negative purposes. However, here and now in our situation, it is my intention to use the reorganization process as a positive tool to shape the school structure to meet the needs of a changing environment.

The purpose of reorganization as I see it is to strengthen our organization and to preserve good talent — not destroy it — by placing people in positions to perform best in response to the ever changing needs of the system.

Our organization must adapt to the world of the 1970s and '80s. It must improve its capacity and increase its pool of skills to withstand the stress and strain it will surely face as the community grows and varies in character and the needs of its children take on new forms.

Neither I nor any superintendent can guarantee any employee of this school system, including myself, an eternal job with eternal growth potential. The best I can do — or, better still, the best we can do working together — is to continue to strengthen, revitalize and improve upon the organization that provides our livelihood. To be effective, the organizational structure must continually be reviewed to assure that it satisfies four major requirements:

First, it must be organized for educational performance and the achievement of learning goals. This is the end which all activities in the school system must serve. In fact, organization can be likened to a river that converts all creeks into one "stream", that is, educational performance. Organization is more efficient the more direct and simple it is. The largest number of administrators and supervisors should perform as educators rather than bureaucrats, and should be tested against educational performance and results rather than primarily by standards of administrative skill or professional competence.

The second concern in reorganizing to improve the organizational structure must be to direct its efforts toward the same objectives.

It must encourage managers to give major attention to new and growing methods and techniques. It must make for willingness and ability to work for the future rather than rest on the achievements of the past, and to strive for growth rather than to put on fat.

A third concern about reorganizing is that the organization structure contain the least possible number of management levels, and forge the shortest possible chain of command. Every additional level makes the attainment of common direction and mutual understanding more difficult.

Every additional level distorts objectives and misdirects attention.

Every link in the chain sets up additional stresses, and creates one more source of inertia, friction, and slack.

Above all, especially in large systems, every additional level adds to the difficulty of developing tomorrow's executives, both by adding to the time it takes to come up from the bottom and by making specialists (rather than managers) out of the men and women moving up through the chain.

Good communication is essential to the process. Vital and valid information must be able to move rapidly through the structure without being altered or diffused. I say **valid** information to make a distinction from the rumors and false communiques which do move rapidly from wagging mouths to eager ears, particularly in large, unwieldy organizational structures.

Without the proper organization principles, levels will simply multiply. Yet, how few levels are really needed is shown by the example of the oldest, largest and most successful organization of western civilization; the Catholic Church. There is only one level of authority and responsibility between the Pope and the newest parish priest: the Bishop. The recent unresolved conflict in the church would indicate that responsiveness to the citizenry or base of support is lacking.

A fourth concern about reorganizing is that the organization structure must make possible the training and testing of tomorrow's top school leaders. It must give people actual management responsibility in an autonomous position while it is assumed that they have an open perspective to learn from their new experiences. Women and men must be put into positions where they at least see the whole of an operation, even if they do not carry direct responsibility for its performance and results. If we are not careful, we begin to think that our own corner is the whole building, or worse yet, we begin to think the corner or the job is ours forever and does not even belong to the taxpayers and the school board.

To satisfy these requirements for changing the structure of an organization, we will apply what we shall term as the principle of **functional decentralization** to set up integrated units with maximum responsibility for a major and distinct stage in the education process.

But this functional decentralization must not lead to levels upon levels of management. It must train and test leaders in educational performance, and it must result in positions where a manager has full responsibility for results. It must not have so many levels that it tends to erode the meaning of each job and to make it appear nothing but a stepping stone to a promotion.

Ideally, a reorganization plan based on functional decentralization would enable school building and program managers to know what is expected of them; for that is determined by the objectives of the units which they helped to establish and must manage. As long as these objectives are supportive of the overall "plan" and are achieved satisfactorily, they will have little difficulty getting across to the superintendent what they want and need.

Any reorganization based on functional decentralization requires both strong parts and a strong center. The term "decentralization" is actually misleading. It implies that the center is being weakened; but nothing could be more of a mistake. Functional decentralization requires strong guidance from the center through the setting of clear, meaningful and high objectives for the whole. These objectives must demand both a high degree of educational performance and a high standard of conduct throughout the school system.

Functional decentralization also requires control by measurements. The measurements must be so precise and so pertinent that a school leader and his performance can be judged reliably by them. The evaluation of goals is as important as the plan itself.

However, functional decentralization must have a kind of "general welfare clause" reserving to the top leadership the decisions that affect the educational system as a whole and its long-range future welfare, and allowing top leadership to override local ambitions and pride in the common interest of all. An effective organization allows for personal goals to be achieved within the organizational goals.

Most school leaders with experience know a healthy school organization when they see it. But they are like the M. D., who knows a healthy person when he sees one, but can only define "health" negatively, that is, as the absence of disease, deformity and pathological degeneration.

Likewise, a healthy school organization is hard to describe. But the systems of poor organizational health can be identified. Whenever they are present, there is a need for thorough examination of the organization structure. To correct this organizational health problem requires reorganization.

One telling symptom of poor organizational health is the growth of levels of management — which shows poor or confused objectives, failure to remove poor performers, over-centralization, or lack of proper activities analysis and job descriptions. Poor organizational health also shows itself in pressure for "frictional overhead" — that is, for more coordinators, expediters, or specialists who have no clear job responsibility and are hired every time a new problem surfaces. Also, poor organizational health is shown in the need for special pressures to co-ordinate activities and to establish communications between managers; coordinating committees; incessant meetings; full-time liaison men and so forth.

Equally telling is the tending to "go through channels" rather than directly to the woman or man who has the information or the idea needed or who should be informed of what is going on. This is particularly serious for it greatly aggravates the tendency of principals, directors, or supervisors to think more of their school building or their job or their subject area or their function than of the school system as a whole and its goal of helping children learn. "Going through channels" is a symptom of poor organizational health.

The reorganization that has occurred in our school system during the past two years has been toward the goal of improving the health of the organization. The McGuffey Report was the initial step in this direction of functional decentralization.

The McGuffey Report was required by a new Superintendent to get a fresh, outside look at both the formal and informal structures of a school organization that had functioned under the same ruling groups for nearly two decades. The report includes recommendations in line with the organizational principles I have been discussing. It calls for a horizontal organizational structure with a reasonable span of control for persons in leadership positions, plus the capability to communicate decisions quickly to the buildings and the supporting staff.

The next step was the study of the instructional department and the recommendations of the task force chaired by Gary DiVecchia. One of the primary purposes of this task force was to produce objective information from supervisors of instruction and principals concerning the instructional and instructional support organization as the basis for determining the direction of needed change.

Future phases in reorganization include further decentralization of the budget process to the local building level, the organization of an instructional support unit, an improved communications and community involvement effort, and more accountability for results on the part of all school leaders.

The School Board itself is undertaking some reorganization of its meeting dates and its structure, for processing information and taking action.

Good organization structure does not by itself produce good performance — just as a good constitution does not guarantee great presidents, or good laws a moral society. But a poor organization structure makes good performance impossible, no matter how good the individual school leaders may be.

To reorganize to improve organizational structure — through functional decentralization — will therefore always improve performance. It will make it possible for good women and men, hitherto stifled, to do a good job effectively. It will make better performers out of many mediocre women and men by raising their sights and the demands on them.

It will identify poor performers and make possible their replacement by better women and men.

Reorganization is not a panacea. It is not the only thing that matters in managing the educational process. Anatomy, after all, is not the whole of biology either. But the right organization structure is the necessary foundation; without it the best performance in all other areas of instruction, support services, school services, or school plant services would be impossible.

What we are talking about here in reorganization is the skill to put together a team which is carefully selected — one in which each person is well qualified, sharply trained, clearly assigned and competently led. It could be described as a tight organization which possesses a high degree of morale, skill and coordination.

Adaptability means that the organization is able to adjust itself quickly to changing conditions. It is flexible. This means that the team is trained in the "T" formation and the single and double wing formations as well as the "L" formation. It means that it can plan a 5, 7, or 9 man defense according to what the competition offense is. It means that it can quickly sense what is needed and shift its defense where it is adequate without disintegration, panic or confusion.

The need for flexibility is a continuous need. But there is resistance to change. As a result, organizations that are progressive leaders at one time can find themselves a few years later dropping lower in competitive positions and dying of obsolescence and complacency. Human beings and human needs are not static, but ever changing. Everything around us reflects that nothing is static. The status quo is comfortable but it can be a dead end.

Keeping an organization effective, efficient and dynamic is a skill requiring conscious attention and vision. The results cannot be left to chance. The public does not continue to support an organization that no longer meets its needs and standards, even though at one time they may have cheered it as a champion.

Therefore, reorganization is our attempt to continue to keep this school system alive and growing and on the field of champions.

Champions arc human, and human behavior is difficult to change.

Those among you who can cope effectively with change by being adaptable and flexible will be the true leaders within the organization whose charge is the future of students and society.

Management Team Concept: Thoughts on Management

Management Team Seminar for Prince William County Public Schools, Virginia

A Presentation by Superintendent Milton L Snyder for the Management Team Seminar, August 15, 1975.

Prince William County has a 3.5 million dollar investment in the management-leadership function of its school system. You are the 3.5 million dollars. Every investment should have a return. Your efforts will determine what Prince William receives in return for its multi-million dollar investment.

Much effort over the past few year has been directed toward the organization of school leaders around a concept called "the management team." If we look toward a definition of this concept, we might say that in team management the manager works with his subordinates as a group or team. **Goals are jointly set and progress towards targets become a joint responsibility of all team members.**

When this approach works, it reduces individual competitiveness and increases communication, mutual understanding and respect, union of resources and joint effort. The skills of team management require a reorientation on the part of the manager who has been trained to supervise subordinates on a one-to-one basis.

The key to Team Management is participation which can be defined as an individual's mental and emotional involvement in a group situation that encourages him or her to contribute to group goals and to share responsibility for them. There are three important points to be made about participation in team management.

First, participation means mental and emotional involvement rather than mere muscular activity. The involvement of a person's self, rather than just his skill, is the product of his mind and his emotions. The person who participates is ego-involved, instead of merely task-involved. Some managers mistake task-involvement for true participation. They go through the motions of participation, but it is clear to teachers and staff that their leader is an autocrat who does not really want their ideas.

A second important characteristic of participation is that it motivates contribution. Individuals are given an opportunity to direct their initiative and creativity toward the objectives of the group. In this way, participation differs from consent, which uses only the creativity and ideas of leaders who bring their ideas to the group for their approval. Participation requires more than mere approval of something already decided. It is a two-way psychological and social relationship among people rather than a procedure imposing ideas from above.

A third characteristic of participation is that it encourages people to accept responsibility for an activity. Because they are self-involved in the group, they want to see it work successfully. Participation helps them become responsible citizens rather than non-responsible onlookers.

As individuals begin to accept responsibility for group activities, they become interested in and receptive to teamwork, because they see in it a means of accomplishing a job for which they feel responsible. Persons who are actively involved in something are naturally more committed to carrying it out. Of their own free will, they create responsibility rather than having it forced upon them by delegation. By making themselves responsible, they gain a measure of independence and dignity as an individuals making their own decisions, even though these decisions are heavily influenced by their team environment.

There are many other contemporary management models in addition to this team management concept. These include:

- Management by objectives
- Budget Centers

- Temporary Systems
- Project Management
- Management by exception

All of the above management models **are** being used or **will be** used as our organization grows and the environment in which we operate changes. You have used the **management by objectives** concept as a part of your evaluation procedures.

Our reorganization for financial planning places a great deal of stress upon the operation of **budget centers.**

In **temporary systems**, a group of team members are pulled together to find solutions to organizational problems. When the problems are solved, the group disbands and group members return to their organizational home base.

In **project management**, a team of experts is formed and directed by a project manager who is responsible for project goal completion. When the project has been completed, the project team disbands. We have used this management model in school plant services and other areas.

In **management by exception**—which is a variation of management by objectives—plans and goals are set by superior and subordinate in advance. So long as the work is going according to plan, the superior is not concerned with its administration. He or she leaves that in the subordinate's hands. The superior re-enters to give technical assistance in the situation only when some exception to the plan is of a magnitude great enough to warrant his or her attention.

The above review of contemporary management models indicates some of the ways in which we are implementing this concept. Perhaps at this point we should discuss the determination of the management team. What is management and the manager's role on the management team?

Before discussing the role of the manager, it must be realized that a general role description does not imply that all managerial jobs are the same or that all managers approach their jobs in the same way. Managing is, to a large degree, an individualized activity, dependent upon the woman or man, what they mentally bring to their jobs, and how they utilize their talents in the uniqueness of their organizational environment. They are not like a machine that responds automatically. They remain distinct individuals, although they may be coping with similar problems and utilizing many shared and learned skills in common with other managers.

With this in mind, we can now examine some of the "in common" aspects of the managerial role. First, the manager is a **leader**. He cannot function without guiding and directing the work of others. His performance is normally dependent upon how well his subordinates perform. He has to motivate, guide, communicate, influence, counsel and, in general, direct the work of other people to maintain his part or unit of the organizational system at a desired level of production.

Secondly, the manager is a **management process specialist** in that, to perform effectively as a manager, he must be specialized and proficient in such common managerial activities (or functions) as planning, organizing, motivating, controlling, evaluating, investigating, and so on, all of which comprise the management process. These are distinct functions present in all manager jobs, and the proficient manager has to be skilled in all of them. Traditional theories of managing explained the manager's job almost exclusively in terms of these functional skills, but more recent theory goes beyond the constricting limits of these activities to include other role aspects as well.

Thirdly, the managerial role is that of a **change agent**. With the rapid changes in the modern world of business and in our society, the manager is principally responsible for continually introducing and implementing new systems and changes within his or her particular organizational unit. Since the successful implementation of change is dependent upon human acceptance, managers need to be skilled at securing such acceptance and support. Likewise, change implies innovation and creativity. The manager should constantly seek new, better, and novel ways of improving organizational performance and minimizing harmful conflict and friction caused by resistance to "the new ways," yet encourage creative conflict and resolution and dissatisfaction with the status quo. So, managers cannot be content with merely sustaining their work domain, but they must measure up to meeting the challenge of generating growth, improvement, and vitality in the work system and in people.

Fourth, the manager must be **achievement-oriented**. Inherent in the managerial job is accomplishment and attainment of organizational goals as well as personal goals. School systems and related institutions can only justify their existence in organized society by accomplishing predetermined and distinct purposes. Satisfying all levels of human needs—including those of the general public and the employee group—necessitates managers dedicated to productive results beneficial in an optimum fashion to all concerned. The manager has to be a "doer," an action-oriented individual prone not to hasty, compulsive, plunging behavior but to persistent and steady pursuit of well thought out and conceived personal and group goals, all integrated into the entire system of learning goals.

Fifth, the managerial role requires people who are **decision activists**. Note the emphasis is not on decision making, but on decision activating. Unfortunately, too many people, including managers, have an erroneous impression that all managers do is to sit back and make "yes" or "no" decisions. Nothing could be farther from the truth, however, such "yes" or "no" decisions are not difficult to make, assuming all the necessary information bearing on the decision has been accumulated and weighed and all the people affected by the decision have been appropriately considered and involved in it.

Furthermore, making a "final" decision is but the starting point in the decision process. Implementing and carrying out the decision to a successful conclusion, perhaps changing it if necessary, is far more difficult to achieve. In all organizations there are managers who fail (or are failing) because they do not perceive the total decision

process, often being incapable of seeing the totality of their decisions over time. These "Edsel" decision makers look more at themselves and their personal benefits rather than at what is good for the organization as a whole.

A decision activist does not concentrate only on a "yes" or "no" solution to problems or on his own personal image, as few of the former exist and the latter is evidence of a misdirected woman or man. The decision activist first seeks full and complete information through sound, comprehensive research for problem identification, then determines a decision incorporating its potential effects on all parties involved, seeking their involvement and support in actively implementing the decision over time. They are also capable of changing their decisions should conditions change, recognizing that they, too, are fallible as are their subordinates.

Decision activists do not decide on a particular course of action because of personal hunch, whim, or fancy, nor do they "delegate" the impossible to others and then pass off failures on the shoulders of "my incompetent subordinates." Their decisions should be based on a realistic appraisal of organizational resources and conditions, present and future, and not on personal benefits to themselves or on what they would like to have happen.

Still another aspect of the managerial role is **negotiation**. Managers spend a great deal of their time negotiating with all types of people inside and outside of the organization. Some of this negotiation is direct bargaining, such as with unions and suppliers where both parties defend certain rights of prerogatives and a compromise settlement is usually reached.

Other phases of the negotiation role are far more subtle and less understood, however. Personal give-and-take centering around career competition with other managers in the same school system is part of life in the working organization. Power plays and jockeying for position highlight this career advancement, and a keen sense of political negotiation is required on the part of the astute manager. This career maze in the school system, and one's ability to cope with it, can often make or break an aspiring manager.

Other forms of negotiating skills are often required to cope with superiors and subordinates making demands which conflict with productive performance on the part of the manager. Hence, many different types of negotiating skills are required as managers devise various strategies to perform in an effective fashion despite many obstacles and/or challenges within the work environment.

Educational managers must, therefore, be career oriented and mutually dedicated to the advancement of the profession, their school board, and themselves. Above all, they have to be able to realistically perceive their roles as discussed above, to gain a true notion of self in a demanding and ambiguous environment.

All managers grapple with continual uncertainty and risk in their work and have to be constantly adjusting conflicting personal and organizational needs and values. The pressures for career development are great and, the ability to adjust to these diverse pressures fundamentally determine individual success or failure as a manager.

Management makes things happen. Management does not wait for the future, it makes the future. Managers are not custodians of the present, they are architects of the future. A famous college president once said, "There are three kinds of people in this world: those who make things happen, those who watch things happen, and those who don't know what's happening." Managers are supposed to be in the first group.

If you wish to know how effective you have been as a manager, list those things that have happened in the last twelve months because you made them happen. Are the services you offer in the school any different? Are the teachers working any better? Are the people who work with you any finer? Is the morale any better? Is the school any cleaner? Are more parents involved? Are you conscious of having any impact upon your environment and what takes place within it?

The president of AT&T once said, "…to have a part in a significant enterprise, to be one of its movers and managers, in industry, in government or in education, is not to fill some nitch every morning and leave it each night as you found it; it is to help build and shape, to plan and to execute, to measure alternatives against the horizon and act on the course that judgment and resolution command."

Vision and skill to seek alternatives are the foundations of management.

Leaders think, act and motivate. Followers do, object to, resist or revolt against what leaders do.

Management is not only the direction of things, but the development of people.

Management is taking people as they are, with what knowledge, training, experience and background they have accumulated and developing those people by increasing their knowledge, improving their skills, and developing their abilities and attitudes. Upon this improvement depends the success of any managerial or supervisory effort. In terms of such improvement, executive ability can be measured.

Therefore, the management team's job is to get people to work well and willingly. A management that can do this is effective management. Any management that cannot do this is ineffective management.

The management process is motivating in itself. When special motivation programs and devices are required, it proves that the management process is not working clearly.

It is necessary at this point to make it clear that there is no attempt in this approach to reduce dealing with people to a pattern. Human relations cannot be reduced to a pattern, but you can have an orderly approach to human relations problems.

The heads of major departments such as instruction, school services, school plant, and personnel have a dual role to play.

Each of these leaders have two major jobs: to run their particular department or operation for which they are specifically held responsible, and to serve as a member of the executive team with the Superintendent.

That means that these leaders must operate their own particular responsibility in terms of what is good for the school system as a whole. The executive team is ultimately responsible to the Superintendent, and for the success of the entire operation as well as for their own particular function.

Some mention should be made about the use of committees by members of the management team. The functions of committees are not clearly understood, and they are frequently misused.

Committees never were intended to be decision making or operating bodies. Someone once observed that Lindberg never would have flown the Atlantic by committee. Some wars have been planned totally by committee. The main purpose of committees used by the management team is to integrate the viewpoint of people, functions, and resources. It is an excellent educational, informational, and advisory device. It is a method by which a manager can secure the suggestions and opinions of all people involved before arriving at a particular course of action. This is a distinct skill necessary for management team members to use in committee work and it deserves conscious attention on the part of every manager.

The management team should always have a definite plan which it uses in dealing with the activities and problems of the future regardless of what those problems may be. The management team should be conscious that the events of the future can, to some extent, be **envisioned, controlled,** and even **created.** A large part of the team's success depends upon the degree to which it plans the direction of the forces which may affect the future of the organization.

Many are inclined to let organizations work rather than to make them work. Due to the inherent ability of human beings, such leadership often gets by. Those organizations live, however, in spite of their leadership; not because of it, which

is similar to the difference between just **existing** throughout life and **living** life!

I call upon you as members of the management team to have a definite program or a plan of operation that will enable you to have dynamic impact upon the future of your organization. It should evoke the best in any person who comes in contact with you. It is a relatively simple matter to find people who can sit on a job, handle events as they come, meet emergencies and get by. It is difficult to find individuals who can plan, who can make events happen as they want them to happen, who through such planning can reduce emergencies, and who can keep this organization in a position of leadership.

Management team members must strive for improvement as an **objective**, and perfection as a **goal**. Perfection in any activity can be attained only through practice. If no one had been willing to fly the original airplane because it was not perfect, where would air transportation be today? What we are flying today is probably not nearly as good as the planes ten years from now will be. The same is true of management methods of dealing with the human element.

The greatest reward any executive, director, supervisor, principal or superintendent can receive is to have those who have been under her or his direction say that they arc better workers, better citizens, better teachers and better students because of his or her influence. That is the reward in being a member of the management team.

To be part of the Prince William Management Team can be the most rewarding opportunity ever offered. It means work, commitment, perseverance, and accountability, but most of all self-satisfaction in the knowledge that you have influenced the future.

If you accept these management team conditions, welcome aboard!

They Did It

Potomac News, August 22, 1975. Opinion Page, A6. Editorial.

Hurrah! Osbourn Park High School is finished.

One and a half years behind schedule and approximately $2.1 million more expensive than originally contracted, Osbourn Park is expected to be ready for students on Sept. 2. Its completion is cause for celebration.

Credit for the success is due to Schools Supt. Dr. Milton Snyder, his staff, the Prince William School Board, expert advisors hired by the School Board and those supervisors who had the wisdom to support their School Board.

For others, a meal of crow is in order; those who said the school could not possibly be finished in September and that cost overruns would be millions of dollars higher than the School Board estimated have been proven wrong.

Osbourn Park should have been finished by Ranger Construction Company in December 1973, at a contract price of approximately $8 million. With the school 75 percent finished, the School Board kicked Ranger off the job in September 1974.

The problem then became how to complete the school as quickly and economically as possible.

At a time when owners in other areas were renegotiating to return Ranger to troubled construction projects, the School Board dared to venture on its own to complete the building by September. A few members of the Board of Supervisors dared to support them.

The School Board's plan was to hire a construction management firm to oversee completion and independently obtain the needed $2.1 million. Travelers Indemnity Co., the bonding company for the school, offered the School Board the money, but the firm attached a number of strings. In any event, Travelers said it would be impossible to finish the job by September.

When the School Board took its proposal and financial requirements the supervisors, Ralph Mauller called the proposal "a wild trip" and predicted that the estimated $2.1 million additional money needed would turn into $6 million.

In the months that followed, Mauller never missed an opportunity to try to repeal the supervisors' financial backing for the school. Because the School Board's plan was unique in Prince William's construction history, other supervisors wavered.

It may even be possible that supervisors who might have lost their nerve decided to vote with the School Board, rather than align themselves with Mr. Mauller's noisy, childish scenes.

From the very beginning, Supervisor Charles Colgan declared his intention of backing the School Board and its administration.

Supervisor Andrew Donnelly quickly made it clear that he would not sit quietly by and let Mr. Mauller be the only vocal board member. His voice answered Mauller's tirades.

In session after session, the supervisors first agreed to provide financial backing, then they reneged and tabled resolutions. Eventually, the finances were approved.

Now, there can be no doubt. The School Board and its advisors chose the right path. They hired CM Associates, with Charles Martini and the project manager. The work was done on time and within the estimated cost.

The School Board, Dr. Snyder and his staff, CM Associates and others who worked on the project have a right to be proud that they had the guts to gamble. Had they proceeded to complete the building in the traditional way, Osbourn students would have been crammed into a too-small school on split shifts for at least another semester.

They all placed their efforts and their votes on the line to serve students, and they won.

Basic skills to be stressed

Snyder discusses his personal educational goals for county

Potomac News, September 2, 1975. Lynne Grandstaff.

Improving student achievement in fundamental skills is, for the second consecutive year, the major goal of Prince William's school superintendent.

Schools Supt. Dr. Milton Snyder discussed his goals with the press this week; in addition, Snyder is stressing special education, post-secondary career skills, human relations, responsible citizenship and accountability.

Snyder explained that, in outlining his personal goals, he does not represent the goals of the School Board: "This is the attempt of the superintendent to collect the needs of the school system and place priorities on them," Snyder said.

Of the six goals for the 1976-77 school year, four were also prime goals last year. They include fundamental skills, career education, human relations and responsible citizenship. Snyder said these goals are continuing concerns: problems cannot be solved in a single year.

On fundamental skills Snyder said, "Setting a goal is one thing, but verifying it is another. The achievement tests should show us something; both we and the community should be concerned about the results. Although we would like rapid improvement in some areas, we are looking for steady improvement in all areas."

Besides the state's standardized testing program, Snyder is looking toward the upcoming state competency requirements as a method of verifying student achievement in basic skills.

In particular, Snyder is looking toward children with "societal, physical or emotional problems, as well as those students who have somehow slipped through the grades. These children have be dealt with in special ways, with individual emphasis like that in special education. The goal is to have achieve up to their level of ability."

Snyder's second goal, special education, is tied to the special education management proposal, which was recently adopted in principle by the School Board. The goal simply keeps education in the forefront and asks for continued concern. Snyder added, "We need to give both the School Board and the Board of Supervisors credit for going ahead with special education in a tight budget year."

Developing programs for career education is a long-term goal, and Snyder expects to see great strides in preparing students for college or jobs. For the current year, the goal is tied to receiving a $450,000 grant for a new career education program. Prince William should find out in the near future whether the school system will receive the money.

Responsible citizenship is a fancy way of saying .discipline. Snyder said, "We are not deaf to the concerns of parents who worry about decline in discipline. We will preserve an atmosphere for learning, and we will not tolerate disruption."

At the same time, Snyder urged people to look at the relative lack of serious discipline problems in Prince William's schools, when compared with other metropolitan area school systems.

Finally, accountability has become a goal for the year. Snyder said accountability has always been an implied goal of the school system, but giving it priority should give it "new meaning."

He added that some aspects of an educational program "Do not lend themselves to (missing text)…"

Nonetheless, this school system must be held accountable for what it does."

A New Spirit

The Journal Messenger, September 9, 1975. Editorial.

The Misses Fannie and Eugenia Osbourn, founders of the Manassas Institute, which later became the community's first public high school and whose memory was perpetuated first through Osbourn and now through Osbourn Park High School, would have been proud of the fine new school which opened last week if they could have returned to see it in operation. They might have been even prouder of the new spirit which seemed to have taken hold, culminating Friday night in a football victory after a long 24-game losing streak. It is doubtful if they would have condoned the acrimonious debate over the school's name or would have felt any less honored by the name in its present form. Most of all, they probably would have been amazed by the big changes in methods of education and in the educational facilities which are in use today.

The new school seems to have generated a new spirit all along the line. The football game may be symptomatic of what is happening throughout the school, among both students and faculty. Not limited to athletics, there also appears to be a new spirit academically with the shedding of the former rundown school building for a fine modern educational structure. This spirit may find its way to some of the parents who previously had been discouraged and disgruntled over the many difficulties which beset the school before it opened. Some of this is already evident as the officials of the cities of Manassas and Manassas Park joined forces to support the football program at the new school. This auspicious beginning bodes well for the future of the new school and provides hope for an end to the animosity between the two cities which had flared up on many occasions.

The best hope of future good relations between the two cities could well be realized through the medium of Osbourn Park High School. When the good people of the two communities get to know each other better through the common interest in their children, the rancor of former years is bound to fade away and disappear. Working together in booster groups and parent-teacher organizations will provide opportunities for contact which never existed before. As relations improve, both cities will be better able to meet common challenges and understand each other's problems. The new spirit at Osbourn Park offers much hope for the future. Let's expand this new spirit to every corner of the two communities.

Appendix D:
1976

Financial Statement

1976 speech by Dr. Snyder, Prince William County Schools Superintendent, to the School Board.

"Since the early 1960s the population explosion in this, nation—synchronized with an expanding economy—created a favorable climate for school budgets in most school districts, this one included.

"In the last year, however, inflation and a cooling economy have put a damper on school budgets. Citizens and their elected representatives more and more tend to look with apprehension at the tax rate and at public expenditures.

"People still want the best possible education for their children. But at the same time, they now demand to be convinced that each tax dollar spent for schools is necessary and spent wisely:

"It is no longer possible to conceive and produce a school budget in a back room at the central office. Every body must be involved—parents, school patrons, school staffs, as well as the central staff.

"The budget and its management is everybody's business. We are all accountable. And all of us who deal with finances must be good will ambassadors and communicators, as well as planners and accountants.

"We are in the process of reorganizing the school financial structure in line with these new needs in a changing climate. Specifically, we are going to start the budget process earlier in the year; we will involve more people—including everybody in this room—and others; and we will produce a final product in time to educate the community well in advance of the time that the Board of County Supervisors sets the tax rate and allocates school funds. And we will assure that all funds are fully and wisely accounted for.

"The function of "Fiscal Services" will be retitled "Fiscal Planning, Management and Control" with expanded responsibilities and resources to operate in the new climate. This does not mean that we will hire large numbers of new people for this function.

"We have the resources. They include you. It's just a matter of redistribution and re-emphasis to meet a changing requirement in the best interest of our school system and the girls and boys that we serve."

School styles change

Potomac News, February 18, 1976. A1. Lynne Grandstaff.

New buildings in Prince Williams probably won't look at all like the current schools, according to Schools Supt. Dr. Milton Snyder.

Snyder could not give a specific description of school buildings proposed for the county; he said designing schools is the job of architects.

However, Snyder said new construction will probably be designed for greater program flexibility, both inside and outside. He explained, "We may have modular buildings; a central area would include services, like libraries as well as some class rooms. Then we could add modules which include more space. These may be relocatable, so that we can move them to other parts of the county as population shifts."

As Snyder explained the idea, the buildings would look different from current Prince William schools: they could be more box-like "and they many not be brick."

Inside, Snyder envisions spaces divided by partitions which could be moved with relative ease to match demands in the instructional program.

He pointed to a wall at Gar-Field High School. "This is a demountable partition; the maintenance people can remove it overnight; however, the staff has not been geared toward moving them around. We want to make new buildings as flexible as possible. There are systems in which you can press a button, and the partition moves. However, those are very expensive."

Snyder does not expect the cost of modular construction to be significantly different from the cost of traditional buildings; in the long run, he said, cost could be reduced because of their mobility.

School Plant Services Director Dr. Paul Trautman explained that modular construction is a relatively new method of building schools. He said the state of Florida recently bought $23 million worth of modular units, which will be used throughout the state. Florida, he said, expects the buildings to last 10 to 20 years rather than the 40 to 60 years for a traditional building. However, he said no one has had enough experience with the units to know exactly how long they will last.

The modular buildings apparently bear minimal resemblance to the trailers now used in Prince William. Trautman said that some types are installed on slabs with anchors and pillars, so they are more like permanent construction than trailers.

No one has made any decision on the type of construction for new Prince William schools, and there could be a combination of permanent construction and modular units.

Schools Switch Signals

The Journal Messenger, February 18, 1976. A1.

In a brief announcement released this morning. Prince William Superintendent of Schools, Dr. Milton L. Snyder revealed the school administration has apparently shelved the idea of creating a sixth high school by phasing in a student body to an afternoon shift at Gar-Field High School in 1976-77. The community will be asked instead to consider other alternatives for easing crowded classrooms in eastern Prince William County pending voter action on a $26.25 million bond issue in June, he added.

Noting the proposed bond issue was passed 6-1 by the Board of County Supervisors Tuesday, provides for construction of four new school buildings, including one new high school. Dr. Snyder said the administration will go ahead with its plan to create jurisdictional boundaries for the new high school at such time as it may be built.

"We appear to be moving away from the idea of using this phase-in plan," a school system spokesman said this morning, pointing to School Board action Tuesday for new community interest surveys of sentiment on year-round schools.

Parents to be polled on 45-15

Year-round interest seen

Potomac News, February 18, 1976. A1. Lynne Grandstaff.

Parents in the Gar-Field and Woodbridge senior high school attendance areas will be surveyed on their interest in year-round school.

Prince William's School Board Tuesday approved the survey, which was requested by the student housing committee. The idea is to allow the board to adopt mandatory year-round school programs at the eastern Prince William high schools without deviating from board policy, rather than create a sixth high school student body.

The School Board's policy, adopted a couple of years ago, states that no community will be placed on year-round school without community input and a formal survey.

The newly approved survey will be mailed to the parents of all students in sixth through 12th grades in eastern Prince William. Parents will be asked to select among the six student housing options developed by the student housing committee.

The options include: year-round school for all eastern Prince William high school students; year-round school for high school students who live in areas where elementary and middle school students attend year-round school; and expanded optional year-round program combined with the creation of a sixth high school student body; creation of a sixth high school student body; expansion of the optional year-round program combined with an extended day, and split shifts.

Forms will be mailed to all parents, and parents will be asked to return the forms in the mail. An outside agency will compile the results.

Making the request to the School Board, Student Housing Committee Chairman Richard Johnson said the request was based on the feelings of parents who attended student housing committee meetings in eastern Prince William. "At these meetings, tremendous interest has been generated in year-round school," he said.

At the same time, the board turned down a staff request to conduct an interest survey on year-round school in western Prince William. Administrators told the boardmen that there has been some interest in year-round school expressed at student housing meetings in western Prince William. Therefore, they requested that families in all schools in the Osbourn Park and Stonewall Jackson high school attendance areas (to include elementary and middle school families as well as high school) be surveyed to determine whether they were interested in a formal study of year-round school. The earliest possible year-round school implementation for western Prince William would be July 1977.

The proposal was defeated, with all four School Board members living in western Prince William voting against it and the three from eastern Prince William in favor.

Schools Supt. Dr. Milton Snyder explained that, although there was only a small amount of interest expressed by the western Prince William community, the proposal was placed before the board "because of pressure from the Board of Supervisors and some citizens to mandate county-wide year-round school in conflict with your policy."

The four western Prince William boardmen apparently felt that the community interest in western Prince William was insufficient to justify a survey.

Bond Issue Gets Supervisor's Support

The Journal Messenger, June 2, 1976. Front Page. Betty Calvin.

DALE CITY — Voters here hold the key to the outcome of Prince William County's controversial $26.23 million school bond referendum, supervisor James McCoart told about 50 listeners last night.

"Apathy, not resistance," will be to blame if the Tuesday vote fails to support the construction program, McCoart indicated. Before the two and a half hour meeting at Godwin Middle School was over, the Neabsco District member of the County's governing body had personally enlisted promises from several persons in the audience, to work at the polls Tuesday and to telephone registered voters to come out and vote for the bond issue. The bonds would provide funds for a high school and three elementary schools, plus renovations and expansions at several other locations.

The high school is to be located in the southern end of the 1-95 corridor, to serve students from the Graham Park and Rippon Middle School attendance zones. The new elementary schools will serve western Dale City, Lake Ridge and the Dumfries-Triangle area.

Regis Lacey, a member of the county's School Board also was on hand.

"I don't feel $26 million is enough for what we need," Lacey said. "The western portion of Dale City will need a high school not too far in the future; we will need to be back to you in three or four years (in another referendum)," Lacey went on.

McCoart was praised by Dr. Milton Snyder, superintendent of schools, for "taking a step forward," in setting up the meeting and working in support of the issue. Snyder called McCoart "a real leader who recognizes needs," in introductory remarks at the opening of the meeting. He also praised Ms. Sheila McDaniel who heads the volunteer Citizens' Bond Committee for her comprehensive work throughout the county pushing the construction program.

Much of the discussion centered around the kinds of schools that had been built with previous bond issues and the kind that are being planned now. Several parents indicated concern over what they felt were unduly wide halls and other open spaces within the buildings. Snyder replied that more conservative plans for construction would be followed this time around.

"It's up to your appointed and elected officials to get involved and to hold professional educators accountable," Snyder said. "We have to accept and bear responsibilities for hard decisions."

McCoart gave a presentation with charts and maps indicating growth areas already zoned in the land that lies between Smoketown Road and Minnieville Road. "Dale City now has 25,000 population," he said, and "there's not much land left for schools. ... Land presently zoned, but not yet containing completed residential construction, will provide homes for 30,000 additional persons," he added.

The current school population is 41,000. Although the growth rate has slowed down "because of the depressed economy," there will still be an increase of at least 1,000 students a year, according to Richard Johnson of the school staff.

Not counting those in Lake Ridge and Dale City, there will be 20,000 new students in eastern Prince William on land already zoned residential but not yet constructed, he said. His charts showed that in the fall Gar-Field and Woodbridge senior high schools, even on year-round programs, will be more than 900 students over capacity. By 1978, the excess will reach more than 1,700 students, enough for one new high school, Johnson added.

A parent asked why, with a declining birth rate, school populations keep rising in the county.

Johnson answered that more families keep

moving into the area and that the bulk of the student-population growth is in the sixth, seventh and eighth grades.

Other parents indicated they felt developers like C.D. Hylton of Dale City should be forced to contribute mere towards public facilities like schools. They are upset that Hylton continues to expand in Dale City, seemingly uncontrolled.

"After many years here. I finally met Mr. Hylton the other day," McCoart answered. "I talked to him about the situation," he went on, "and he has what I would call a businessman's view; he feels he has done his part... I feel it is not enough." But McCoart said taking Hylton to court would be fruitless; "He's won 15 out of 16 cases."

Dale seen as bond key

Growth to heavily hit schools, McCoart says

Potomac News, June 2 ,1976. Front Page.

DALE CITY — "Dale City will be the key in the election next week," Richard Johnson of Prince William County's School Housing-Task Force told an audience of 50 Dale City residents Tuesday.

Johnson joined Neabsco Supervisor James McCoart and School Superintendent Dr. Milton Snyder to answer questions on the $26.23 million school bond referendum facing county voters June 8. Johnson, estimated a 50-50 chance for approval on the bond and emphasized the importance cf Neabsco and Coles residents voting.

McCoart shocked Dale City residents with the magnitude of projected population growth figures in the Dale City area and their impact on the over-crowded schools.

McCoart used graphics to illustrate how land in or adjacent to Neabsco district is already zoned for a total of 30,000 people, and he speculated that the current growth rate of 2,500 people a year in Dale City will increase.

McCoart pointed to Forestdale Apartments on Darbydale Road, with 1,333 family units, and Greenwood Farms townhouses with 492 units on Minnieville Road, as either approved or awaiting final site plans approval, and said over 3,000 additional family units have been zoned to be built in the immediate Dale City area. All of these units, according to McCoart, will have an impact on Dale City schools. "The point is, we have a lot more people coming in," he said, predicting Dale City students would be bused to Manassas if the school bond doesn't pass.

"Why can't you just say, 'Stop building new homes building new houses, the schools can't handle it,'?" asked a Dale City citizen, and McCoart explained that legally the school are the responsibility of the community and zoning is already final.

The total capacity for all county schools in September 1976 is 40,300 and enrollment is projected at 42,163. By 1960 projections are for over 46,000 students.

"We need the space as desperately as any school district ever needed space," Snyder told the group. He cited population growth cycles and economic recessions as causing school problems beyond the control of professional educators and called upon citizens to participate in solving these education problems.

The proposed school bond would provide for construction of one new high school along the I-95 corridor and three elementary schools, including one in Dale City, and provide for modernization of certain existing schools.

Johnson emphasized that projected student figures were based on the last two years with a depressed economic state. Any upswing in the economy would throw the projections out the window, he said, and indicated evidence is already pointing toward an upswing.

A Dale City resident asked the Citizen School Bond Committee about school bond opposition in the county, and committee member Ilona Salmon responded, "We don't have opposition, we have apathy." She continued to explain that most of the resistance to the bond has come from western Prince William and those who say, "Go ahead and bus, it's not affecting my children."

Citizen School Bond Committee chairperson Sheila McDaniel explained in response to questions by Dale City residents that the proposed bond has a built-in inflation figure and there is legal precedent to compel the Board of Supervisors to build the schools if the band is passed.

The Citizens Bond Committee handed out fact

sheets illustrating the growth rate in student enrollment, school capacity, and a table outlining the estimated impact of the bond on the county real property tax rate for the next five years. According to the sheet, the real property tax would go from 3 cents in 1976-77 to a high of 36 cents in 1979-80 and then decrease until the proposed 20 year bonds are repaid.

Another citizen said he was concerned about wasted space in school design, and Mrs. McDaniel said citizens are urged to tell the school board what they want in their schools. She cited the smaller size of the proposed new high school (1800 students) as a partial outcome of citizen rejection of huge schools like Gar-field.

School Planetarium Vetoed

The Journal Messenger, June 3, 1976. Kristy Larson, JM Staff Writer.

MANASSAS — Students will not be gazing at the stars, unless they are the real ones, following the County School Board's decision Wednesday turning down a planetarium.

Half of a $50,028 federal tax grant would have funded the planetarium instruction equipment, which was to be located in Gar-Field High School, with the other portion going to library resources.

The planetarium would have cost local taxpayers $26,200 for finishing the room, student transportation and a teacher in the first year, according to figures from the school board staff.

In a 4-3 vote, the board asked the staff to draft another proposal to the federal government asking that all of the $50,0283 go to library resources, textbooks and other instructional materials.

Supt. Dr. Milton L. Snyder urged the board to carefully consider the request for planetarium equipment.

"I must emphasize the importance of our solar system. Science is an important part of cur curriculum," Snyder said.

The planetarium would be used as a tool for instruction, like a microscope, said J. Earle Phillips, associate superintendent for instruction.

"It is another aid to identify with space," Phillips said.

Board member Thomas 0. Beane also urged his board members to vote in favor of the planetarium.

A recent trip to a planetarium in Alexandria by Herbert J. Saunders. Mrs. Emily M. Rosenberg, and Beane apparently showed the board members that the facility was not being used because of a lack of interest.

"The equipment we saw there left a lot to be desired, but I think a planetarium offers a lot to students," Beane said.

However, the majority of the beard felt that the cost to the school system would be prohibitive.

Saunders said that, even though he represents the Gar-Field High School area, he could not vote for the facility.

"I feel we can ill-afford to go to this expense," he said.

Board member George P. Mullen said he would rather see the money go towards books, and the space which would be taken up by a planetarium used for another purpose.

Board Members Question Unexpended School Funds

The Journal Messenger, June 4, 1976. A1. Kristy Larson, JM Staff Writer.

MANASSAS — Although the County School Board recently has been working to cut funds, some members Wednesday turned their concern to an apparent surplus estimated at between $1 million and $2 million.

James 0. Allison, fiscal planning, management and control director, said an accurate estimate will not be available until next week.

From figures presented by Allison, 70 percent instead of 75 percent of the budget was spent in the third quarter.

"If that money was there, why wasn't it spent," asked board member Herbert J. Saunders.

"Maintenance at the school plants have been badly needed. I know this board would have loved to have expended there," added board member George P. Mullen, referring to the 65 instead of 75 percent of the funds spent in that category.

Allison stressed that the amount of surplus will not be known until next week. The school system may not be able to assess whether or not it has under-expended even by June because of delay in the computer processing of bills.

The budget at 70.24 per cent spent by the third quarter is closer than it has been in the past, noted board member Mrs. Emily M. Rosenberg.

In fiscal year, 1974-75, 69.5 percent had been expended, and in 1973-74, 68.72 spent by the third quarter, according to the figures.

Surplus in the school budget goes into the county general fund.

"I have had the worst fear of being over-extended," said Supt. Dr. Milton L. Snyder. "There is a legal problem. I can go to jail for that."

Snyder said he had heard that the state was planning to make another cut in its aid to the school divisions, which can be done up until June, or the end of the fiscal year.

"We need to have some leeway left for contingencies," said Mrs. Rosenberg.

In other business at its meeting Wednesday, the County School Board approved an alternate housing plan in case the air conditioning at five schools is not installed on time. The air conditioning at Saunders, Washington-Reid, Dumfries and Triangle Elementary School and Graham Park Middle School is expected to be completed by July 1, the opening of year-round instruction, said Paul Trautman, school plant services director.

But a contract has been negotiated with the Quantico school system in case there are any delays, said Richard Johnson, student housing task force chairman.

In meetings, patents and administrators favored an early start and release at the local schools, but in a prolonged delay Dumfries and Triangle students would be moved to Quantico schools, said Johnson.

The County School Board also:

- Agreed to pay $50,000 of a long standing $303,000 sewage bill for Gainesville and Tyler Elementary Schools. Supervisor Donald White appealed to the school board to straighten out the nine-year bill so that the Greater Manassas Sanitary District can be merged with the Gainesville-Haymarket Sanitary District.

- Approved a $86,697 bid by S&J Associates to replace an air conditioning unit damaged in the Gar-Field High School fire.

- Approved the submission of a proposal to the U.S. Office of Education for funds for an experience-based career education program, in which students learn about jobs by observing at work sites.

- Approved a variety of policies to bring the school system into compliance with Title IX, the federal law mandating that institutions receiving federal funds may not discriminate on the basis of sex.

- Agreed to have the school board's policy committee look into students' carrying of weapons in schools. Two recent knifing incidents have created a need for a policy on the matter, said board member William Dunn.

- Approved a six-year plan, which is a statement of goals. Fundamental skills, post-secondary career skills, accountability and decision making will receive the top emphasis out of the 10 goals.

Woodbridge

The Journal Messenger, June 7, 1976. Betty Calvin.

WOODBRIDGE — The Bicentennial Class of Woodbridge Senior High School was graduated Friday evening in a sunny ceremony under smiling blue skies at the school's stadium.

They numbered about 550, this "leadership class" as they were termed by one of the speakers, Dr. Milton Snyder, superintendent of schools for Prince William County.

Snyder recalled how the class had begun its high school sojourn in crowded "old Woodbridge," on York Drive, on split shifts. But, he added, the class had helped the 1976 year at Woodbridge become a historic one with the school taking lop awards in nearly every field of endeavor, more than any other school in the county.

Henry Tannenbaum, the zany news commentator of WTOP-TV, captured the interest of the graduates with a short but relevant speech, the substance of which was "Think more." He told of his days at New York's Stuyvesant High. "We were incredibly naive—when someone mentioned 'the pill' we generally meant aspirin. I suspect many of the things you take for granted are things we found very hard to learn."

Tannebaum said his station's research department had studied typical high school graduates. Among its findings young people "are not terribly involved in national issues, in politics… it frightens me that you young people aren't watching the news."

He added "perhaps the news doesn't show THE REAL WORLD—we do crazy stunts in the news—but people in the real world also do funny things; do enjoy themselves." He summed it all up with "The better informed you are, the better person you will be."

Three honor graduates were introduced by Eliis Hawkins, School Board chairman. Tied for valedictory honors were Catherine Louise Coulter and Deborah Monne Johnson. Johnson earned the salutatorian honors.

The $500 Gregory Peal Memorial Scholarship went to Matthew Trowbridge, who also received scholarships from the Woodbridge Lions Club and the Woodbridge Womans' Club.

Alice Woodworth, whose proud father, the Rev. Robert Woodworth of Covenant Presbyterian Church gave the benediction, received the American Legion Citizenship award and a $1,000 regional scholarship to Mary Washington College.

Anna Woods won a $200 VFW nursing scholarship and a Woodbridge Lions Club scholarship. Kevin Weeks received a citizenship award as well as a $350 Norsemen scholarship.

The $500 Kiwanis Club scholarship went to Mary O'Connor who also received a Lake Ridge Lions Club scholarship. A full scholarship to Lincoln Technical Institute was earned by Ames Miller who also won the SAE award of $600.

National Merit Scholar Cameron Smith won a Merit Scholarship to Michigan State University. A $1,000 scholarship to the University of Missouri was presented by the Marine Officers Wives Club to Miss Coulter. Other scholarship swards went to: Karen Ann Heffner, Woodbridge Lions Club and American Legion Auxiliary; Richard Butts, Richard Legere and Lawrence Lavin, NROTC; Marie Smith, Woodbridge Jaycees; Sheree Zerby, Business and Professional Women's Club; Harry Dashiell, Dale City Art Guild; and Elizabeth Cantu, a $250 scholarship from Hardee's Food Service.

The grads—from Kenneth Lee Abbott to Paula Renee Zimmerman—filed in and out of the packed stadium to music by the school's Symphonic Band lead by Dr. J. Zuill Bailey. The Rev. James Little of Ebenezer Baptist Church gave the invocation.

Among the administration members presenting awards and diplomas were Haynes W. Davis, principal; William Stephens, Ray Norris, Dr. Sarah Jerome, and Wayne Mallard.

The class showed its final burst of exuberance at the close of the ceremony with a flurry of green and white mortar boards tossed high into the air amid cheers from the class and the crowd.

Too much or too little money?

School Board members complain of budget surplus

Potomac News, June 9, 1976. C6. Lynne Grandstaff

Two Prince William School Board members complained Wednesday that school administration is either spending too little money or has budgeted too much for the current fiscal year.

In addition, Boardman William Dunn claimed later that the school administration has withheld financial information from the board in an effort to secure passage of the bond referendum.

The board received a newly-devised report, which shows only 70.24 percent of the current operating budget had been spent by April 1. If all the school budget were to be spent at an even rate for the year, the percentage of expenditure should be 75 percent.

Boardman Herbert J. Saunders asked why the percentage was so low. A staff member replied that the low expenditure rate was the result of the hiring and purchasing freeze, which was instituted in November. The freeze was lifted after the board determined areas in which they would cut to meet the five percent reduction in state funds imposed by Va. Gov. Mills E. Godwin.

Saunders growled, "I can't buy the idea that the freeze accounted for it; a freeze will not save $2 million. It would appear that more money than was needed was included in the budget. It appears that there is going to be a great surplus."

On the other hand, board member Emily Rosenberg maintained, "We do not have any information concerning rates of expenditure for the last quarter of the fiscal year. Besides, we're closer to a schedule for spending 100 percent of the money than we were in the past two years."

The report shows that, on April 1, in the 1974-75 year, 69.5 percent of the budget had been spent.

On the same date in the 1973-74 fiscal year, 68.72 percent had been spent.

Nonetheless, Boardman George P. Mullen directed the board's attention to the budget category which includes maintenance funds. He said, "Everyone is always screaming that there are insufficient funds to maintain the schools, but we're underspending by approximately 10 percent in this quarter (of the fiscal year)."

School's Supt. Dr. Milton Snyder defended the rate of expenditure: "Our intent has been to conserve. We have been on a freeze plan for almost all of the three years I have been here. The staff has been almost afraid to go to zero (spend all the money). If we overdo our conservatism, I know we're going to be criticized; if we overspend, we're in real trouble. I can go to jail for that."

At the end of the discussion, Allison told the board he would have an update of spending patterns at the June 9 special meeting. He said the computer run had not been completed in time to provide current information at the June 2 meeting.

After the meeting, Dunn charged that the updated information was being withheld until after the bond referendum, so that no one would know how much money remained in the maintenance category of the budget. Major maintenance projects are included in the bond proposal; Dunn has consistently said that maintenance projects should be funded from operating money. He said there might be sufficient unexpended funds in the budget to handle some of the maintenance projects included in the bond. Dunn maintained, "There are a lot of things which haven't been brought out; things have been held back."

Voters Reject School Bonds

The Journal Messenger, June 9, 1976. Kristy Larson, JM Staff Writer.

MANASSAS — Prince William County voters took advantage of the fine weather Tuesday to defeat a proposed $26.25 million school bond issue by a wide margin. Unofficial results showed 4,406 voters against the bonds and only 3,146 for the issue.

Residents in the eastern magisterial districts of Occoquan, Coles and Neabsco, who stood to gain three elementary schools voted in favor of the issue by good margins: Coles 454 for, 325 against; Occoquan 588 to 505; Neabsco 745 for, and 522 against.

Western Prince William County voted overwhelmingly against the bonds. Brentsville District turned down the issue 1,085 to 131, with Gainesville District citizens voting 975 to 183 against it.

The other two districts, Dumfries and Woodbridge, rejected the construction and maintenance bond by smaller margins.

Surprisingly, Dumfries voters, who were promised a new high school and elementary school to relieve their crowded schools, turned down the bond by a vote of 660 against and 532 for.

In Woodbridge, the voters cast 536 ballots against and 300 ballots for.

Reactions to the bond's failure were mixed according to the positions taken on the issue. But school officials agreed that they would like to submit another bond issue in November, the earliest possible date.

"I'm disappointed with the results, but I'm certainly not discouraged or disheartened," said County School Board Chairman Ellis B. Hawkins, who represents Occoquan District.

"The real need for more buildings will not go away with the vote," Hawkins said, promising a new bond issue.

William T. Dunn, the school board's most outspoken critic of the defeated proposal, said he was surprised at the results of the vote, thinking that the issue would pass.

"I understand (the voters) reluctance and I understand their concerns," said Hawkins. "I have listened to what they, the voters, have to say and I will look very closely at the results of the election when a new bond is introduced, as surely it must be."

Dunn said he felt the voters were saying that they wanted more concrete answers about the package, do not want maintenance of buildings financed for 20 years and were asking for a less costly issue.

He said he plans to propose a bond which would contain no frills.

"I think the people are putting the onus back on us," Dunn said, referring to the board members who opposed the bond. "They were saying that the minority shot their mouths off so come back with something that will work."

The cochairman of the Citizens School Bond Information Committee expressed their disappointment with the results.

"I don't think (citizens) voted it down for what it was," said Mrs. Shiela McDaniel, western county cochairwoman. "I think they were trying to let the supervisors and school board know about their general dissatisfaction."

"I don't think it was a vote against the bond, but the discontented feeling with things in general," agreed Andrew C. Tainter, east-end committee cochairman.

He said he felt that the bond had many "soft spots" which could not be satisfactorily explained to the public, like why old Osbourn High School was not being used to house students, and the alternative of busing children to the west end.

"The people who said they were against this bond but would support the next one are going to have to produce results," said Tainter.

He added that he was disappointed with the

turn-out at bond information meetings held throughout the county.

"We probably didn't get the message across, but it's difficult to make a case when you don't have the people to listen," Tainter said.

The committee's work was commended by Hawkins and Supt. Dr. Milton L. Snyder.

The school superintendent also expressed his regret that the issue failed.

"From the lessons learned by this experience, I hope that we will find the common ground to work with those who were opposed to the last bond, as well as those who favored it," Snyder said.

Hawkins said he was not sure of the reasons behind the bond's failure in Dumfries and Woodbridge districts.

A sixth high school costing $14 million was planned in the southern I-95 corridor, with three elementary schools costing $2.7 million which would have been located in the eastern end.

The rest of the money would have gone for repairs and renovations in the western Prince William County schools.

Hawkins speculated that the rejection in Woodbridge was due to an older, more stable community which has less of a need for schools or because students were already being housed in year-round facilities.

The board chairman said he was puzzled over the defeat of the bond in Dumfries District and attributed the results to the voters' general dissatisfaction.

School planetariums nixed

Potomac News, June 9, 1976. Lynne Grandstaff.

There will be no planetariums in Prince William's schools, at least in the near future.

The School Board Wednesday, by a 4 to 3 vote, rejected a $25,000 federal grant to provide equipment for a planetarium, which would have been placed in Gar-Field High School.

Boardman Herbert Saunders, who cast the deciding vote, said he would not vote for any program, except in emergencies, where were not budgeted.

Although the federal funds would have provided the equipment, the schools would have been required to staff the planetarium with a teacher, provide transportation to it and provide funds for connecting the equipment. However, the administration had proposed that the teacher not be hired this year. Boardman Thomas Beane suggested students could pay 25 cents each for transportation making the only expense for the 1976-77 year a $5,000 installation fee.

Board member Emily Rosenberg maintained, "This is an extravagant way to teach about the solar system."

On the other side, Schools Supt. Dr. Milton Snyder defended the need for planetariums. He explained, "This is an integral part of the science program. Although it is not the three R's, science is an important part of our program. We haven't been able to educate the public or the staff to the need."

Voting against the proposal were Saunders and Mrs. Rosenberg, as well as board members George Mullen and William Dunn. Those in favor were Beane, Ellis Hawkins and Regis Lacey. Basically, these who favored the planetariums pointed to educational need, while those opposed discussed expense.

The board directed the staff to return with suggestions for reapplying to receive the same federal money for something else. Under the federal requirements, a variety of types of instructional equipment may be purchased with the federal money.

Paperwork Hunters Find Plenty of It

The Journal Messenger, June 21, 1976. A1. Kristy Larson, JM Staff Writer.

MANASSAS — The county school superintendent's paperwork committee has completed a survey to determine in which areas teachers' administrative workload can be reduced.

The committee was established Mrs. Mack, by S u p I. Dr. Milton L. Snyder to investigate paper work which may be reducing classroom time, said chairwoman Mrs. Lyle Mack.

Problem areas identified by elementary teachers include the collection of money, student permanent records, and forms required for special education evaluation, said Mrs. Mack.

In high schools, teachers protested that mandatory interim reports for all students and attendance checks take away from instructional time, she said.

Individual schools can also make unreasonable administrative demands upon teachers, she added.

Ironically, said Mrs. Mack, about half of the teachers objected to the paperwork committee's survey distributed during the last week of school, a typically prolific time of year for administrative forms.

The committee has suggested a clearinghouse to avoid duplication of forms, and a master timetable so that required tasks may be scheduled throughout the year, she said.

Teachers complained that paperwork seemed to flow in cycles and was unusually heavy at times, said Mrs. Mack.

The advent of year-round schools also created additional administrative requirements, she said. For instance, 45-15 high school teachers find they are filling out report cards or interim reports every week and a half.

As the school system has grown and centralized, the paperwork demands have also grown, explained Mrs. Mack.

"Dr. Snyder was getting an abundance of phone calls from teachers saying they didn't have time to teach," she said.

The committee is tailing a closer look at the administrative workload and plans to make its final recommendations before September.

Another school system committee, this one reviewing films, has completed its recommendations, said chairwoman Mrs. Marianne Durst. The results will be made public after review by the school administration, she said.

Board Told Pupil Loss Doesn't Mean All Costs Reduced

The Journal Messenger, June 25, 1976. A3.

MANASSAS — The school system's first quarter appropriation and the reduced costs associated with the withdrawal of Manassas Park students was discussed recently in a joint meeting of the County School Board and Board of County Supervisors.

A three-month budget of $19,474,229, or 30.29 percent of the budget, which was adopted by the school board was presented to the supervisors. No action was taken.

This did not include any reduction in the costs required with 2,100 Manassas Park students, said James O. Allison, fiscal planning, management and control director.

The city's decision to start its own schools came too late to make the appropriate adjustments in the budget through the computer, Allison said.

He suggested that $338,000 could be cut out of the first quarter appropriation based upon the estimate of the loss of federal and state tax revenue. The total revenue reduction is expected to be about $1.6 million.

"Any quick or arbitrary moves to make instant reductions in school funds could be harmful to Prince William students remaining in our system," said a statement handed out by Supt. Dr. Milton L. Snyder.

With the increased number of students now on a year-round schedule, more money for supplies, personnel and other items must be spent in the first quarter, said Allison.

Five additional schools begin 45 15 July 1, putting about half of the system's 42,000 pupils on that schedule:

Past year's budgets do not give enough information on which to base expenditures needed for schools to operate July 1, he said.

"We're asking for the full appropriation to find out as exactly and precisely as possible the impact of the withdrawal," added Allison.

He explained that fixed costs make it unacceptable to reduce the budget $1,230, for each lost student.

Fixed costs, he said, are expenditures that are required regardless of the number of students in the system.

Utilities, custodial service based on the amount of building space, security and other items are examples of costs necessary, for any number of pupils, said Allison.

Supervisor James McCoart asked whether supplies would be in the year-round schools by July 1.

Snyder said he could not guarantee that the suppliers would come through with the material by the July 1 school opening dale. Mark Rothaeker, school service associate superintendent, added that he thought the equipment would be in the schools on time.

State May Withhold County Schools' Aid

Planning Time at Issue

The Journal Messenger, June 28, 1976. A1.

RICHMOND — Virginia's State Board of Education has warned local school systems their state aid is in jeopardy if they dismiss school early to give teachers planning time.

Board members meeting in Richmond Friday unanimously adopted a resolution calling for strict adherence to a state requirement for schools to have a minimum of five class-hours a day for at least 180 days a year.

Preston C. Caruthers, who drafted the resolution, said an Arlington youngster was routinely dismissed at. 1:30 p.m. each Wednesday, after being in school only four hours.

Caruthers said he had been informed that some other Northern Virginia school systems also released elementary school students early to give teachers planning time.

The resolution said the "apparent trend toward reduced time spent in the development of basic skills, particularly at the elementary level, must halt. Evidence suggests that more, not fewer, hours of basic instruction and practice are required if we are to improve reading, writing and arithmetic skills."

Prince William County school officials recently approved a demand by the Prince William Education Association (teachers' union) that elementary schools be dismissed early on given days to allow planning time for the teachers

Prior to the arrangement by the State Board of Education, the Prince William County School Board adopted in principle, the early dismissal planning time generally as implemented during the 1974-75 school year, according to Richard G. Neal, employee relations specialist for the county school system.

Neal said the superintendent, Dr. Milton L. Snyder, was to recommend to the School Board on July 7 exactly how planning time would be implemented in Prince William County during the 1976-77 school year.

"I would guess the State Board of Education's action clouds the issue," Neal said thus morning. "If the State Board did pass such a resolution, it will be reported to the Prince William County School Board on July 7, and a decision would then be up to the School Board," he added.

School Superintendent Gets $800 Pay Increase

The Journal Messenger, June 29, 1976. A1.

MANASSAS — School Supt. Dr. Milton L. Snyder received his annual evaluation from the County School Board in a 4.5-hour executive session Monday night.

At the end of the meeting, the board voted to increase Snyder's salary by $800 to $37,700.

Chairman Ellis B. Hawkins would not comment on the board's discussion except to say that it was a "very good evaluative (sic) process."

"As in any evaluative process there were pluses and minuses," said Hawkins. "I think it was constructive for the board and superintendent alike."

"It was an extensive review and I compliment the Board for giving so much of their time," said Snyder.

Neither the chairman or superintendent would comment on whether or not the evaluation might result in any changes in direction for the school system.

The purpose of the discussion is to appraise the performance of the superintendent based on the School Board's goals.

The board followed a state form, said Hawkins, which rates the superintendent on relationship with the board, community relationships, staff and personnel relationships, educational leadership, business and finance, and personal qualities.

In voting on the pay raise, only Thomas Beane abstained from the $800 increase, saying he thought Snyder should have received more.

Saunders Leads Attack on Hiring Methods

Potomac News, September 23, 1976. Lynne Grandstaff.

School Boardman Herbert Saunders, former head of Prince William's personnel department, led the attack Monday on the current method of hiring professional employees.

In response to previous complaints by Saunders and other board members, Associate Supt. Earle Phillips outlined the current method of hiring professional personnel. In response, Saunders grilled the staff members on the current practice; although he did not spell out his proposals, he appeared to favor a return to the system as it existed under his direction.

Under the former system, all responsibility for hiring was vested in the personnel department; when he became superintendent in 1973, Dr. Milton Snyder changed the system, so that personnel became part of the instructional department. Saunders, who had been assistant superintendent for personnel, became director of professional personnel, a less powerful position in the organization. The following year, Saunders retired.

Basically, the change in hiring means that building principals have an active role in selecting teachers for their individual schools, and final personnel responsibility is vested in the instructional department. The function of the personnel department is in locating candidates, selecting those with proper background, setting up interviews and making recommendations.

The current administration favors the system because, as Phillips explained, it is oriented to the instructional program and the individual building.

As Saunders questioned the staff, an apparent problem with the current system emerged: the personnel department, which does not have full responsibility, has more precise budget information concerning teacher hiring than the instructional department.

Although Phillips promised more precise budget information from instructional administrators in the next couple of weeks, Saunders was not impressed.

Boardmen were nowhere near finished their questioning of hiring practices when Chairman William Dunn called the meeting to a halt. The session began at 5 p.m., and the personnel item came up at 11:45. Saunders looked as if he had many remaining questions when Dunn announced that the meeting would be adjourned at 12:30.

Neither Dunn nor George Mullen was pleased with the hiring system, although their questions and concerns were nowhere near as many or as precise as Saunders'.

At one point, Mullen groused, "With this system, you have 140 personnel directors (roughly the number of total administrators in the system)."

Dunn was concerned that the administration was recruiting in academic areas where they had no vacancies.

Both complained that they had asked for changes and the staff presented a compendium of current practice. There was one change proposed in college recruiting.

The discussion will continue at a future board meeting.

Changing School Board

Unanimity, agreement give way to long discussions

Potomac News, October 25, 1976. Lynne Grandstaff.

At a recent Prince William School Board meeting, members haggled for one half hour over whether a unanimous vote would be needed to add an item to the agenda.

The board recessed, listened to tapes of the previous session and called the lawyer.

Boardman Thomas Beane objected to adding a personnel item to a special meeting; boardman Emily Rosenberg announced that she would walk out if the item was not added.

After the half hour of research and caucusing, Beane withdrew his objection; the agenda was unanimously approved and the meeting proceeded.

It was a minor incident over a minor matter, but the proceedings highlighted a frequent situation at the board. At times, members seem incapable of agreeing on anything. Tempers flare, and concern for issues gives way to haggling over procedure.

On the other hand, once the procedural matter had been settled, the board moved rapidly through its agenda with total unanimity. The board varies from meeting to meeting. Sometimes, the sessions move relatively smoothly; at other times the board has difficulty accomplishing anything.

The dissension and tension on the board are relatively new. In the past three years, there has been a near-total shift in the board's method of doing business.

At the first board session in September of 1973, the board members made eight motions, of which seven were unanimously adopted. The meeting ran from 10 a.m. until 4 p.m.

At the first September meeting this year, 23 motions were offered. Only one was not approved, but the boardmen failed to get a unanimous vote on six of them. The session began at 10 a.m. and adjourned at 8:35 p.m.

During the first meeting in October 1973, 11 motions were offered and eight were unanimous. The session lasted from 10 a.m. to 4:30 p.m.

For the same meeting this year, only eight of the 22 motions were unanimously approved. The meeting began at 9 a.m. and was adjourned to a special session at 8 p.m.; even so, several items were dropped from the agenda.

The board now takes official action on all sorts of matters for which no formal action was previously taken. For example, the board formally approves the agenda at the beginning of each meeting: new items during the meeting must be added to the agenda through a special unanimous resolution.

Minutes were formerly ruled approved by the chairman; now the board frequently has lengthy discussions about the minutes before taking a formal vote.

In addition to procedural matters, the board is also acting on a variety of items which were previously handled administratively. For example, at the first October meeting, the board approved bids on meat for the school cafeterias. Board approval of such bids is part of a new policy which reflects increasing activity in relatively small board matters.

Other matters, which had previously been handled as routine, are now the subject of lengthy discussions and split notes. For instance, at the Oct. 6 meeting, boardmen Beane and Regis Lacey voted against approval of the minutes, while Lacey and Herbert Saunders opposed payment of the bills and Beane abstained.

There is no way to be sure why the board has undergone such rapid or complete transformation. It was not long ago that the School Board was criticized as a "rubber stamp" for the administration.

Currently, board members talk about hassling and belittling the staff.

It was not long ago that the board members seemed to be nearly anonymous members of a unified body. Now, boardmen frequently project themselves like politicians giving lengthy justifications for their votes on minor matters.

There are various possibilities within the framework of board members' appointments which may, at least in part, account for the changes.

Most obvious is the altered method of appointing board members. Until the change in form of county government in 1972, all School Board members were appointed by the Circuit Court.

Under the current county executive form of government, School Board members are appointed by the Board of Supervisors; the supervisors have made the appointments under a gentleman's agreement that each individual would receive his fellow supervisors' backing on his choice for School Board.

Because the School Board and the previous supervisors spent 1-1/2 years in court to settle questions on the method of appointing School Board members, only five of the seven current School Boardmen have been appointed by supervisors. Boardmen William Dunn's and Ellis Hawkins' appointments expire on March 13; supervisors will appoint school Boardmen to their seats for the first tie. Of the board men appointed by supervisors only Beane was reappointed. He was appointed on March 13 to fill T. Clay Wood's seat, after Beane had been previously unseated when former supervisor C. Scott Winfield appointed George Mullen.

Thus, the board has had five new members in the past three years including Beane and Robert Boyd, who resigned when Manassas because a city.

The high degree of turnover on the board is, in itself, a substantial change; two of the boardmen who were replaced in the past year had 24 years' seniority each.

Another potential cause of change is the philosophy of the previous Board of Supervisors, which made appointments for three School Board seats.

Mrs. Rosenberg, who was appointed by the late supervisor Roy Doggett, said she believes she was appointed "because I said I wanted to blow up the schools. I went onto the board with the idea that the schools were using too much of the tax dollar. There was an atmosphere of suspicion and distrust. We were put on the board because we had a negative attitude toward education."

Although Mrs. Rosenberg said her attitudes have changed since becoming a board member, the transition in the board may be related to the ways in which board members view each other and their jobs.

Some board members told the Potomac News privately that they are not sure whether their fellow boardmen are heading toward the same, ultimate goal. Others said the goal is the same, but the proposed methods of reaching it are different.

Boardman Lacey said, "I don't think the divisions on this board are as deep as they appear to be."

Mrs. Rosenerg said, "I think we're beginning to come together."

Beane said, "I think this board can solve its problems, if the members work together and put their minds on the issues."

There is also talk among board members about a split board; the most often cited example is the split vote on the recent school construction bond referendum. However, some members do not see a definable split; instead, they look at the members as individuals who are voting their personal philosophies on each matter. The question is whether board men have personal alliances with influence their votes.

To try to find out what board members think and how they approach various issues, the Potomac News conducted lengthy interview with each of the seven members. Members' comments are the subject of the following articles.

Next: housing high school students
(end of article)

Area educators ask state to OK block planning time

Potomac News, October 29, 1976. Lynne Grandstaff.

RICHMOND—Prince William Schools Supt. Dr Milton Snyder headed the list of educators who asked the State Board of Education to reconsider its five-hour school day requirement at a public hearing Thursday.

The majority of the speakers were from Prince William, Fairfax, Arlington and Winchester; all those school systems had instituted an early release program for elementary school students, so that teachers could have block planning time.

The five-hour day requirement, which has existed since at least 1942 but was not enforced, would put an end to the early student release system. When early release was being used in Prince William, students were sent home early on Thursdays and did not receive five hours of instruction.

Prince William's School Board asked that the state modify its requirement, so that each week would average a minimum of 25 hours.

At the conclusion of the hearing, Dr. W.E. Campbell, state superintendent of public instruction, recommended the state board adopt a minimum requirement of 27.5 hours per week instructional time, with a maximum of one day for early release.

He said he had found no attempt in the early release programs to cut the number of instructional hours. He recommended that the early release day have a maximum of four instructional hours.

In general, the speakers at Thursday's public hearing supported the idea of a minimum instructional week, but they asked for flexibility to organize their instructional time.

Snyder said. "I think we should be increasing, not decreasing, the amount of instructional time children receive; however, I think it is important that we be allowed flexibility."

James O'Cain, executive director of the Prince William Education Association, concurred. He said, "We found that parents would rather their children had 28 hours of well-planned instruction than 30 hours of poorly planned instruction. We also found that planning periods of one or two hours each week were more valuable than whole days a couple of times during the year."

The education association has pushed for the block planning time since 1972, when it was first instituted. If the State Board of Education changes its five-hour day ruling, Prince William will apparently return immediately to the early release system, since the School Board has already given its concurrence to the idea.

Snyder has always opposed early release of elementary students

Outside the hearing room Thursday, he told the press that he still opposes early release. He said, "I do favor flexibility, and I favor block planning time. My objection is to automatically releasing students every Thursday. If we release them early on Thursday, pretty soon we'll be sending them home early on Tuesdays, too."

Only one speaker opposed changing the State Board's regulation. An assistant superintendent of the City of Richmond schools said she favored the requirement because children need the instructional time.

Others joined Snyder in suggesting that the regulation address the number of total instructional hours in a year; he said it might be possible to increase the current requirement from 900 hours to 950 or 1,000 hours.

The Campbell plan would not conflict with the Prince William proposal for early release.

Campbell said his proposal would increase the amount of instructional time for elementary children in 15 school systems; none of those are school systems which use the early release system.

The board's stated reason for deciding to enforce the five-hour day requirement was concern that the amount of instructional time for elementary students was being reduced. Campbell's plan would meet the average instructional time in the state; he said it would be an unfair financial burden on the school systems to increase the minimum requirement.

The board will discuss the problem and the proposal at Friday's regular State Board of Education meeting.

The Right Decision

The Journal Messenger, (exact date not mentioned, photocopy says October/November 1976).

The School Board of Prince William County is scheduled to meet in executive session next Monday to discuss the superintendency of Dr. Milton Snyder. The simple fact that such a meeting is taking place has launched some degree of speculation on the part of those who like to speculate on matters of civic interest. There is really nothing unusual about this meeting being held at this time since the School Board is required by law to make superintendency appointments between March 1 and May 1. Since Dr. Snyder's contract expires June 30 the subject of its renewal must be faced by the board in the near future to permit a final decision in advance of the deadline.

The customary rumor mills are bound to grind out all manner of speculations about something which very little is known. Prince William County politics being what it is, the rumors include suggestions that there is a deep division among school board members on the subject of contract renewal. It is known that there was a good deal of controversy between the old Board of County Supervisors and the School Board in the wake of the former body's attempt to unseat the old School Board *en masse* so that the supervisors could name their own selections as replacements. After a fairly bitter court battle which was ultimately resolved by the State Supreme Court, the supervisors were forced to wait until previous terms expired before they could make those replacements.

With the replacement of the old County Board by new faces in the 1975 elections, it is doubtful that there is any connection between the composition of the School Board and any effect it may have on the retention or dismissal of Dr. Snyder. It would indeed be a sad state of affairs if the school superintendency were to become the focal point of a political tug of war. Dr. Snyder's contributions to Prince William County are too great to be subjected to such treatment. He must be judged on his record of positive achievement.

Dr. Snyder took office under conditions which were far from perfect. Not too long after he came on the scene he was faced with a tangled mess involving the construction of Osbourn Park High School, a mess which was not of his own making. Standing firm against a wide variety of proposals of doubtful merit, the new superintendent charted a sound course which enabled the school to be finished in the shortest possible time with a minimum of hardship as far as the county and its taxpayers were concerned. The greatest beneficiaries were the students at the old Osbourn High School who had been forced to endure intolerable conditions for too long a time.

His tenure in the post has spanned some very difficult years in the life of the Prince William County schools. Adverse economic conditions coupled with a continuation of rampant growth forced him and his staff to make some hard decision forced on the schools by greatly curtailed county budgets. Although not always in agreement with the manner in which budget cuts were applied, we came to realize that may of these cuts were forced on the School Board and administration by decisions originating with the County Board. State mandated programs also contributed to the difficulties faced by the schools.

Dr. Snyder has gone to great lengths in the years he has been our superintendent to open the decision-making process to the influences of county citizens. The annual school-community seminars have been invaluable in guiding the administration to provide the kind of school programs desired by a majority of the citizens. Special questions of concern to groups of parents have been addressed through community involvement and participation in special committees to consider these controversial matters. Parent objections to certain teaching materials were considered in this manner.

Public information has been made readily available under Dr. Snyder's administration without any attempt to hold back facts requested by the press.

On occasion we have not seen eye to eye with the school administration regarding some policies and programs, but we have never been denied full access to the information we sought. We have never felt that there was any attempt to be less than candid on the part of Dr. Snyder and his organization.

If the School Board is contemplating any replacement of Dr. Snyder, it would do well to consider that in making such a replacement it will be dealing with an unknown quantity. Snyder's knowledge and experience in running a school system must be the nub of any discussion. These positive qualities have been amply demonstrated during the period of his incumbency. The wonder is that he has put up with the pressures to which he has been subjected without giving up on Prince William County.

Before taking any rash actions based on individual likes and dislikes, the School Board would do well to weigh the good accomplished by Dr. Snyder and to ask themselves what alternatives he had in the face of the conditions which he had to meet. In our opinion, Dr. Snyder should be kept here if he will have us. We are indeed fortunate to have a man of his stature.

Our Viewpoint: An evaluation of Dr. Snyder

Potomac News, November 11, 1976.

We have taken our own advice.

Last week we detailed a process for evaluating the performance of Prince William Schools Superintendent Dr. Milton Snyder. It is an exercise made necessary by the expiration next June of Dr. Snyder's four year contract.

Applying our own evaluation guidelines, we found that Dr. Snyder scored well in nearly all categories. And we would wholeheartedly recommend that the School Board offer to renew Dr. Snyder's contract.

Our guidelines had three basic standards for weighing Dr. Snyder's contract renewal: the known problems facing the system and his qualifications for meeting them; the School Board's own standards for measuring professionalism; and the record regarding Dr. Snyder's leadership on major problems in the past.

—Dr. Snyder is eminently qualified for his job and his credentials are as good as we could hope to find.

As foreseen problems, school space needs, quality of education and teacher contract negotiations rank high.

None of these is a new problem; all are ongoing ones for which Dr. Snyder has already helped to develop solutions.

Perhaps the most controversial of these will be school space needs. In this area, while the administration has made proposals and provided necessary study, the School Board has become intricately involved. Both the School Board and the administration have proven to be highly susceptible to public opinion—willing to discard unpopular ideas. This attitude should help to east the controversy as the problem continues to be addressed in the future.

—On the School Board's evaluation form, Dr. Snyder would score very well. The form basically establishes the way in which a really professional school superintendent should carry out his job. It includes divisions of relationship with the School Board, with the community, and with staff, as well as his reputation as an educator and his personal code of ethics.

We could find only one weak area in the entire evaluation sheet; that has to do with staff. Dr. Snyder has met with some difficulty in his relationship with teachers. Although he does not deal directly with the teachers, it is important that teachers respect the school superintendent.

We're not certain just how the strained relationship developed. We suspect it is the result of what teachers saw as a failure on Dr. Snyder's part to use his influence to push for a higher teach pay scale. The problem is not insolvable.

There have been indications of philosophical differences between Dr. Snyder and individual members of the School Board. But using the criteria of the School Board's own evaluation sheet, Dr. Snyder has conducted himself in a highly professional manner in dealing with the board.

Over the years he has had very good rapport with the news media and has made himself as open to questioning as his schedule would permit.

When the state announced severe cuts in the funds Prince William would be getting for schools and when the Board of Supervisors cut the school budget, Dr. Snyder reacted professionally, not emotionally, and managed to absorb the cuts without (missing text).

—Dr. Snyder has a record over the past four years of which he can be justly proud. He has dealt with a number of major and minor crises.

Last week we listed two areas in which Dr. Snyder has not been completely successful—in providing a long-term solution to school space needs and in his rapport with teachers.

The matter of school space needs has been an

unbelievably complex issue during the past four years. It has been complicated by the withdrawal and proposed withdrawal of Manassas and Manassas Park students, leaving the county with unused classrooms in one end of the county and crowded schools in the other.

The one big plus in Dr. Snyder's favor throughout his tenure in dealing with housing needs, has been that proposed solutions have been taken to the public in time for the public to influence the proposals. We would guess that not since the very early days of the school district, has the community had a greater opportunity of influencing planning.

So, according to our evaluation system, Dr. Snyder has proven himself a capable superintendent. The School Board would do well to ask him to stay on and provide the continuity of leadership which only he can give.

We Salute Them All

The Journal Messenger, November 16, 1976.

At this time every year a week is set aside to pay tribute to American education and its accomplishments. We are now in the midst of this special occasion, American Education Week. In this particular area of Virginia several significant changes are taking place in the educational picture. The dedication of a new public school system in the City of Manassas Park reflects one of these changes. Another is the development of an independent school system by the City of Manassas to be unveiled next year. The county schools are striving to cope with problems of growth and overcrowding.

At one time or another we have found it necessary to be highly critical of some aspects of the local educational picture. We have been equally as critical of some national trends in education as they affect our individual school divisions. This does not necessarily make us opposed to education, its practitioners or the good which it has accomplished. More often than not, our disagreement relates to matters of policy which are often imposed by federal and state government through mandated programs. Frequently we must wonder how our local educators are able to do the fine job that they do in spite of this outside meddling.

Many schools in the area have prepared special programs to make the public aware of the aims and accomplishments of public education locally. Most of these program stress the educational programs and opportunities provided and offer a glimpse at what is going on in our public schools. Teachers and administrators are on hand to furnish this insight to those who are willing to take the time to visit the schools during this very special week.

It is fitting during American Education Week that we take special note of the remarkable achievement of Manassas Park in dedicating a functioning school system only six months after the decision was made to set up an independent educational program. This accomplishment is a tribute to the school board, city council and the mayor and to the devoted citizens who stood behind them and backed them every step of the way. In blazing a new trail in school construction with a $2.1 million price tag for the construction of two elementary schools and a junior-senior high school, the Park has opened new vistas which other school systems would do well to explore.

As the City of Manassas prepares to implement its own school system next fall, it will have the opportunity to blaze some trails of tis own in the months ahead. Steps have already been taken to provide the necessary physical plant for housing the city schools and preparation of the administrative and teaching staffs is going forward. When American Education Week rolls around next year, Manassas should have a functioning school system to show off to a proud community.

Prince William County has somewhat of an advantage over the two cities in that its school system has been long established. This is not to say that it is without its problems which a hard-working administrative staff is working diligently to solve. The educational accomplishments can be explored by visiting many county schools this week. The problems of school housing are in the process of being considered by the school board and administration. Meanwhile, the county's dedicated teachers continue to do a good job in providing an education for thousands of Prince William students.

When one considers the dramatic difference in the county school system today from what it was more than three years ago when Dr. Milton Snyder took the administrative helm, much that is positive has been accomplished. Dr. Snyder found a way out of the mess that surrounded the construction of Osbourn Park High School. His solution of the problem paved the way for its completion in the fall of 1974. Under his administration, there has been a greater openness in dealing with the public and a greater accessibility for those who have concerns about school methods and policies.

Citizen input has been sought and received through the school-community seminars held all over the county to permit the public to give its views on the operation of the various schools. Areas of special concern such as the controversies over certain teaching materials have been met directly by making these materials available for examination by parents and other concerned citizens. Special committees have been enlisted to study these problems and arrive at satisfactory solution.

All in all, Prince William County and the cities of Manassas and Manassas Park can take pride in the accomplishments of their school systems. While differences of opinion may exist with regard to specific aspects of school operations, the citizens cannot question the sincere dedication of those who have the responsibility for providing public education. On balance, there is far more that is positive than negative on the local educational scene. We salute them all on the occasion of American Education Week.

School Board vote backs Snyder 4-3

Potomac News, December 7, 1976. Lynne Grandstaff.

Prince William's School Board Monday night, by a 4 to 3 vote, expressed its intent to hire Schools Supt. Dr. Milton Snyder for a second four-year contract.

The resolution has no legal effect. As boardman Thomas Beane explained, "It is an expression of the intentions of the seven people who are currently on this board."

Under the provisions of state law, a superintendent can be hired between March 1 and May 1 for the four-year contract period which begins on July 1.

Between now and March, there could be two new School Board members, since the terms of Ellis Hawkins and William Dunn expire on March 13. Although it was not stated, it is the apparent intent of the board to wait until those appointments have been made before officially hiring a superintendent.

Boardmen Beane, Hawkins and Regis Lacey had previously indicated their support for Snyder; the opposition of George Mullen, Emily Rosenberg and Herbert Saunders was also clear.

Thus, Dunn constituted the swing vote. He said, "I weighed it and weighed it and weighed it. I even made a list of the pros and cons. I voted for Dr. Snyder with some qualifications; there are areas about which I am concerned. One thing I asked him (in executive session) was how he could even tolerate this kind of split, much less lead the district. He answered the question."

Dunn continued, "I felt like I was making the decision all by myself, and I have to live with the decision."

Saunders, whose opposition to Snyder dates from the time when Saunders was director of personnel, said he voted against the resolution because he wanted the opportunity to choose among candidates for superintendent; the other option before the board was to advertise the position and invite candidates to apply for the job.

Saunders said, "I felt that, with a split board, we ought to have looked at other applicants and made a definitive decision at an appropriate time."

Lacey, who backed Snyder's reappointment, came to the meeting with a lengthy list of particulars. He cited various accomplishments, including completion of Osbourn Park High School, development of a comprehensive special education plan, expansion of the year-round school program, implementation of a kindergarten program and development of a program for gifted and talented students.

Lacey continued, "People of his caliber come along only once in a great while. We have afforded him four years of Prince William's multitude of problems; now that he knows us and some of our unique problems, I encourage you to extend Dr. Snyder's contract for four more years."

At the conclusion of Lacey's remarks, Saunders replied, "That is a personal opinion; some of us do not agree with any or all of what he said."

Before the 6 p.m. executive session on the superintendent's contract, Snyder met with his executive team of administrators to announce to them privately, his decision to seek a second four-year contract.

In a prepared statement, Snyder said he had decided to seek reappointment, in part, "because I wish to complete the projects I have started and see the county school system achieve its full potential."

In addition, Snyder outlined several goals for a second four-year period: decentralization of the school staff, solution of school facilities problems, completion of a program to assure competency in basic skills and assessment of the year-round school program.

Staff Development and Strategies for Change, Innovative Learning Theory

EDAE 5780 Graduate Seminar in Education, Winter Quarter, 1976.
Taught by Milton L. Snyder, Ph.D., at Virginia Polytechnic Institute and State University, Blacksburg, Virginia.

Introduction

In an attempt to understand learning processes at an advanced graduate class level this course will give special consideration and emphasis to readings relating to Man and theories of innovative learning practices. Using group study interaction and the analysis of basic innovative learning theories as basis, special designs and strategies will be developed for practical application by individuals participating in the class.

Course Goals

The major purpose of this course is to review the current literature on the concept of man, and theories of innovative learning practices (including basis of theories) and relate them to curriculum designs for class analysis and evaluation.

Specific goals are:
- To review established concepts of man
- To review learning and program needs of special concern groups (minorities, economic factors,etc) and individualized hopes and aspirations of present society
- To identify and review current innovative learning practices and models
- To identify and analyze actual situations in which different concepts of learning are applied
- To study and report on a learning plan that is conducive to achieving learning objectives
- To establish a learning goal consistent with course goals and planned to meet the individuals interest and needs

Course Requirements

- Special readings
- Group interaction — dynamics
- Presentations by instructor, students and outside speakers
- Design on the basis of present job assignment and or professional need, a curriculum program of study

Present report on self-designed curriculum to class (with written report for instructor) in the following organized manner.

1. Review of Literature
2. Rational
3. Design
4. Implementation Process
5. Evaluation
6. Significance of Approach (Strategies for Change)

Evaluation

Evaluation will be based on individual and group participation in and outside of class, termination of class project, readings, and satisfactory completion of the final examination.

Course Outline

I. Concept of Man
II. Learning Theories
III. Curriculum Needs—women, minorities, economic individualization
IV. Individual Design (strategies for change)— Group Project.

I	II	III, IV	V	VII, VIII, IX	X
Introduction of Prospectus Review of Individual Students Needs & Concerns Class Interaction Review of Books & Materials	Concept of Man Philosophies Program Example	Learning Theories Analysis Identification Relationship of "Man" to "Theory"	Special Concern Group Minority, Women, Vocational	Individual Reports on Curriculum Design Developed for Individual Areas of Interest Review of Literature, Rational, Design, Implementation Process, Significance of Change	Final Exam: Written & Group Exam

1976 EDAE-5780 seminar comment

1976, personal journal entry, Milton L. Snyder, Ph.D.

As a result of teaching a graduate-level course on Staff Development, Winter Quarter during 1976, the following took place.

Herb Saunders, newly appointed, accused me of a failure to gain School Board approval to teach an evening class at VPI. I had gained prior approval from Ellis Hawkins, President of the Board, but Mr. Saunders noted that approval should have been approved by the entire Board. So, based on legal advice, I resigned my position as Supt. and the Board offered me a new contract.

This antic on Herb's part was to showcase his new authority, but was viewed as "petty" on the part of the district. Most staff and parents were impressed about my work as a part-time Adjunct Professor at VPI and University of Virginia.

In fact, teaching the class and Herb's actions gave me a new sense of credibility for teachers at the graduate level.

MLS

Appendix E:
1977

Snyder to leave June 30

Potomac News, March 22, 1977. Lynne Grandstaff.

Dr Milton Snyder, who has served as Prince William's school superintendent for the past four years, resigned Monday night.

His resignation is effective June 30, the end of his four-year contract period.

In his three-paragraph statement to the board, Snyder cited "personal reasons" as his reason for deciding. "At this time, it is impossible to consider a continuation of the contract for a continuation of the contract for a new four-year period," he said.

There was no board reaction after Snyder made the announcement.

The board unanimously accepted the resignation, although Thomas Beane said, "it is with great personal reluctance" in making the motion.

The board will now appoint a three-member screening committee to review the applications of those who would like the job. The committee, to be composed of professional educators outside Prince William, will select no fewer than 10 candidates for the position.

Under state law, the board has until May 1 to make a decision. Should the board, which has been divided on many issues in the past two years, be unable to choose a superintendent, the State Board of Education has the power to select a local superintendent after May 1.

When the School Board last searched for a superintendent, the selection process began in October.

Snyder has been the target of dispute for at least the past year.

In December, the School Board as it was then constituted expressed its intent to rehire Snyder for a second four-year contract. At that time, the vote was 4 to 3, with Herbert Saunders, Emily Rosenberg and George Mullen opposed.

Since then, boardmen Ellis Hawkins and William Dunn, both of whom voted for Snyder, have been succeeded by Michael O'Donnell and Phyllis O'Toole. Neither new board member cast a vote on the superintendency.

Snyder made his announcement at the beginning of Monday's session. For the remainder of the meeting, it was as if a different board were sitting.

For at least the past year, the board has disagreed on the majority of the items on its agenda. Monday, all votes were unanimous, and there was minimal discussion. The meeting, which was slated to end at 11:20 p.m., ended at 9:15.

Following the meeting, Snyder was unavailable for comment.

The Snyder years

Potomac News, March 22, 1977. A1.

Prince William County schools have changed substantially since Dr. Milton Snyder was hired four years ago.

During his four-year term, the number of children in public schools has increased through a state-mandated kindergarten program and through expanded county special education programs.

Only one member remains of the school board that hired Snyder. New board members have brought a different, more conservative, philosophy of education to school affairs.

Board member Herbert Saunders, who retired from his 30-year career in school administration and teaching after Snyder reorganized the top level of school administration, has fought for Snyder's removal.

Over the years, Snyder's critics have charged him with everything from personal aloofness to excessive spending for education. Under Snyder's leadership, Osbourn Park High School was completed. School officials are awaiting a court decision they hope will force the contractor for that project to pay compensatory damages for construction delays

Although no school construction bonds have been approved by county voters during Snyder's term. Snyder has found ways of housing the increasing number of students in eastern Prince William.

Snyder started a new method of making student housing decisions, so that the community is informed about potential boundary changes and given time to react.

During the first two years of Snyder's tenure, virtually the entire top level of school administration changed. Snyder hired many teachers, assistant principals and principals in his four years. The number of women and blacks in management positions has increased.

Through the four-year period, nationally standardized test scores for county students have improved.

A curriculum, which was first designed for Dale City year-round schools, was expanded to all elementary schools. New programs, such as alternative education and the ExCel Career Education Program, were begun.

Search for Superintendent Begins

The Journal Messenger, March 22, 1977. A1. Kristy Larson, JM staff writer.

The search for a new county school superintendent is on.

Following School Supt. Milton L. Snyder's announcement Monday that he will resign as of June 30, the board has set in motion a procedure to hire a new chief administrator.

A screening committee composed of three superintendents has been selected to review applicants, said school board chairman George P. Mullen.

Letters have been sent to the educators from outside the county asking them to participate. But since none have accepted yet, their names will not be released until they do, said Mullen.

The vacant position will be advertised through several associations such as the National School Boards Association, Virginia School Boards Association, and administrators' associations, said Mullen.

A general range salary has not been discussed by the board. Snyder presently makes $37,700.

The screening committee will then submit at least 10 names to the County School Board so that they may be interviewed by the board.

This process of selecting a superintendent is often used throughout the country and has been practiced before in the county, said Mullen.

By state law, a new superintendent must be chosen by April 30, but the county may request 60 day extensions, said Mullen. He estimated that a new superintendent could be hired within the time allowed in an extension.

A temporary superintendent, which would probably be someone from within the system, could also be appointed, he explained.

The school board members gave a wide range of reaction to Snyder's announcement to resign and not seek another four year term.

The board voted 4-3 in December giving its unofficial intent to rehire Snyder. He also announced his intent then to seek a renewal of his contract.

But since then, new board members — Phyllis O'Toole and Michael O'Donnell — have replaced two board members who voted for Snyder.

O'Toole said that, if given the opportunity to vote, she would have voted to rehire. But O'Donnell would not say.

"You know that type of answer is something I'm not going to give," be said. "It's academic now. It doesn't matter one way or another."

He said the board must now concentrate on the future.

"We've got a task of getting programs in the budget, running the school system… and taking off in a new solid direction," O'Donnell said.

"I think Milt Snyder is a decent man. I wish him well in whatever he does," said O'Donnell.

"I never had the opportunity (to vote to rehire Snyder), but I would have been proud to," said O'Toole. "I'm very saddened by his resignation. It is a loss to the community."

Regis Lacey said that given the opportunity to vote he would have reaffirmed his position in favor of Snyder.

"I have all the confidence in the world in Milt," he said. "He came in under some trying times and spent a great deal of time with the litigation of Osbourn Park High School.

"I think he pulled us through extremely difficult times and could have brought us much farther ahead," said Lacey.

Thomas O. Beane also said he would have voted for Snyder again. He said it was with "reluctance and sadness on my part" that he voted to accept Snyder's resignation.

Emily Rosenberg said that she did not vote in December to renew the superintendent's contract and would have voted the same way again if given the opportunity.

She said she is looking forward to the chance to hire a new superintendent.

"He sure put up one heck of a fight. The man has a lot of courage. I wish him well," Rosenberg said.

Herbert J. Saunders, who voted giving his intent to rehire in December, said he is also looking forward to the opportunity to pick a new leader.

"His resignation now opens the door to do the thing I felt we needed to do," said Saunders.

He said in December that he wanted a chance to interview applicants, which would not have excluded Snyder from applying.

Mullen said that "in all probability" he would have voted the same — against giving intent to rehire — as in December if the issue had come before the board.

In selecting a new superintendent, the board members mentioned many qualities that they would like to see in the new leader.

The members said they want a person with honesty and integrity, who has the ability to communicate with students, teachers and the community and can carry the educational system forward.

"I would like someone like Milt who is strong, able to take a lot of criticism that may have to be taken," said Lacey.

"I would like someone, who in private session with the board is willing to tell them to go to hell," sale O'Donnell. "I would like someone willing to take a strong position and point out the good and bad aspects of what he and the board are standing for and still work in harmony."

"It's a difficult job. I wouldn't have it for the world," O'Donnell added.

Among the qualities listed by Saunders, who said that it doesn't necessarily mean they were lacking in the present administration, is knowledge in curriculum.

Who will speak for education?

Potomac News, March 22, 1977. Our viewpoint.

Prince William's School Board shoulders the responsibility of providing the best possible education for the county's children. It went a long way toward abdicating that responsibility two weeks ago when it took upon itself to cut $2.4 million from an already bare-bones proposed school budget. Now we don't see how it helped the cause of education by forcing the resignation of Schools Supt. Milton Snyder.

Dr. Snyder's departure won't restore educational programs which have already been cut or which already are doomed by the budget frugality. These steps backward were not so much his, but the School Board's.

Admittedly, Dr. Snyder has not been the darling these past few years of some functionaries of the Prince William Education Association. They say, for one thing, that he hasn't fought on their side for a better teacher pay scale. But it was the School Board, not Dr. Snyder, which this year pulled back a proposed 9.6 percent hike to 5.5 percent.

And in the matter of providing the physical facilities to house Prince William's growing school enrollments, it was not Dr. Snyder, but the School Board, with its divided stance, which last year scuttled a $26 million bond issue providing a long- range program to handle needs without waiting for crises.

The School Board has by no means been unanimous in these matters. Some members have divided votes, in fact, indicate the concern of some members at the direction the board has taken the past year or so. Four months ago. Dr. Snyder was able to hold the board's confidence by the barest of margins. But now, it is apparent, though not mentioned last night, even that has slipped away.

The validity of that concern has been symbolized by the board's decision to reduce the budget by $2.4 million. Of this figure, $1.4 million was identified as money which would have boosted teachers up to the 9.6 percent increase level. The remaining $1 million, however, was cut without identifying budget items which would have to go. The school boardmen voting for this cut had no idea—at least none which they made public—of which facets of the educational program were expendable.

In short, the board relinquished its role as the protector of the education system and became, instead, the advocate of lower taxes.

Certainly, fiscal responsibility is expected of the School Board. But its prime responsibility is to determine what constitutes a quality education program for our young people and recommend it to the county supervisors for funding. Making the county budget balance is the job of the Board of Supervisors.

The cuts made in the school budget, even before it was sent to the supervisors, were not made in the name of efficiency, nor did eliminated programs and positions constitute "fat." The cuts touched the heart of progress made over the past decade.

Already eliminated by the tax-cutting fervor have been summer school for middle and high school students (with the exception of make-up courses for high school students), summer music, elective high school courses in social studies, English, advanced science and physical education.

Because $1 million of the $2.4 million also trimmed from the budget by the School Board has not been identified, other programs are seriously threatened—the fifth grade string music program, remedial classes in math and science at middle schools, adult education, $200,000 worth of special education programs, replacement buses and bus drivers and certain arts and typing classes.

And as serious as these cuts are, some members of the Board of Supervisors say they want to cut up to another $2.5 million from education.

With Dr. Snyder gone, who will speak out for the education needs of Prince William County? The School Board has relinquished its voice and no new superintendent can be expected to be very vocal against the folks who have just hired him.

We may be entering dark days for quality education in Prince William.

The County's Loss

The Journal Messenger, March 23, 1977.

The resignation of Dr. Milton L. Snyder as superintendent of Prince William County schools may have taken many people by surprise, but in retrospect it is surprising that he did not take this step at an earlier time. It has been no secret that many people, both in and out of the school system, have been highly critical of his performance in directing the county's sprawling educational establishment.

Occupying a most sensitive position at a very critical time, Dr. Snyder has been put in the unfortunate position of being made the personification of many people's frustrations and discontent with this or that aspect of the county schools.

The Journal Messenger has not always agreed with the superintendent and his staff, but in evaluating his record since he took over the reins almost four years ago, we have found that there is much more that is positive than negative. Our assessment Jias been echoed by dedicated teachers who were in the system long before Dr. Snyder came here and were in a position to make professional judgments comparing what he has done with the old ways. In restoring professionalism to the Prince William County schools, he undoubtedly stepped on the toes of some individuals who may have availed themselves of every opportunity to get even

The school board and the superintendent were spared the embarrassment of a showdown which was expected to come at the Monday night meeting when he resigned, citing personal reasons. The unwarranted abuse which bordered on personal vilifications at times would have forced a less strong individual to throw In the towel long ago. The protracted struggle which seems to have forced Dr. Snyder out has done the county schools no good. All the citizens of the county will be the losers for his leaving the system, but those who will suffer most are the students whose interests have been the object of Dr. Snyder's efforts.

In finding a successor with equal qualifications, the School Board will undoubtedly be interviewing professionals who have been stamped out of the same mold. Whoever follows Dr. Snyder will be fortunate in coming into a system which has gone a long way from the state it was in when be took it over in 1973. The new superintendent will have to operate within the framework of the educational superstructure directed from Richmond. The funds at his disposal approved by the School Board will have to run the gauntlet of the Board of County Supervisors. Parents, students and teachers may find him a convenient scapegoat when things are not to their liking. History could repeat itself. For the sake of the new superintendent and the county schools, we hope that it does not.

A final vindication

Potomac News, May 18, 1977. Our Viewpoint.

The recent court order awarding Prince William's School Board approximately $2.75 million in damages from the Osbourn Park High School construction case may not mean immediate money in the county coffers.

It does, however, mean the final vindication of those once-scorned educational leaders who dared to take a major contractor and a huge insurance company to court, then proceed to build a high school themselves.

The six-year history of construction and litigation over Osbourn Park can be described as a huge series of small actions and reactions to contract law.

Over the years, it meant late-night meetings and the ongoing vilification of those who thought it could be done. More important, the history of Osbourn Park is a story of courage and a commitment to children.

It would have been simple for the School Board to renegotiate its contract with Ranger Construction Company. With a $13 million lawsuit hanging over its head, many boards and administrators would have buckled.

There is no way to know if Osbourn Park would have been completed if the School Board had taken the easy route. Instead, the board decided to fight in court for the concept that a contractor is required to complete the building he has agreed to construct. The board also decided that a construction management approach, which had never before been used in Prince William, would be the fastest way to get children off split shifts and into their new building.

The board was right. The first vindication came when a jury ruled that construction delays at the school were the fault of Ranger Construction.

The second vindication came when the building opened in September 1975, long before Ranger or the county's more timid people said it was possible.

Last week's court order, which will reimburse the county for the additional cost of building the school, completes the process. The list of those who deserve this community's accolade is long:

- Former Schools Supt. Dr. Milton Snyder, who recognized the magnitude of the problem shortly after arriving in the county. By moving decisively toward a solution, he took the largest share of scorn and disbelief.
- Dr. Paul Trautman, who coordinated the complicated process of completing the building and subsequently worked with the lawyers on the court case.
- The previous School Board, led by Ellis Hawkins and Thomas Beane, which trusted its professionals. Those men, faced with huge antagonism, held to their primary goal of providing a school for children.
- St. Sen. Charles Colgan, who worked from his place at the Board of Supervisors to assure that the supervisors would provide the financial guarantees which the School Board required.
- The Osbourn Park parents and student who, after initial discord, backed the staff and board in their efforts.
- All those professionals, from school employees to outside specialists, who worked doubly hard to assure the success of the project.

All these people were willing to take a chance. No one can ever predict the outcome of a court case. No one could assure that new problems would not force further delays in construction.

What provided the courage was the conviction that the needs of high school students came first. Those students' needs made everyone willing to take the chance.

Before the school opened, Dr. Snyder said, "Getting the kids into the school is the goal. After that, the money from the litigation, which we're going to win, will be the icing on the cake."

That icing is sweet, indeed.

Osbourn Park Money Should Go to Schools

The Journal Messenger, Vol. 109, No. 35. May 19, 1977. Opinion page.

A court case begun nearly three years ago by the Prince William County School Board against Ranger Construction Company and Travelers Indemnity has reached its culmination except for the determination of the settlement and possible appeal by the defendants. Federal Judge Oren Lewis has awarded the School Board almost everything it asked in the litigation over the construction of Osbourn Park High School.

The decision reinforces the rightness of the course taken by the board at that time on the recommendation of the then superintendent of schools, Dr. Milton Snyder. In spite of the mess which fell into his lap after coming to the county, Dr. Snyder and his staff managed to get things moving to complete the school in time for the fall term in 1975, only one year after its originally scheduled completion date.

By hiring a management firm to supervise the completion of the school and borrowing $1.1 million from the Virginia Public School Authority, the School Board was able to make the best of a bad situation and resume construction activities. At the time there was much criticism of the additional funds needed to complete Osbourn Park. The court's award, when it is finally determined, should serve to reimburse those funds.

According to law, any money so received must be paid into the general county funds. The same was true of money received by the county for the sale of school properties to the City of Manassas. A legal opinion stipulated that in the latter case monies so received should be used for school purposes. The Board of County Supervisors did make these proceeds available to the School Board for school construction.

If and when the judgment in this court case is received by the county, it would be hoped that the same would apply. These funds should be used first to wipe out the loan made from the school authority and then go toward any other additional costs incurred to get the high school finished. The county board has a moral — if not a legal — obligation to see that money originally designated for school purposes by the voters continue in such uses.

Those in the school system — both board and staff — who worked so hard to bring order out of chaos in the Osbourn Park construction, must be gratified by the direction their court battle has taken. The turn of events certainly warrants their commendation for seeing this matter through to a successful conclusion.

Letter of Appreciation

April 27, 1977. Ronald L. Snyder, handwritten on letterhead.

Neabsco Elementary School
3800 Cordell Avenue
Woodbridge, Virginia 22193

Dear Dr. Snyder,

I would like to take this opportunity to express my sincere appreciation for the outstanding work you have accomplished over the past four years. Through your dedicated efforts the children of Prince William County have benefited greatly. I have never seen a man do so much, for so many, with so little. You can reflect with a sense of pride on a job well done.

I would like to personally thank you for assisting me in my professional growth. It has been a valuable learning experience as a member of the management team under your supervision.

I regret your decision to leave, but I'm sure you have many new avenues to pursue. Best wishes to you and your family.

> Sincerely,
> Ronald L. Snyder

Letter of Appreciation

May 10, 1977. Harold A. Hayden.

Dear Dr. Snyder:

In August of 1975 you recommended me for the position of principal of the Ann Ludwig School. At that time I was an administrative unknown and I realize that you were placing your trust in me. I want you to know I've worked hard to live up to the opportunity and challenge you gave me and am deeply appreciative of your trust.

I have seen a great deal of good happening in special education because of your interest and intervention and, on behalf of the students here at Ann Ludwig, I wish to thank you for all you have done.

I am personally and professionally sorry to see you leave the system, but realize that change is inevitable. I hope your next experience will bring you great reward and that you will remember all the good things that have happened to Prince William County because you were here.

> Harold A. Hayden

Appendix F:
1980-2012

Thank-you, a bit belatedly!

Potomac News, 1980. Our Point of View, editorial page.

When the decision finally came a couple of weeks ago, Prince William reacted to the $3.1 million court settlement from the Osbourn Park litigation as if the money is just another addition to the capital improvement fund.

The discussion centered around the best possible means of spending the money; no one seemed to remember the years of anguish or the immense courage which this money represents.

The file photographs are brown with age, but the memories they engender are clear. In the pictures, Osbourn Park High School stands, half-finished, with scaffolding up the sides and a sea of frozen mud around it. We remembered the inside, too: puddles of water on the floor and rusting pipes lying around, walls torn out to expose faulty mechanical work and the famous alligator pits, where workmen dug holes in the concrete floor looking for grease traps that were never installed.

It was 1973 when Prince William's School Board recognized that the construction of the fourth large county high school was in desperate trouble. The first major attempt was to re-negotiate the building contract with Ranger Construction Company, but school officials seemed to realize that the effort was futile even before the altered contract was signed.

The students of Osbourn High School were on double shifts; they needed a new school building, and there was no quick solution to the problem.

What followed is history—a massive federal suit against the School Board, charging that it breached the construction contract; a School Board decision to kick Ranger off the job; another resolution, in which the School Board became the general contractor for the project and hired subcontractors under the emergency provisions of state law; ongoing wrangling with the Board of Supervisors to secure additional funding to complete the building while the complicated court case was being tried.

By September 1975, the building was completed, so that you have to know exactly where to look to find evidence of the construction problems. The students moved in, and Osbourn Park became a place for education. Then, after a mistrial, came the jury decision that Ranger Construction was responsible for the construction problems. The case was appealed and the original decision upheld. Finally, 5.5 years after the original suit was filed, Ranger Construction and its bonding company, Travelers Indemnity, decided to end the controversy and pay the county.

It is the ultimate vindication of the wisdom of former Schools Supt. Dr. Milton Snyder, as well as former School Board Chairman Ellis Hawkins. There were many others involved, but these people led the way. They convinced others that the dangerous course of suing Ranger and completing the school alone was correct.

Many were fearful, and others saw political advantage in continuing the problems at Osbourn Park. Mr. Hawkins and Dr. Snyder set a simple goal—to get students into the building as quickly as possible, then fight the legal battle to its conclusion. They sought the best professional help they could get, and they coaxed and coerced to bring School Board colleagues and their own staff and lawyers to join their battle.

The effort did not make them popular. Mr. Hawkins was not re-appointed to the School Board when his term expired in 1976. Losing support among new members of the School Board, Dr. Snyder took a post in California the same year.

Prince William did not exactly reward these gentlemen for courage, insight, and concern for children. We can, at least, say thank-you. Thank-you for the money, for the high school, and for the courage to take an unpopular and dangerous course aimed at providing education for students.

Snyder era left us ready for next one

[refers to Snyder's tenure in Federal Way, Washington]

The News, Federal Way, Washington, School District, June 21, 1987.

A superintendent of school must have the shell of a turtle, the soul of an elephant, and the plaintive call of the loon. That's an exotic animal. No superintendent in King County fits the description more completely than Dr. Milton Snyder of Federal Way.

He announced Friday that he will leave the district after eight years of service. Finding someone eager to take his spot should not be difficult. He has been a competent caretaker who restored public faith in our district. He leaves his successor with a good board, favorable public relations, and a sound academic program that has earned respect for the district.

That is not to say there are no problems. Basic education funding never has been delivered by the state [Washington] as promised. Though levy campaigns under Snyder have been consistently approved, deferred maintenance from previous years has left us with some schools that still need rehabilitation.

Because the state did not meet teacher demands for salary hikes and reduced class sizes, teachers are likely to come to the bargaining table with persistent calls for local support for their cause.

Snyder's board will probably escalate its demands for accountability.

That means the same exotic traits Snyder showed here must be a part of the repertoire of the new superintendent.

The turtle shell will help in dealing with public demands for quality schooling without increased cost.

The elephantine soul is required equipment for anyone who tackles the endless task of managing a suburban school district that lies in the path of growth.

The call of the loon? That's for going to Olympia, where Snyder spent many hours pushing for the financial commitment public schools need to handle their diverse and demanding load.

He did well enough that he was recognized nationally for his excellence, and was elected as president of the state's school administrators. His effervescent energy, his determination, and his deep devotion to public schools have been a welcome and rejuvenating part of our district's difficult history.

We thank him and wish him well.

Former superintendent Stuart Beville dies

The Journal Messenger, April 7, 1990. A8. Betty Curran, JM Staff Writer.

Stuart Beville, 77, a former superintendent of Prince William County schools and a lifelong educator, died of a heart attack Thursday in Blacksburg where he moved after he left the county.

A memorial service is tentatively being planned for 3 p.m. Sunday in Blacksburg.

Beville served as Prince William's schools superintendent for 18 years, from 1954 through 1982. When he arrived in the area there were slightly more than 3,500 students in the county. When he left the position in 1972 there were more than 32,000 students.

Under Beville's watch, the county built and opened 30 new schools to take care of the ever-growing population and year-round schools were implemented in Dale City. During his tenure, he was responsible for the hiring of nearly 50 percent of the principals now working in the county schools.

Beville was born in Blackstone and earned both a bachelor's and master's degrees from Duke University.

Before he came to Prince William as school superintendent in 1954, he had taught and coached and served as an elementary and secondary principal in the counties of Halifax, Danville, Crewe and Farmville.

Several of the county's school principals plan to attend the service for Beville this weekend. In addition to the memorial service in Blacksburg, there will be graveside services Monday at 1 p.m. at the Lake View Cemetery in Blackstone.

"I knew him slightly when he was in Crewe but I first knew him well in Farmville," said Norborne Beville of Nokesville, nephew of Stuart Beville. "I remember every year when he would bring his budget over to the supervisors and Supervisor Roy Doggett used to fuss and cuss about the schools spending all that money and my uncle would just ignore him and not pay any attention to Doggett ranting and raving.

"He also was pretty much a basketball and football fan of Duke and VPI."

In October 1972, Beville became the director of off-campus activities for the College of Education for Virginia Tech.

He retired in 1978, but continued to teach at Virginia Tech for a few years.

Most recently he served for six months as acting superintendent of Montgomery County Schools.

"He was a good family man and became the patriarch of the family, but he had lived a good life and he was healthy and sharp right up until his heart attack," the younger Beville said of his uncle. "We'll all miss him on the one hand but on the other hand we recognize that he lived a long and healthy life."

Beville is survived by his wife, Rosa Beville of Blacksburg, and two daughters, Alice Bostrom of Grafton, and Kitty Miller of Covington, KY. He is also survived by four grandchildren. Hoy-McCoy Funeral Home in Blacksburg is handling the funeral arrangements.

Thomas O. Beane Obituary

July 14, 2005. Source: http://covenantfuneralservice.com/obituaries/thomas-beane/

Thomas O. Beane, 73, of Fredericksburg died Thursday, July 14, 2005, at the Woodmont Center from complications of Parkinson's disease. He and his wife, Elizabeth, had just celebrated their 50th wedding anniversary.

He was born August 8, 1931, at the family home in Manassas. He was a track star and graduate of Osbourn High School and was awarded an athletic scholarship to the University of Richmond, where he majored in political science, held the university track record for the 220 that remained unbroken for many years, and played two seasons on the Spiders football team.

After graduation he joined the U.S. Army and was stationed at Arlington as an Army intelligence specialist during the Korean War.

Tom was awarded a master's degree in history by the University of Virginia. He received his law degree from the T.C. Williams School of Law, where he was a member of the McNeill Law Society and the student council. He joined the staff of Attorney General Albertis Harrison in 1960. In 1964 he joined the Manassas law firm of Owens, Thornton and Underwood, where he practiced for 31 years.

A great deal of his life was dedicated to serving the community. Tom served as commissioner in chancery for the Circuit Court of Prince William County; was appointed to the Prince William County School Board for almost a dozen years, including a term as chairman from 1977 to 1979; and served on the board of directors of the Virginia School Boards Association.

Tom served on the Prince William County Electoral Board for 16 years, including terms as secretary. He was a member and president of the Manassas Kiwanis Club and served as president of the Prince William County Bar Association.

He was a lifetime member of Manassas Baptist Church, serving as chairman of the Board of Deacons, Sunday-school teacher and superintendent, choir member and soloist.

In 1998 Tom was commended by the Virginia General Assembly for his singular dedication to serving his community and the commonwealth. An editorial that appeared in the Potomac News on his retirement from the School Board stated that "his wisdom and commitment will not be easy to duplicate. His departure should be seen by all as a loss; his years of service should remain as a model."

He is survived by his wife, Elizabeth Bright Beane; three children, Betsy Fowler of King George County, Victoria Coogan of Roanoke, and Samuel Beane of Spotsylvania County; six grandchildren, Eric Fowler, Kate Fowler. Bryan Fowler, Erin Coogan, Madeline Beane and Riley Beane; four sisters, Julia Summerlin, Betty Dietler, Barbara Wright and Marjorie Fortuna; and a large extended family.

A service will be held at 11 a.m. Wednesday, July 20, at St. George's Episcopal Church at 905 Princess Anne Street in Fredericksburg. Interment will follow in Quantico National Cemetery. Following the interment, the family will receive friends at the Crossroads Inn, 3018 Russell Road, Quantico Marine Corps Base. Memorials may be made to the Parkinson's Foundation, 1505 N.W. 9th Ave., Bob Hope Road, Miami, FL 33136-1494.

Herb Saunders Dies at Age 92

Potomac News, March 17, 2007. Obituary.

Herbert J. Saunders, who died early Friday at age 92, was always a teacher.

His career with the Prince William County Public School system spanned five decades. He served as a teacher, football coach, principal, superintendent and School Board member.

"He was always teaching. Whether he was at home or at school," his grandson, Hunter Woods, said.

Even late in his life, when Saunders moved to the Potomac Place assisted-living facility; he remained a teacher, family members said Friday.

"He would teach people to play cards and games. One lady called him the professor," his daughter, Barbara Woods, said.

Family members recalled his fun-loving spirit and his sense of humor. Community members may best remember him for his name.

Herbert J. Saunders Middle School, on Spriggs Road in Woodbridge, was named after him.

"He always felt it was such an honor to have a school named after him while he was still alive," his daughter, Mary Brawley, said. "He saw how much the students enjoyed it when he was there, and he felt that was very special."

At the school, students observed a moment of silence in Saunders' honor Friday morning, principal Catherine Puttre said. In the spring, the school plans to plant a tree in his honor, she said.

"He was multi-talented and a perfect gentleman and a great role model for the students," Puttre said Friday. "He has visited here a number of times, and he loved to come to school events. He was very proud to have a school named after him."

A picture of Saunders hangs in the school's hallway, she said.

A plaque in Saunders' honor hangs in the front lobby of Gar-Field Senior High School, where he served as the school's first principal in 1953.

That plaque dubs Saunders the "Father of Gar-Field," but students had a different name for him at the time, family members said.

"They called him the 'Gray Ghost' because he always seemed to show up where the kids were getting ready to get into trouble," Hunter Woods said with a laugh.

Saunders' two daughters, Mary and Barbara, and three of his grandchildren sat in Barbara's house Friday evening, thumbing through newspaper clippings from throughout Saunders' life and trading stories and memories of him.

"I didn't live here as a kid and whenever I would visit in the summers I was always amazed that everyone knew my-grandfather," James Brawley said. "Wherever we went, everybody knew who he was and he knew everybody. I always found that impressive."

During his time with the schools, Saunders saw many changes. He started the area's first high school football team in Manassas in 1939 — a team that included the late long-time Virginia House of Delegates representative Harry J. Parrish on its roster.

In the 1960s, Saunders was there when Prince William County Schools opened their doors to black students for the first time.

And, as personnel director, Saunders hired many of the long-time teachers who still work in county schools today.

Saunders retired from the school system in 1975, but never fully left.

In 1976 he was appointed to fill a four-year term on the School Board. After that Saunders remained active in the community, visiting Saunders Middle School and other schools when he could.

He made one of his last visits to the school in April 2005 when students interviewed him about his life and accomplishments. An audio clip of that interview was placed on the middle school's Web site Friday — "I want the kids to know that you have to set goals. Know where you're going and how to get there," he said. "I want to tell the students that if I can do it, you can."

Saunders is survived by two daughters, Mary and Barbara, six grandchildren and eight great-grandchildren. He was preceded in death by his wife of 66 years, Augusta Ross Saunders.

The family will receive friends from 6 to 9 p.m. Monday and from 2 to 4 p.m. and 7 to 9 p.m. Tuesday at Mountcastle Funeral Home, 4143 Dale Blvd., Dale City. Funeral services will take place at 11:30 a.m. Wednesday, March 21, at Dumfries United Methodist Church, 110 Cameron St., Dumfries. Interment will follow at Quantico National Cemetery.

Herbert J. Saunders

Obituary, March 20, 2007.

Herbert J. Saunders, 92, died peacefully at his home in Potomac Place in Woodbridge on Friday, March 16, 2007. Mr. Saunders, the eldest of five children, was born in Nuttallburg, W.Va., July 16, 1914, to Edward and Maude Saunders.

After graduating from Woodrow Wilson High School in Beckley, W.Va., Mr. Saunders received an athletic scholarship to Lynchburg College where he participated in basketball, baseball and track, earning eight athletic letters. He graduated in 1939 with a degree in history, math and physical education. It was there that he received the honor of being inducted into the Lynchburg College Sports Hall of Fame.

In 1939, Mr. Saunders began his long career in Prince William County schools with a teaching and coaching position at Manassas High School. In 1943, Mr. Saunders joined the U.S. Navy during World War II. He was stationed in Iowa and was an instructor in the Naval Pre-Flight Program.

After returning from active duty to Prince William County, Mr. Saunders was a coordinator at Manassas Vocational School. It was there that he started and coached the first football team in Prince William County.

In 1949, Mr. Saunders became principal of Occoquan District High School, which was the only high school in Eastern Prince William County. In 1953, he became the first principal of Gar-Field High School and served in that role for 10 years. At Gar-Field he was affectionately known as the Gray Ghost by students and staff. The Herb Saunders Football Trophy, sponsored by the Potomac News, is still awarded to the winner of the Gar-Field vs. Woodbridge football game.

Saunders became director of personnel of the Prince William County school system and later served as interim superintendent of schools.

In 1973, Mr. Saunders received the Outstanding Educator of the Year Award for Northern Virginia, which was presented by the Fairfax Chapter of Phi Delta Kappa.

Mr. Saunders retired from Prince William County schools in 1975, at which time he was appointed to the Prince William County School Board. He held this position for four years.

His many contributions to the Prince William County school system left their mark and touched the lives of many students and teachers who kept in touch with him throughout his lifetime.

It was a great honor to Mr. Saunders to have Herbert J. Saunders Middle School named after him. He always enjoyed visiting the school and speaking with the students.

Mr. Saunders was a member of many civil organizations within the county. He served 57 years with the Quantico Lions Club, where he was the recipient of the Melvin Jones Fellow Award. He also served many years on the Quantico Town Council. In addition, he was a member of the Woodbridge

Kiwanis Club and a longtime active member of Dumfries United Methodist Church.

Mr. Saunders enjoyed golf, fishing, goose hunting, duck hunting, woodworking and tending to his beautiful rose bushes.

His wife, Augusta, preceded him in death in May 2003. He also was preceded in death by his parents and three siblings, William, Margaret and Edward Jr.

Dorothy Mae Hamilton, and her husband, William, of Sumter, S.C., survive him, as do several nieces and nephews. He leaves two daughters, Mary Brawley of Livonia, Mich., and her husband, Monty, and Barbara Woods, wife of the late Sam Woods of Woodbridge. Also surviving are Mary's two daughters, Lisa Brawley and Julie Brawley Seale and her husband, Rodney, and their two children, Kyle and Olivia Seale; and two sons, James Brawley and John Brawley and his wife, Van, and their child, Jason Brawley.

Also surviving are Barbara's son, Hunter Woods and his wife, Christine, and their children, Hunter Jr. and Samantha Woods, Michael Hicks and his wife, Nicole; and a daughter, Suzanne Woods Hawes and her husband, Ronnie, and their children, Holden and Skylar Hawes.

The family received friends at Mountcastle Funeral Home, 4143 Dale Blvd., Dale City, on Monday, March 19, from 6 to 9 p.m., and also will receive friends Tuesday, March 20, from 2 to 4 and 7 to 9 p.m.

A funeral will be celebrated at Dumfries United Methodist Church, 3890 Cameron St., Dumfries, on Wednesday, March 21, at 11:30 a.m. A committal service will follow in Quantico National Cemetery.

In lieu of flowers, memorial contributions may be sent to Dumfries United Methodist Church, 3890 Cameron St., Dumfries, Va., 22026; or to the Quantico Lions Club, c/o Brad Meyer, 4507 Kingston Road, Dale City, Va. 22193.

Lynn Grandstaff's passing a major loss to all of us

Letter to editors of the Potomac News & The Manassas Journal Messenger

December 4, 2008, from Milton Lee Pritchard Snyder, Ph.D.,
Former Division Superintendent, Prince William County Schools, 1973-1977.

CC: Herald Grandstaff

Please allow me the opportunity to express deep condolences to the family of Lynn Grandstaff, her many friends and fellow staff members. Lynne Grandstaff's passing is a major loss to all of us who knew her and had the privilege of being associated during her long career in the communication field.

During my four-year term as Division Superintendent of Prince William County Schools during 1973-1977, I worked closely with Lynne when she served the Potomac News as an executive news reporter covering the County School Board. During this period of the 1970s, Lynne's writing and reporting assignments covered all of the conflict matters regarding school board and county board of supervisors debates.

Several major issues that Lynne and editorial staff at the Potomac News followed and wrote extensive documents about concerned the political strife and war-like negotiations that took place between county government officials, school board members and my administrative staff during this period. In my opinion, Lynne's work and writings were significant in helping communicate news to parents/patrons and create a more transparent scene for the public regarding schools and county government activities. Her work was significant in helping achieve the opening of kindergarten programs in Prince William County Schools for the first time. Also, I believe that the Osbourn Park High School construction project was finally approved and opened on time due to the work she and the Potomac News provided during the warlike debacle between the school board and county supervisors. The kindergarten and Osbourn Park feuds coverage were major achievements of Lynne's early reporting years.

A lasting tribute must be extended to Lynne Grandstaff for her factual and tireless communication reporting during the years I served as Superintendent of Schools. An Academy communication award to you Lynne for superior excellence in reporting the facts. You will be missed!

Milton Lee Pritchard Snyder, Ph.D.
Seattle, WA

Prince William County Schools Planetarium

Letter sent from William Helton to Dr. Milton L. Snyder, Jun 23, 2010, with included news release.

Dear Dr. Snyder,

I am enclosing a news release from the Prince William County schools about the planetarium located at one of the high schools. It brought back some memories of the battles you fought in the early 1970s to have a planetarium at a high school in each end of the county. I describe my memories and the irony of the school board's action after the article.

Prince William County Schools Planetarium Re-opening Ceremony Set for May 20, 2010

"Hylton High School in Woodbridge will hold a re-opening ceremony at 4:30 p.m. on Thursday, May 20, to unveil its recently renovated planetarium and to formally name it the Irene V. Hylton Planetarium. Prince William County School Board and other elected officials are expected to attend. The education foundation, SPARK, will host a reception following the event in the foyer of the school.

The renovation and technology upgrades in the planetarium were made possible through a grant of $246,225 from the Cecil and Irene Hylton Foundation. The planetarium has been closed since March 24, 2010. Hylton High School is located at 14051 Spriggs Road in Woodbridge.

Prince William County Public School (PWCS) students and the public will enjoy shows with new all-digital projection, a new laser projection unit, and new LED cove lighting. The planetarium holds two shows daily during the school year for PWCS students.

Shows for the public occur year-round. "Christmas, Halloween, and Valentines Day are my biggest shows," said planetarium director Anthony Kilgore, M.Ed.

Kilgore also welcomes birthday parties, private groups, and summer camps with a minimum of 30 customers.

Upon reading this recent story about the high school planetarium in Prince William County, I remembered that you had proposed building one for each end of the county back in 1974. You fought the good fight with some board members to include these buildings to enhance the science curriculum for the benefit the William County Schools Planetarium future generations of students, but four board members led by Herb Saunders argued that the cost of around $600,000 was too expensive for the budget and voted it down.

Later, after you convinced the voters to pass a bond referendum to build Potomac High School in the Dumfries area, the same board members again led by Herb Saunders, voted to add $750,000 to the cost of the new high school in order to build a football stadium at the site.

The football stadium and stands are used at the most seven times during the entire school year for football games and require constant maintenance and upkeep. What a contrast between your and the board's priorities on what was most important to the future education of the youth in the county!

We were so pleased to see that you were honored by the Lewis-Clark State College Alumni Association to receive the Marion Shinn Lifelong Achievement Award. It was also doubly meaningful that the award was named for a dedicated high school teacher at Lewiston High School. The College has acknowledged that you had applied the education you received there to a lifetime of service and leadership in the public schools of this nation. Your accomplishments reflect well on the College and on its mission.

I also enjoyed reading the article that Craig sent me about your work in the community being recognized in an award by the Rotary Club. I especially enjoyed the photo of your surprise at being so honored. After a lifetime of devotion to serving others and to implementing improvements in all the communities that were fortunate enough to have your leadership, it is satisfying to know that you are receiving some of the awards and recognition earned in a career of outstanding achievement.

Be well and keep in touch.
Warmest regards,
Bill Helton

Berkshire cuts 105 jobs, shuts paper bought by Buffett

Bloomberg News, November 14, 2012. Noah Buhavar, Zacharv Tracer.

Warren Buffett's Berkshire Hathaway Inc., buyer of more than 60 newspapers in the past year, will close the Manassas News & Messenger in Virginia amid a review of operations acquired from Media General Inc.

The News & Messenger has a circulation of 10,000. This is actually the closing of two newspapers, since the Potomac News and the Manassas Journal Messenger merged in 2008.

Job cuts include 33 employees of the News & Messenger, which is published five days a week and has a circulation of 10,000, according to a letter posted today on the Web. Another 72 positions will be eliminated, mostly corporate staff added as part of the Media General deal.

"We looked at a bunch of different scenarios and I sent multiple teams up there," Doug Hiemstra, chief executive officer of the World Media Enterprises unit, said in a phone interview. "We just could not get to a sustainable profitable operation for a daily newspaper there."

Buffett, 82, has said that newspapers with local readerships could withstand an advertising slump. The News & Messenger, which traces its history to 1869, serves a northern Virginia suburb and faces competition from papers including the Washington Post.

"It's a suburban newspaper to a metro area and we don't really have that at our other operations," Hiemstra said. "It makes it more difficult for the community to be engaged."

World Media is still "bullish" on the prospects for community newspapers, Hiemstra said in the letter.

Berkshire agreed in May to pay $142 million for 63 newspapers from Media General. The deal also included a $400 million loan to the media company at 10.5 percent interest.

Berkshire plans to sell the News & Messenger building, surrounding downtown Manassas property and a nearby parking lot, he said. The final edition will be Dec. 30, 2012, according to the letter. No other job cuts are planned.

Manassas News & Messenger and InsideNoVA.com, top Prince William news sources, closed down

All newspapers in Prince William County closed

By Tom Jackman.

The Manassas News & Messenger and its Web site, InsideNOVA.com, closed at the end of December, 2012.

When investor and newspaper fan Warren Buffett bought the Media General newspaper chain last year, there was hope for all of them, including the Manassas News & Messenger and the Richmond Times-Dispatch.

But Buffett's company announced today it is shutting down the News & Messenger after 143 years, as well as its highly informative website, InsideNoVA.com. It is the only paper in the Media General chain being shuttered by World Media Enterprises, a division of Buffett's Berkshire Hathaway Inc.

This is horrendous news for everyone in Prince William County and those who care about Prince William news. The News & Messenger and InsideNoVA are the definitive source of news in Prince William. Their reporters and editors work extremely hard to cover government, breaking news, high school sports, the latest lottery winners, everything.

InsideNoVA also has a Facebook page with more than 26,000 followers, and when they post stories there they get plenty of reaction. Reaction that isn't standard anonymous-crazy comments because people must use their Facebook accounts to post, which makes a lot of sense.

World Media chairman Terry Kroeger told me this morning there was "a lot of competition for the ad dollars." I whined and complained about losing the biggest news source in a county of 400,000 people. "It is too bad," Kroeger said. "We didn't see a way to take the negative financial momentum and turn it positive. We didn't take this lightly. We worked very hard to develop their plans, and we just could not get there."

I pointed out that InsideNoVA had a large following on Facebook and seemed to be working well in the digital world. "They put a lot of emphasis on their digital products," Kroeger said, "so their print circulation fell even further." The print circulation is about 10,000.

When Buffett bought the 63 papers in the Media General chain, he said: "In towns and cities where there is a strong sense of community, there is no more important institution than the local paper. The many locales served by the newspapers we are acquiring fall firmly in this mold and we are delighted they have found a permanent home with Berkshire Hathaway."

This is actually the closing of two newspapers, since the Potomac News and the Manassas Journal Messenger merged in 2008.

World Media said all 33 people working for the paper and website would lose their jobs, along with 72 others in the Media General corporate structure.

There are a lot of talented and hard-working journalists at the News & Messenger and InsideNoVA and they deserve our respect and thanks. They didn't deserve to be shut down after 143 years of public service.

UPDATE, 5:30p.m., from Jeremy Borden in Manassas:

Prince William County Board Chairman Corey Stewart (R at Large) said that he noticed that as the News & Messenger and Washington Post newsrooms have shrunk over the years, fewer people approached him to ask about county issues. He said residents are less informed about local issues than they once were.

"People will always be interested in local news," Stewart said. "But where do you go for local news? Right now there just aren't a lot of resources for that other than the local papers. As those are withering away, I'm not sure what's going to replace them."

Tracy Conroy, a parent who advocates on schools issues, said it's likely that more people will start blogging to try to fill the void. But politicians and officials are often dismissive of blogs, she said, and the media has an authoritative voice that school leaders feel they must respond to.

Appendix G:
2014-2015

2014 Regional Dinner Meeting Invitation

Invitation from Milton L. Snyder, January 18, 2014.

To:

Dr. William & Cindy Helton
Helen P. Warriner Burke & Pat Burke
Dr. Jerri Mills Sutton
Bill & Marilyn Dunn
Richard & Callie Johnson
Regis & Donna Lacey
Ellis & Jane Hawkins
Herald Grandstaff
Senator Charles Colgan

I am planning to be in the Virginia region in March 2014 and wish to see you during my visit to the Commonwealth of Virginia. Please consider being my guest for dinner and joining in conversation from a period long past.

As William Jennings Bryan once penned, "Destiny is not a matter of chance, it is a matter of choice; it is not a thing to be waited for, it is a thing to be achieved!" For a number of years, I have desired to return to the area by choice to be with former friends and associates. So as a result, I wish to be with you the leaders and associates who gave me so much help during my term as Division Superintendent of Schools in Prince William County Schools in 1973-1977 and during "The Third Battle of Manassas."

I invite you and a small group of friends to assemble with me for cocktails and dinner at and during the following event.

Date: Saturday, March 15, 2014
Tie: 4:00 p.m. for cocktails
Dinner: 6:00 p.m.
Place: Thomas Jefferson Hotel: The Ginter Room at 101 West Franklin in the City of Richmond, Virginia.

Regards,
Milton Lee Pritchard Snyder Ph.D
Seattle, WA

Obituary for Ellis B. Hawkins

July 23, 1929 – March 10, 2014

sourced from Cunningham-Mountcastle funeral home website, March 2014.

Ellis B. Hawkins, 84, of Woodbridge, VA, passed away on March 10, 2014.

Beloved husband of 5 years to Jane Hawkins. He was predeceased by his late wife Frances.

Loving father of Frances Olds (Michael), Nancy Chryst (John), Diana Hawkins, and the late Ellis B. Hawkins Jr., stepfather of the late Scott Mercer, Theresa Wilhide (Brian). His daughter-in-laws Denise Hawkins and Teruyo Mercer still survive.

Cherished grandfather of Venus Denk (Dennis). Step grandfather of Zachary Wilhide, Gregory, Bethany and Andrew Mercer, Jonathan and Marshall "Cody" Chryst. Great grandfather of Maddilynn Denk.

Step great grandfather of Evan, Isaac, Aiden and Cade Mercer. Dear brother of the late Clagett Hawkins. Also survived by numerous nieces and nephews.

Mr. Hawkins was actively involved in the St. Paul United Methodist Church Building Fund.

Interment will be on Monday, March 17, 2014 at Fairfax Memorial Park.

Tribute to Hawkins from Herald Grandstaff

Posted on website, April 18, 2014. http://www.mountcastle.net/obituaries/Ellis-Hawkins-2/

While chairman of the Prince William County School Board, Mr. Hawkins was a soft-spoken titan who towered among men for his knight-like strength and determination in combating the sheer madness of the 'Four Horsemen' of the PWC Board of Supervisors as they tried to replace all seated county School Board members on Jan. 1, 1972. Mr. Hawkins led the School Board with a firm, steady hand. The School Board prevailed in keeping their seats. The court established a reasoned, staggered appointment process to name successors as terms expired.

Mr. Hawkins assisted in the first integration of the school system. He shared his brilliant vision for the school system with the hiring of Milton L. Snyder, Ph.D., as county schools system superintendent. The county was fortunate to have Dr. Snyder for his four-year term. From the combined efforts of Mr. Hawkins and Dr. Snyder, kindergarten was launched for Prince William County girls and boys. Mr. Hawkins also helped ensure that the troubled construction project of Osbourn Park High School be completed.

Dr. Snyder is leading an effort to have donations made to the Drs. Milton L. Snyder/Delores J. Gibbons Endowment Scholarship in honor of Mr. Hawkins at: LCSC Foundation, Lewis Clark State College, 500 8th Ave., Lewiston, Idaho 83501.

Respectfully,
Herald Grandstaff
Potomac News reporter, 1971-77.

Re: Tribute to Ellis Hawkins

Email from William Helton to Milton L. Snyder, April 21, 2014

Hi Dr. Snyder,

Thanks for sharing the tribute by Herald Grandstaff about Ellis Hawkins and about his and your fortitude working together to protect the school system against the adverse and unwise actions of the governing body. It is well done and captures the steady hand of Mr. Hawkins in guiding the school board in a turbulent period of the county's history.

Thank you also for sending a copy of the information about your and Dolores' endowed scholarship in Ellis's honor at Lewis-Clark State College. It is a most generous gesture on your part to honor a man who did so much for the Prince William County schools. You and he made a great team for leading the school system in a united effort that stands as a model for policy making and executive action to the benefit of the future of the County and its young children.

The Washington Post recently published an editorial about the policy direction of the current Republican school board in Prince William County in which I thought you may be interested. It brought back echoes of similar battles fought by you and Ellis over forty years ago.

Bill Helton

Communications gone to dogs in PWC

Letter from Charles J. Colgan, Virginia State Senator. April 21, 2014.

Dear Dr. Snyder:

You are quite a guy, so thoughtful and kind. How nice you are to pay tribute to our old friend Ellis Hawkins. Communication has gone "to the dogs," in Prince William County during the last year. Both The Journal Messenger and the Potomac News are gone and local news is hard to come by. I did not know Ellis had passed away until I got your letter. Had I known, I certainly would have paid my respects to his family.

I should add Warren Buffett bought up about 100 newspapers, and then proceeded to close the small ones which were not making money; this included both of our newspapers. Well, so much for Mr. Got Rocks.

It is always good to hear from you. Ellis succeeded in stirring up great memories.

Thank you again my friend. One last thing, I am in my 39th year as a State Senator. God willing, I will begin my 40th year in January 2015. Three years ago, I became the longest-serving Virginia State Senator in history. I wouldn't recommend anyone sticking around as long as I have, I am now 87 years old and that's too old for a rundown state senator like me.

My best to you and your family, and God Bless You.

Sincerely yours,
Charles J. Colgan
President Pro Tempore Emeritus
29th Senatorial District

Letter from Senator Colgan

Hand-written letter on Senate of Virginia letterhead. September 30, 2014.

Dear Dr. Snyder,

You named the four best of the school board—Hawkins, Dunn, Beane and Lacey—they were my favorites too.

I thought the way you delivered Osbourn Park High School was a classic—you delivered on the day school began, just as you promised. I was happy to be your cheerleader. This was a great victory. The skeptics ran and hid. You were an excellent superintendent.

My best to you always, you were a great example for all of us to follow.

Sincerely,
Charles Colgan

Pr. William's schools plead poverty in failing to offer pre-K to disadvantaged students

The Washington Post, April 18, 2014. Editorial Board.

PRINCE WILLIAM County's school system, with 85,000 students, is the second-largest in Virginia and among the 40 biggest in the United States: its annual budget is almost $1 billion. By contrast, the school system in Grayson County, in rural southwest Virginia, is one of the state's smallest, with a budget of barely $20 million. The combined population at Grayson's seven schools — just 1,763 students — easily would fit inside any of the dozen or so high schools in Prince William.

So why is little Grayson doing its utmost to provide pre-kindergarten classes to its most disadvantaged children while Prince William is doing so little? In fact, as a percentage of its school spending, Grayson is doing vastly more.

In Grayson, school officials allocate enough money to unlock all available state matching funds for the 33 children from low-income families who qualify for Pre-K funding. The rationale for tapping those funds is sound: Pre-K classes improve learning skills, including reading readiness.

Meanwhile, in Prince William, the Republican-led school board has all but ignored low-income 4-year-olds, more than two-thirds of them minorities, who could benefit from the state-funded program. The county ponied up only enough to garner state funding for 72 children, just four percent of the 1,663 who were eligible for the program.

Incredibly, Prince William has found no more money in its $1 billion budget for disadvantaged 4-year-olds than Grayson has found in its $20 million budget.

In both cases, the state required only a modest local contribution to release matching funds that would cover all qualified children — a little over one-third of one percent of each county's annual allocation for K-12 education. Grayson came up with the cash; Prince William mustered less than one one-hundredth of one percent of its overall budget

Prince William's median household income, about $100,000, is three times greater than Grayson's. Prince William was a leader among big school systems in introducing all-day kindergarten in 2007 for 5-year-olds. And it's true that the county has been struggling with rapid growth; classroom crowding is a problem. But Grayson faces its own challenges: With a dwindling student population, schools have closed and teacher salaries have been frozen. "We get every penny we can and utilize it to the best of our ability," an official in Grayson told us.

The attitude in Prince William is different. Some county leaders and school board members barely acknowledge a problem; others are overtly hostile. The school board chairman, Milton C. Johns, has pleaded poverty, citing state cuts to education funding and arguing that the county's priority is to maintain existing programs and services.

But Prince William's stingy attitude is more a matter of priorities than budgets. Other large school districts around the state, both richer and poorer, do a much better job at tapping state dollars. Richmond, Norfolk and Newport News, to name just three, secure state funding for virtually all children eligible for Pre-K. Prince William's Northern Virginia neighbors, Fairfax and Loudoun counties, secured funding for slightly more than half.

No major school system in Virginia is even close to Prince William's miserly participation rate of four percent in the Pre-K program. In turning its back on its poorest children, the question for Prince William is this: What kind of place does it want to be?

© The Washington Post Company

Condolences, loss of Ellis B. Hawkins

Letter from Dr. Steven L. Walts, Superintendent of Schools, Prince William County, VA. April 25, 2014.

Milton Lee Pritchard Snyder, Ph.D.

Dear Dr. Snyder:

Please accept my condolences on the loss of your dear friend, Mr. Ellis B. Hawkins, who was a distinguished chairman of the Prince William County School Board from July 1972 – June 1976. Although I did not have the privilege of knowing Mr. Hawkins, I am aware that he led this School Division through an amazing time of explosive growth in the county, and had many achievements to his credit.

I noted in your letter of April 10 your intentions to make a memorial gift to a scholarship fund established at Lewis Clark State College in Lewiston, Idaho, in honor of Mr. Hawkins. This is admirable and a fitting tribute to his legacy.

Our School Division has an In Memoriam page on its website, and we have posted a fitting announcement on Mr. Hawkins. You may view this by going to our website, pwcs.edu, and clicking on the tab on the left, "News & Updates," and scrolling down to "In Memoriam."

Additionally, your request that the current School Board consider naming a school facility in honor of Mr. Hawkins has been noted and will be forwarded to school naming committees as they are formed in the future.

I wish you the best, and if you are ever here on the east coast, please come by to see how we are "Providing A World-Class Education" for students in Prince William County Public Schools.

Sincerely,
Steven L. Walts
Superintendent of Schools
Manassas, VA

Obituary for T. Clay Wood

August 1, 1919 – May 1, 2015

Thomas Clay Wood was born August 1, 1919 in Nokesville Virginia to Nettie Gertrude (Herring) Wood and Henry Clay Wood. He worked on his family's farm, where he developed his love of farming and passed that love on to future generations. He attended a small, one-room schoolhouse, which he walked to each day and later graduated from Nokesville High, which is the present day elementary school. At a young age he remembers driving his mother into Washington DC to sell the family's produce and meat at a farmers' market.

After graduating from Strayer College in Washington DC, he returned to his family farm and in 1941, married Winifred (Winnie) Elizabeth Swank and moved to her family's farm where his beautiful bride had been born and raised. It was there he started his farming career with ten cows and would later purchase the farm from his father-in-law.

Over the next 70 years, Clay Wood would devote himself to this church, family, community and state. An active member of the Nokesville United Methodist Church, Clay held many leadership positions, including a faithful delegate to the United Methodist Conference even up into his senior years.

He was 22 years of age when he joined the Nokesville Ruritan Club where he was an active member for 64 years, and the District Governor in 1952. In 2001, Clay received an award for perfect attendance of 60 years. He was involved in numerous community activities, including Nokesville Day celebrations, and the annual Brunswick stew fund-raiser.

In 1952 he became a member of the Prince William School Board, a position he held for 24 years. Knowing that Prince William County's population would continue to grow, he saw the need for a new high school in Nokesville, and with determination and hard work, petitioned for the funds which were subsequently approved in 1964 to build the Brentsville District High School on Aden Road in Nokesville. Clay was also instrumental in getting special education introduced into the school system.

Clay was elected to the Prince William Board of Supervisors, a position he held for four years, deciding not to run for a second term in order to spend more time with his family. During all of these years of public service, Clay continued his farming operation and became a well-respected home builder in the county. Clay also served 19 years on the Prince William County Soil and Water Conservation Board. He was appointed by four Virginia Governors to serve on the Commonwealth Council on Aging, and was a personal friend of Governor Godwin and Virginia State Senator Chuck Colgan.

But ensuring a promising future for the county's young people was always his main concern, which is why in his later years, he negotiated to sell to the county his boyhood home farm, which is now the site of the county's newest High School. In appreciation of Clay's dedication and service to the county's educational system, the Board of Supervisors voted to name T. Clay Wood Elementary School in his honor, a dedication service held in 2011.

Clay died on May 1, 2015, at his home farm, in the same house where Clay and Winnie began, and lived out their life together. Clay is survived by three children, Linda Hingorani, Diane Elizabeth Wood, and Lanson Clay and wife Galina Wood. He is also survived by six grandchildren, seven great grandchildren and one great, great grandson.

Question, re: Mr. Beville's Tenure

Email from Milton L. Snyder to William Helton.

Please help me on a history question: The PWC Schools web site lists Edward Kelly as the longest serving Supt. of Schools in the history of the county at 18 years. I believe that Supt. Stuart Beville, who I followed also served 18 years and should be listed along with Kelly. Am I correct?

Milton

Email from William Helton to Milton L. Snyder. April 3, 2014.

Good morning Dr. Snyder,

Good to hear from you and thanks for your kind notes which we received in the mail. Your recollection of Mr. Beville's tenure is the same as mine. I have always been under the impression that he arrived in 1954 and resigned in 1972 which would be 18 years. However, it was only what I had heard, and I don't recall seeing official records on the dates.

It seemed to me that after Mr. Beville left, the school board received special permission from the State Board of Education to extend the time for a superintendent search (because we had two boards in a legal challenge), which enabled Mr. Saunders to serve as interim superintendent for a year before you were selected.

If Mr. Beville departed earlier in that process, that may have reduced his total time as superintendent by a few months which could account for Dr. Kelly's longer tenure. One would assume that the current school board staff would have researched the dates accurately before posting the information on the building.

That was the period during which the 'Four Horseman of the Apocalypse' were elected to the Board of County Supervisors and were proceeding to carry out a "scorched earth" policy to reduce all programs and services (especially the costly expanding school system) to rubble and to return the county back to its pre-Civil War rural agricultural roots. As you know, a major part of the plan was to throw out all existing boards and appoint new members to carry out their directives. When you arrived in the midst of this battle, little did we realize we were witnessing the birth pangs of the future Tea Party!

Therefore, while I can't verify Mr. Beville and Dr. Kelly's years in Prince William County, my impression has always been the same as yours that Mr. Beville served 18 years as Division Superintendent. If I find any information to determine accurately the dates of their service, I will forward it to you.

I am very glad that you returned safely home after your trip to Virginia and West Virginia and thank you again for the wonderful dinner and the welcome opportunity to visit with you and our faithful friends of 40 years ago.

Be well and keep in touch.
Warmest regards, Bill

re: The Proposed Prince William County Project

Email to William Helton from Milton Snyder, May 26, 2014.

Dr. Bill Helton

Thank you so much for your insightful review of the tenure of Mr. Beville. Please include your description of the PWC Board of County Supervisors' escapades prior to my arrival as Superintendent in any or all of your writings about our accomplishments during my four years of duty.

I really like your words in describing the activities of the four county "horsemen"! And, the description you composed in your email would be a super foreword on a Dr. William Helton document of our accomplishments during the Snyder four years, which remains in my rear brain lobes! Please note that your document written as Deputy Supt. to Snyder and also as Superintendent of PWC following my departure to Oakland, CA, would be extremely credible as an addendum to a final book I am presently writing regarding the stay in Manassas.

Also, would seek your approval in the distribution of the book to individuals like Regis Lacey, Bill Dunn, Senator Colgan, Lillie Jessie, School Board members, Deborah H. Urban, Clerk and Milton C. Johns, Present Chair PWC at Large, of the School Board. Should you have concerns about my plans for distributing an book that includes your addendum, please let me know. Naturally, I would show you a draft of my comments prior to any or all distributions.

Bill Dunn called this week to express his concerns for being in Florida on March 15, and unable to attend our dinner event.

I do need to tell you more about my telephone conversation with Ellis Hawkins, four weeks before his death. He described in detail information about the Grey Fox Plan in the pursuit and hiring of a California-based Superintendent candidate.

I had forgotten that the Fox had an official one year Interim Contract as Supt. following Mr Beville and thanks to you for mentioning this important fact. During my initial interview at the NSBA Conference in LA, March 1973 with The Fox, Ellis Hawkins & John Pattie, it was somewhat confusing why an Adjunct Professor at Pepperdine and USC would rise to the top of the food chain.

Milton Lee Pritchard Snyder, Ph.D.
Division Superintendent, PWC, 1973-1977

Letter to Lillie Jessie

Letter from Milton Snyder, August 8, 2014.

Dear Lillie Jessie

Finally, and many thanks to you for correcting me regarding my error of listing you as my first black female principal appointment upon my arrival in Prince William County as Division Superintendent of Schools in June of 1973.

Dr. William Helton, my former Deputy Superintendent (and Superintendent following me when I left the District to accept the job of Deputy Superintendent of the Oakland City, California School District) responded to my request to complete research on the issue. Bill checked on the actual appointments of principals during my term of duty in the district and reported the following information back to me. I quote Dr. Helton on the actual appointment of the female principal in question.

"As I recall, you, Milt Snyder appointed a black female principal to replace a female white principal by the name of "Happy Boozer" who was returning to her home state of South Carolina. Her former school was the scene of a tragic accident when a Halloween display of dry corn stalks caught fire and killed a parent inside the display. The principal, you named was Ruby Strickland to replace Happy Boozer at Washington-Reid Elementary School. You, Milt, went to the school to specifically meet Ruby to tell her about the decision to appoint her to the principal position at Washington-Reid."

Again, Lillie, I thank you and Dr. Helton for correcting my previous error. However, I am truly pleased that Ruby Strickland's appointment has come to light again. She was a wonderful person, a gifted principal and one that I am so proud to have appointed to the position at Washington-Reid Elementary School. Do you have information regarding her present location?

If you were hired in Prince William County schools in 1976, I was Superintendent and able to claim credit for your first appointment, please let me know if I am correct in claiming the year you were hired.

My deepest commendation to you for your past and present work. Your writings and now as an elected school board member, I am extremely proud of you. Please keep up the great work you are doing in representing the students of the Prince William County Schools.

Regards,
Milton Lee Pritchard Snyder, Ph.D.
Seattle, WA

Letter to LCSC Foundation

October 13, 2014

Lewis Clark State College
500 8th Ave.
Lewiston, Idaho 83501

   re: Donation to Milton L. Snyder/
      Dolores J. Gibbons Scholarship Fund

   In honor of Senator Charles Colgan, President Pro Tempore Emeritus, 29th Senatorial District of the Commonwealth of Virginia and regional area of Prince William County located at Manassas, Virginia.

   Please inform Senator Charles J. Colgan of our donation… and that the major purpose of the scholarship is to support and provide college-level scholarships to Idaho High School Graduates to attend college at Lewis-Clark State College in Lewiston, Idaho.

   Senator Charles J. Colgan served as a member and Chairman of the Prince William County Virginia Board of Supervisors located in Manassas, Virginia during the period of 1970-1975. Senator Colgan was elected to the Virginia Senate in 1976 and presently is the longest serving Senator in the History of the Commonwealth of Virginia. As Chairman of the Prince William County Virginia Board of Supervisors, Senator Colgan was instrumental in supporting the school district during my term as Division Superintendent of Schools. He was crucial in his support of the construction of Osbourn Park High School and for assisting in creating Kindergarten programs in the County Schools of Prince William as a first in the Commonwealth of Virginia. He continues to provide major leadership in creating and promoting legislation in the Commonwealth of Virginia for education, health and social issues.

- Please accept the enclosed donation to our scholarship fund in honor of Senator Charles J. Colgan, 29th District, in the Commonwealth of Virginia.
- Request that Senator Colgan be informed via mail of our donation to the Snyder/Gibbons Scholarship Fund.

Regards,
Milton Lee Pritchard Snyder, Ph.D.

Letter from Senator Colgan to Snyder

June 16, 2015

Dear Dr. Snyder:

I feel sure this letter will come to you as a surprise. So—get ready, here it comes. The Prince William County Board of Supervisors has collaborated with the Prince William School Board and joined forces and decided the Counties 12th High School will be named Charles J. Colgan High School. The Board of Supervisors voted unanimously to recommend Colgan and about 10 days later the School Board confirmed the Supervisors action.

I will send you the details on the school later; it will be located directly across Route 234 from Coles Fire House and will house 2400 students. The school will open in September and is about 25% completed now. I know we will make our deadline because I once had a Superintendent who taught me how to do it.

My best to you dear friend. I am in the process of winding up my 40th year in the State Senate and when my time is over I will hold fond memories of a great man who I was so proud to know.

Sincerely yours,
Charles J. Colgan

Senator Charles Colgan High School

Prince William's 12th high school to be named for Sen. Charles Colgan

InsideNOVA, Northern Virginia Media Services, Leesburg, VA. May 20, 2015. Jill Palermo.

Prince Williams' county 12th high school will be named for the county's — and commonwealth's — longest-serving state senator, Charles J. Colgan, Sr.

The school board voted unanimously Wednesday to name the new high school for Colgan, who several board members praised as a humble and effective legislator who always championed public education in Richmond.

"Senator Colgan always made his decisions based on what was best for Prince William County," said School Board Chairman Milt Johns, At Large.

"He voted across the aisle on many issues," Johns added. "Especially when a compromise was needed to move the state forward. His contributions were enormous."

Since first elected to the state Senate in 1975, Colgan, now 88, changed the landscape of higher education in Prince William County by helping secure state funding to open both the Woodbridge and Manassas campuses of Northern Virginia Community College.

Colgan was also instrumental in opening the Manassas campus of George Mason University.

Four of Colgan's children attended the meeting to watch the board's vote. They said their dad was home watching the meeting on TV with other relatives and friends.

Colgan and his late wife, Agnes, have eight children, 24 grandchildren and 19 great-grandchildren, most of whom still live in the county.

"This is just the highest honor he could have gotten because education and children mean so much to him," Colgan's daughter, Mary Finnigan, said in an interview after the meeting.

Finnigan said today was also their late mother's birthday. "We considered that a good sign," she said.

The school board conducted two meetings in April to collect suggestions for the new high school from the community. Forty-nine names were submitted for consideration.

Johns and other school board members said the decision was especially difficult because many residents expressed support for naming the school for Kyle Wilson, a Prince William firefighter who died while fighting a Woodbridge house fire in 2007.

Several other community members lobbied to name the school for Dr. George Hampton, the namesake of a local foundation affiliated with the Omega Psi Phi fraternity.

Hampton is a retired U.S. Army lieutenant colonel and longtime Woodbridge resident who was professor of military science at Virginia State University and served on the county's parole board and advisory board to the juvenile and domestic relations court.

"All had had significant contributions and are all worthy of recognition in a significant way," Johns said.

Johns noted that the school board had already dedicated the playground at Fanny Fitzgerald Elementary School for Wilson and that the county Board of Supervisors was making preparations to name a new fire station for him.

"So I take comfort in the fact that the school board has named something for [Wilson] and that the board of supervisors is planning a significant honor for him," Johns said.

Johns called Hampton "a tremendous contributor to our community, someone who has given his adult life to serving this nation, this community, this county."

Johns also said both would be kept in mind when the school board considers naming future new schools.

"Hopefully that is something we can consider at another school board meeting soon, before the end of my term," Johns said.

Colgan began his political career in 1972, when he was elected to the Gainesville seat on the county board of supervisors. He served as board chairman for one year before being elected senator of the 29th district in 1975.

In his professional life, Colgan founded a professional airlines, Colgan Air, from the Manassas Airport in 1965.

He is also the last living Virginia lawmaker to have served in the U.S. military during the World War II era, which he did after earning his wings as a U.S. Air Cadet in 1945 at 18.

When announcing his retirement last summer, Colgan said he hoped to spend more time with his family and take a few long-delayed vacations to Europe and the western U.S.

But family members at the school board meeting Wednesday said Colgan remains busy as he finishes out his 40th year in the state Senate. Finnigan said he plans to head down to Richmond Thursday for a committee meeting.

"He's still very busy," Finnigan said.

The new high school, under construction near the intersection of VA 234 and Hoadly Road, is expected to be completed in time to open in the fall of 2016.

•

InsideNoVa.com is Northern Virginia's news, traffic and weather website, owned by Leesburg-based Northern Virginia Media Services, which publishes Prince William Today and four other weekly newspapers. The papers, including Leesburg Today and the Sun Gazettes of Arlington and Fairfax, reach close to 200,000 households every week in Loudoun, Ashburn, Prince William, Manassas, Manassas Park, Great Falls, McLean, Vienna, Oakton and Arlington.

Colgan school naming no surprise to Snyder

June 30, 2015

Dear Senator Colgan:

Your letter of June 16, 2015, did not come as a surprise to me. I have championed the naming of a high school in your honor for over 42 years, since serving as Division Superintendent of Schools in Prince William County during 1973-77. Commendations to you, Charles J. Colgan, for being designated as the titleholder of the 12th High School planned for opening in the Fall of 2015. I still believe that your name should have been added to the Osbourn Park High School building many years ago. However, the School Board and County Board of Supervisors decision to place your name on the new high school will be even more important, in my estimation. Naturally, this is a major decision for you and the County, but I know that former school board members for Prince William County Schools, Ellis Hawkins, Thomas Beane, Regis Lacey, Clay Wood, Bill Dunn and John Pattie will celebrate your name on the 12th and newest high school.

Finally, Prince William County leaders are recognizing your performance, not only as the longest serving Senator in the history of Virginia, but for all of your service to the parents, students, patrons of the County and the citizens of the Commonwealth of Virginia. Naming the next high school in your name is an honor that you so richly deserve is beyond all hopes and aspirations! For example, your leadership exerted during the 1970s as chairman and member of the Prince William County Board of Supervisors should be written in stone.

Your Calm, Collected and Conceptual leadership skills were severally tested while handling the affairs of the County and in controlling the "Four Horsemen of the Apocalypse," during the 1970s. Some parents and patrons will remember the leadership you gave to the opening and final construction of Osbourn Park High School. The counsel and courage that you gave to the school board and me in adding kindergarten classes for all of Prince William County students in 1975, for the first time, was one of the commendable actions of that century.

I have completed a book to be published in August 2015, entitled, THE THIRD BATTLE OF MANASSAS. The book deals with much of the conflict that occurred between the School Board and County Board of Supervisors in the 1970s. I have given you considerable credit in the book for assisting the School Board in retaining their policy management responsibilities for which they were charged and responsible. I have recommended in this book that you, Charles J. Colgan, plus Ellis Hawkins and Thomas Beane, former school board chairs have schools named after each of you.

In the meantime, I plan to distribute my book to you, Bill Dunn, Regis Lacey, Phyliss O'Toole, Bill Helton, Richard Johnson, the School Board Secretary, Superintendent Steven Walts, Herald Grandstaff and several news media groups in the Virginia area.

Thank you again for all of your support during my stay with the County Schools of Prince William in 1973-1977. May I include your recent letter? Your June 2015 letter would make my book, THE THIRD BATTLE OF MANASSAS, more credible. Also, I certainly would like to be in attendance at the ceremony when you are honored for opening the doors of Charles J. Colgan High School in the Fall of 2015. Please stay in touch.

Sincerely,
Milton Lee Pritchard Snyder, Ph.D.
Seattle, WA

About the Author

Milton Lee Pritchard Snyder Ph.D., is a direct descendant of grandparents John Wesley Snyder, Mary Elizabeth Cooper, Walter Icen Pritchard and Jesse Lee Jordan—all born in the State of West Virginia. Three of his grandparents moved to the State of Idaho in the 1890s and early 1900s, while one, Walter Icen Pritchard remained in the Buchannon and Weston area much of his life.

Snyder, who was born in Weippe, Idaho in 1929, spent his early life on the farm and his education changed the course of his life. Following the death of his father, Milton Cooper Snyder, he moved to Lewiston, Idaho, graduating from Lewiston High School in 1947. He then received a BA in 1951 from Lewis Clark State College, known then as Northern Idaho College of Education.

Service in the Korean War, 1951-1952, interrupted Milton's educational plans, but following the war he earned a Master's degree from the University of Washington, followed by a Ph.D. in 1973 from United States International University, known now as Alliant International University in San Diego, California.

Milton has had a long career in education, serving as teacher and principal in Sunnyside and Richland, Washington; Superintendent of Schools for Anacortes, Marysville, and Federal Way School Districts in Washington State; Deputy Superintendent of Schools in Oakland, California; and Division Superintendent for Prince William County, Virginia School District in Manassas, Virginia.

He also served as Deputy Executive Director for the American Association of School Administrators in Arlington, Virginia. During his work in Virginia as superintendent, he taught graduate courses in educational administration as Adjunct Professor for the University of Virginia and (VPI) Virginia Polytechnic Institute and State University at their northern Virginia centers. He continues to work for several educational technology firms from his home office in Washington state.

While attending college in the period of 1947-1951 at Northern Idaho College of Education, now known as Lewis Clark State College in Lewiston, Idaho, he had the great fortune to meet Robert Frost. As student body Vice President at the college, he assisted in co-hosting Robert Frost while he lectured to English and poetry classes on campus. It was truly an honor to be with him and in his presence.

Snyder's experience in the Prince William County Schools has made a great deal of difference for him and Frost's words have been and will continue to be an inspiration for a lifetime!

In 2009, Dr. Snyder self-published a memoir, *Maybe Milton Should Work In The Woods*.

www.ingramcontent.com/pod-product-compliance
Lightning Source LLC
Chambersburg PA
CBHW080700110426
42739CB00034B/3346